LONDON SCHOOL OF ECONOMICS
MONOGRAPHS ON SOCIAL ANTHROPOLOGY
No. 26

Kinship and Marriage
in a New Guinea Village

by
H. IAN HOGBIN

UNIVERSITY OF LONDON
THE ATHLONE PRESS
1963

First published by
THE ATHLONE PRESS
UNIVERSITY OF LONDON
at 2 Gower Street, London WC1
Distributed by Constable & Co. Ltd
12 Orange Street, London WC2

H. Ian Hogbin, 1963

Printed in Great Britain by
ROBERT CUNNINGHAM AND SONS LTD
ALVA

DATE DUE

Oct 8 '65			
Nov 30 65			
Mar 30 '66			
19 6			
Dec 7 68			
Apr 10 '72			
GAYLORD			PRINTED IN U.S.A.

KINSHIP AND MARRIAGE
IN A NEW GUINEA VILLAGE

Preface

I WISH to express my thanks to Professor J. A. Barnes, Dr M. J. Meggitt, Dr C. Jayawardena, and Mrs W. M. Balding, each of whom read and criticized parts of the MS of this book.

The work was finished in 1960, and the delay in publication has been beyond my control. Had I been writing the concluding sections of Chapter 2 now I would not have lumped all non-unilineal systems together. Certainly they have factors in common, but there are also important differences. Among the To'ambaita of Malaita a man is free to choose his district group, and among the Busama he can choose his club group. In Malaita, however, the limiting factor is still descent, as in societies with a unilineal system—although the descent is not restricted to a single line—whereas in Busama descent does not enter into the situation. Here the limiting factor is the existence of a relationship tie, which may be genealogical or affinal, with some person already accepted as a member of the desired group.

I. H.

Department of Anthropology
University of Sydney
19 *March* 1962

Contents

Plates

MAPS

I

The Setting

AN earlier publication of mine, *Transformation Scene*, dealt with changes in the economic organization, political system, legal code, and religious beliefs of the people of the New Guinea settlement of Busama during half a century of European contact. The present volume is a companion study concerned primarily with the kinship structure, which, in contrast, has survived almost unaltered. I shall begin with a brief general description and proceed to a detailed account of the different groupings and relationships of the members. Then I shall give the life history of an average native from birth through infancy, childhood, adolescence, and marriage to maturity and in the process show how the community gradually tightens its grip.

Busama is situated on the western shore of the Huon Gulf. Germany had annexed the whole north-eastern quarter of New Guinea in 1884, but the Gulf region did not come under full administrative control till after 1900. An Australian Force drove the Germans out in 1914, and since that date, except for the period 1943-4, when the Japanese Army was in possession, the country has been ruled by Australia, after 1921 under Mandate from the League of Nations, more recently as a Trust Territory of the United Nations. The Government station for Busama is at Lae, less than twenty miles away by canoe to the north. Certain native residents act as permanent official representatives, known as the 'luluai' and the 'tultul', and from time to time European officers carry out patrols.

German Lutheran missionaries were on the scene by about 1907 and set up a local headquarters four miles to the south at a place called Mala'lo. Soon all the Busama were Christians. They built village schools for the Mission, and here the children learned reading and writing. American missionaries replaced the Germans in 1946.

By 1907 the males had already begun seeking employment as wage labourers on the coconut plantations that white settlers were establishing on the neighbouring islands of New Britain and New Ireland. The youths departed at the age of sixteen or seventeen and mostly came back in time to marry six years later. Then in 1926 gold was discovered in the hinterland. This led to the opening up of a deep-water port, Salamaua, a couple of miles beyond Mala'lo and subsequently to the establishment of an aerodrome at Lae. Native workers were in keen demand on the goldfields and

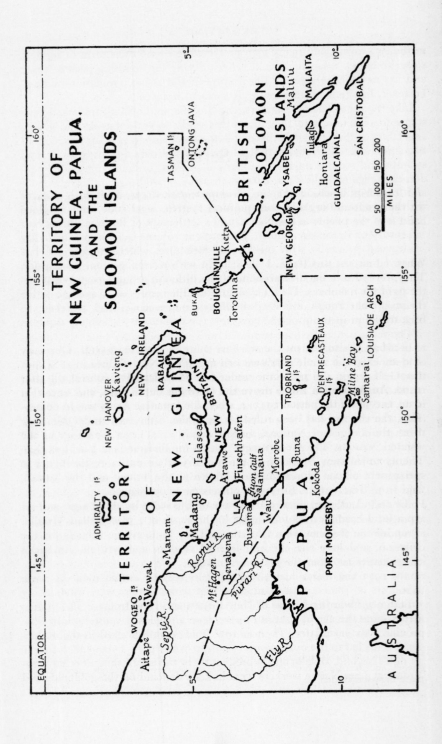

TERRITORY OF
NEW GUINEA, PAPUA.
AND THE
SOLOMON ISLANDS

in the two towns, and many men preferred to spend their term of service closer to home. Salamaua was destroyed during the bombing raids of 1944 and has never been rebuilt. The European and Asian population of Lae, however, has gone on increasing. At present it exceeds 3,000.

Like the other Pacific islanders, the Busama are horticulturalists. Their staple food is taro, and they also plant yams, sweet potatoes, and green vegetables, a few fruits (the banana is the most important), and coconuts. Sago provides additional carbohydrate, but the palms grow wild in the swamps and require no special attention. Animal protein comes from the domestic pigs and chickens, from such game as wild pigs and bandicoots, and from fish. These last the people catch by a wide variety of methods— with spears from the shore and, in canoes, with baited hooks, lures, poison, hand nets, and heavy seines.

THE VILLAGE

When I first reached Busama, in 1944, there were about 600 inhabitants. They were then living in a forest clearing whither they had retreated during the fight for Salamaua and Lae. Not for another year, when, at the end of the war in the Pacific, the Civil Administration was restored, did they go back to the proper site on the coast.

The reconstructed village is now in outward appearance much as it used to be. It stands on a narrow shelf of flat land between the beach and a row of steep jungle-clad cliffs. At two points the high ground advances across the shelf towards the sea and forms a pair of headlands. One of these, unmarked on the charts, forms the southern boundary, and only the cemetery is on the far side. The other, known to Europeans as Schneider Point (Ho'tu to the natives), is approximately in the centre. In the olden days these promontories could each be successfully defended by a handful of warriors, and the original settlement was confined to the strip in between. The name Busama, or Bu-samang in its correct form, is actually that of a spring at the base of one of the cliffs (bu = 'water', 'spring', 'river', or 'lagoon').[1] Today the houses extend from the lower headland to Schneider Point and thence north-westwards for another 500 yards. They are not arranged according to any coherent plan but seem rather to be scattered at random on the seaward side of a shrub-fringed pathway. Here there is a cluster of perhaps a dozen, then one or two stand separately, then an open space intervenes, then there is another cluster, and so on. Even the orientation is not consistent, and while some face the beach others turn sideways to it.

Before the war fourteen of the buildings, distributed at intervals of from fifty to eighty yards, were raised up ten feet or more on wooden columns to provide a sitting platform underneath. They were the clubs, each with a

---

[1] Busama is the Europeanized version. Missionaries alone learn the local languages, and the other white settlers in New Guinea invariably mangle native words, place names included.

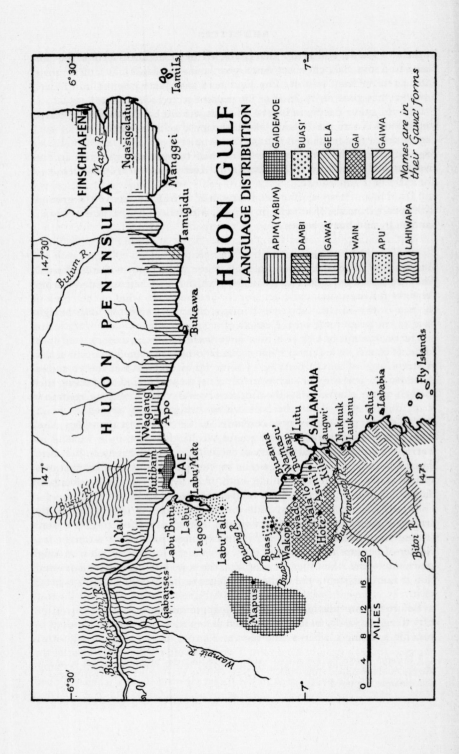

HUON GULF
LANGUAGE DISTRIBUTION

APIM (YABIM)   GAIDEMOE

DAMBI   BUASI'

GAWA'   GELA

WAIN   GAI

APU'   GAIWA

LAHIWAPA

Names are in
their Gawa' forms

FINSCHHAFEN

HUON PENINSULA

Mape R.

Ngasigelatu

Tamils.

Manggei

Bulum R.

Tamigidu

Bukawa

147°30'

147°

Busu R.

Yalu

Wagang
Apo
Butibam
LAE
Labu'Mete
Labu'
Labu'Butu
Gabanses

Busi Markham R.

Markham R.

Buang R.

LabuTali

Buasi
Buasi

Mapus

Wakop
Gwadom
Malo
Hote
Asini
Maia
Kile
Laugwi'

Busama
Wamasu'
Wamasu'
Buakap
Lutu

SALAMAUA

Nuknuk
Laukanu

Salus
Lababia

Fly Islands

Bunu (Francisco) R.

Bitoi R.

147°R.

Waruku R.

MILES

0   4   8   12   16   20

6°30'

7°

6°30'

7°

special name, reserved for the males of the community. Here the men gathered to smoke, chew betel-nut, chat, and sometimes take a meal during the late afternoon and evening, and here also the bachelors and elderly widowers slept at night. In 1945 the people erected fourteen new structures to serve similar purposes but failed to procure the tall columns. Today's clubs look from the outside like ordinary dwellings. They are of such modest dimensions that they could be completed without outside help. No formal celebration took place to mark their completion, and they are un-named. Whether there will eventually be a return to the architectural style of the past I cannot say.

The houses rest on low piles from three to five feet above the ground. Entry is by means of a flight of steps or a notched log. Most consist of a single room about twenty-four feet long by fourteen feet wide with a verandah either in front or along one side. A few are rather larger and have two rooms but are then like a pair of our semi-detached cottages, each one occupied by a separate household. A father and son, or a maternal uncle and nephew, or an older and a younger brother may as a temporary measure choose to live in such close proximity. The outer covering of the trunk of a species of wild palm serves as flooring. Strips are split off, fixed at right angles, and then interlaced. Leaflets of sago palm make excellent thatching material, though one or two men have preferred to buy corrugated iron. The sides are walled in with sawn planks carefully planed smooth, and as a rule blinds of woven bamboo or some other cane protect the verandah. The thatch and timbers have to be constantly repaired, but even then deterioration is rapid. Usually after six or seven years buildings become so dangerous that they must be pulled down and new ones erected.

Although the Busama were converted to Christianity so long ago, they lack a church of their own and attend the Mission station at Mala'lo for services on Sundays. The Elders of the village congregation conduct brief morning and evening prayers either in the open or in the village schools. There are two of these buildings, both of European type with corrugated iron roofs, one on either side of Schneider Point.

Other village structures include pit latrines more or less hidden in the bushes at the base of the cliffs (these are a recent innovation and are seldom visited even during the day and never after sunset), small huts where house-holders who own fowls can shut them up at night for protection from dogs and snakes, and a few sties for confining the sows after they have farrowed. There are no sheds for the canoes, which are simply pulled high up beneath the trees at the edge of the beach beyond the reach of the tide. All the craft are of the same type, a dugout with a single outrigger float attached, but they vary considerably in size. The small fishing canoes can be handled by two or three men, whereas the big vessels that carry goods up and down the coast may require half a dozen. Two masts are permanently fixed in the latter to carry canvas sails, and the outrigger booms support stout decking.

I lived with the people first in the forest clearing. Later, when they had moved, they built me a house alongside the path near the tip of Schneider Point. From here I could see practically the whole village, one end from the front, the other from the back. Subsequently, after I had left for the last time, in 1950, the building became the Government rest house and was used by administrative officers on patrol.

The whole site has been planted in between the houses with coconut groves, and there are also areca palms, pawpaws, oranges, and numerous bush trees preserved for the shade they offer. Drinking supplies come from springs, and persons wanting a freshwater bath need only walk a short distance northwards to find four or five streams, two of which plunge over the cliffs into pools below.

Inland the country rises in a series of ridges to a mountain barrier over 10,000 feet at its highest point. The section immediately behind Busama is known as the Buang Range. A number of rivers have cut broad flat-bottomed valleys through the foothills, and here the people grow their food crops. In gardening they follow the slash-and-burn method, and after each harvest the ground must be allowed to lie fallow until fertility is restored. Earlier I said that seven years elapsed before the next planting (*Transformation Scene*, p. 70). I now know that this was an under-estimate. The minimum is ten years, and some areas require even longer. To support themselves the villagers therefore need more than ten times as much land as they have under cultivation during any one season.

LANGUAGE

The Huon Gulf country is made up of no less than eleven distinct linguistic divisions. The most important language from the point of view both of the number of speakers and their distribution is Gawa', the mother tongue of approximately 7,000 persons. The majority of them are to be found in the villages on the north coast of the Gulf from Lae eastwards, though a group of about 1,200 live on the west coast in the four settlements of Busama, Buakap, Lutu, and Asini'.[1]

In the foothills immediately behind Busama and in one settlement right on the coast, Wamasu', just above Buakap, the language is known as Gai. Further inland still the natives speak Gaidemoe. To the north-west the 200 villagers of Buasi' have a language peculiar to themselves, and beyond, in the three communities on Labu Lagoon at the head of the Gulf, the speech is Apu'. We then cross the Markham River (known to the natives as the Busi) to Lae and reach the Gawa' belt on the north coast, though this

---

[1] For a short account of Gawa' (and Apim) see A. Capell, 1951, pp. 184–99. Gawa' has two forms, that used on the west coast in the Busama village cluster, and that current on the north coast. The speakers of each think of their own version as the standard and of the other as corrupt. In this account I shall give the other languages their Busama names, though generally the peoples whose mother tongues they are have a different word. Thus speech that the Busama call Apim is referred to by its users as Yabim (Jabêm in the orthography adopted by the Lutheran Mission).

gives way to Dambi in one mainland village, Tamigidu, and afterwards to Apim in the extreme east and again to Dambi in the Tami Islands. Two other languages, Gela and Gaiwa, are spoken to the south of Busama, Buakap, and Asini'. Gela has always been confined to villages on the coast, but although the Gaiwa speakers originally all lived in the hills many of them have lately come down to the beach. Along the seaboard today Gela and Gaiwa communities are therefore intermingled.

In earlier times speech differences must have been a barrier to social intercourse. It seems that most men who had close relatives in two areas were bilingual and that others, if they did not actually speak a second language, took pains to understand it—in the native phrase, 'to hear it'. Inter-village trade was therefore possible. Cooking pots came from the far south; Lutu provided stone for tools; Busama and Asini' produced surplus foodstuffs; the hill country exported tobacco; the Labu villagers made all the baskets; the inhabitants of the north coast supplied most of the mats and bags; and the Tami Islanders excelled in wood carving. Any given community, however, restricted its trading to certain others and had little to do with the remainder. Further, the groups that engaged in mutual exchanges often formed temporary alliances and attacked the places with which they were not economically linked. Such unions had nothing to do with language. The Busama, for example, were prepared to welcome almost anyone from the villages around Labu Lagoon, where Apu' was spoken, but would have killed on sight many people speaking their own Gawa'. In one of the last wars before the arrival of Europeans they enlisted Labu help to raid their near neighbours in Asini', whose speech and even dialect they shared. The latter in turn then sought the aid of warriors from a community where Gela was spoken.

Today the language difficulties have been largely overcome. Everybody over the age of about twelve, male or female, from anywhere around the Gulf is fully literate in Apim (Jabêm), the medium of instruction adopted by the Mission; and the youths and men are, in addition, completely at home in pidgin-English (sometimes referred to as Neo-Melanesian), the general New Guinea lingua franca.

BUSAMA ORIGINS

The account that the people give of their past may well be wrong in many of its details. They have only recently become literate, and when traditions are transmitted orally it is easy not only to make mistakes unwittingly but also to incorporate deliberate inventions. Formerly, too, there was no way of recording long intervals of time. The movements of the stars in the heavens, the seasonal changes in the prevailing winds, and the flowering of some of the forest trees were useful indicators when work had to be planned for a few months ahead, but even today, with printed calendars readily available, nobody knows how old he is or how many years have gone by since such notable events as the coming of the first European and the setting up of the earliest Mission school. For the purpose of our study, however, the accuracy of the stories matters little: the important fact is that the natives fully accept them as the truth and hence find in them justification for the conditions of the present. Why is the village located at Schneider Point? Why do certain groups have rights to particular areas of land? Why is there a linkage between some places and not others? These and similar questions are answered by an appeal to the accounts of the doings of the ancestors.

Busama history begins with a group of immigrants from nobody knows where establishing a village on the north coast of the Huon Gulf at a place called Bukawa' (Bu-Gawa' in the Busama dialect, the place after which the Gawa' language was named). If any earlier inhabitants occupied the area they were either absorbed or else driven away. As the years passed and the population increased, so new hamlets were started westwards towards the Markham River and eastwards to the edge of the Apim country. In time all the present northern communities were begun. Each one took over the same structural pattern and even called several of the club houses after those in the parent settlement. The groups that hived off peaceably kept up friendly relations with the Bukawa' by means of visits, invitations to ceremonies, and occasional intermarriage: those that departed in anger after a disagreement generally became enemies.

The only source of stone suitable for making tools in the whole Gulf was an outcrop on the Salamaua Peninsula down the west coast, and thither expeditions journeyed regularly. The northerners soon became familiar with the neighbouring territory, and when at some stage the Bukawa' gardens withered during a severe local drought several families decided to make a home near the quarry. So Lutu was founded, as usual with the familiar structure and many of the old club names. These folk also retained the friendships and enmities of their Bukawa' cousins.

The soil on the Salamaua Peninsula proved to be poorer than was expected, and the settlers soon took possession of a strip of vacant ground on the mainland opposite. They made gardens here but always returned home during the afternoon for fear that the inhabitants of Kila village to the south might attack them (Kila, another European barbarism, should properly be Gela: it is the homeland of the natives who speak the Gela language). But eventually an incident took place that led to a permanent split. One of the youths had become attracted to a betrothed girl from a neighbouring household and persuaded her to marry him. He and his near relatives then fled to the bush at the back of the gardens to avoid the vengeance of the injured parties. This was the origin of Asini'. The ill-feeling continued till the dawn of the European era, and although the descendants of the fugitives preserved their Gawa' language and Bukawa' social structure, they and the Lutu often raided each other. The Kila people, already opposed to the Lutu, looked upon the new community with greater kindness and offered extra land for cultivation.

Later still, perhaps in about 1835, when a further rise in population made another move advisable, a second Lutu group settled on the mainland, on this occasion without a precipitating quarrel. The first site selected was difficult to fortify, and the party eventually shifted slightly north to Schneider Point. This, as has been explained, proved to be ideal. Busama was now in being. The land round about belonged by right of prior occupation to a small Gaiwa community living at a place hard by known as Gaiwaku. These folk had no hope of throwing out the newcomers and quickly came to terms with them. Indeed, before long they had joined them on the beach and lost their separate identity. Today no-one in the village speaks Gaiwa.

Busama was organized on the usual structural model, and, as before, several of the clubs bore Bukawa' names. The people maintained intimacy with the Lutu and constantly visited them. Further, they kept up the ties with some of the north-coast villages and the same hostility to Asini'.

Once the place was well established people came in from the villages around Labu Lagoon, Kila, and other areas. These persons arrived as single individuals or as families, not as complete groups like the Gaiwaku. The majority sought a haven after quarrels had occurred or their homes had been destroyed by enemies and their closer kinsfolk killed. They placed themselves in the care of a protector, who gave them plots to cultivate and, if they were single, found them a spouse. Today villagers descended from such foreigners are in no sense at a disadvantage.

One more Lutu offshoot came to the mainland in about 1907. The Lutheran Mission had not long before set up its Mala'lo station, and some of the householders preferred, for the sake of the children's schooling, to live close at hand. Their village became known as Buakap. Much of the land nearby had already become Lutu territory, and the members of a Gaiwa group made available further areas that they themselves were not using.

We must now return to the Bukawa' colonies on the north coast. The most westerly of them, near where Lae is today, was located at the mouth of the Markham River adjoining country occupied by natives who spoke the Lahiwapa language (Laewamba is their own term). These were notorious as fighters and tolerated no strangers near them. They attacked the Gawa' settlers, and eventually the survivors crossed the river into the swamps surrounding Labu Lagoon. The natives here, the Apu'-speakers, were also hostile, and the refugees fled further south still. Even then they found no rest, for they had to face the Gaidemoe-speakers of the Buang Mountains. Fight after fight took place, and always the Gawa' lost. Pushed ever southwards, they reached a hill called Awasa a couple of miles beyond the spot where Busama was shortly to be built. They and their descendants retained a precarious foothold on this area for the next couple of generations, though they had to submit to raids from Gai hillmen, the Lutu, and the Busama. Finally, perhaps in about 1880, the Busama took pity on them and sent an invitation to join their community. People speaking of the incident give no other reason for the change of heart than sympathy, but it is possible that self-interest also played a part. At that stage each new resident was an extra warrior.

During five or six decades it seemed that the Awasa party might be assimilated as completely as that from Gaiwaku earlier. Intermarriage, to judge from genealogies, was rare, but there was no residential segregation, and the new arrivals, and their sons also, built houses in among those of their hosts. The senior men today say that in their youth everything ran smoothly and nobody sneered at others for having forbears who came from a different place. 'We didn't think about Lutu and Awasa origins. No, we were one people, all Busama.' But it must be remembered that for many years the settlement was still small and that the inefficient stone tools were in use till after 1900. General co-operation on a village scale was accordingly essential not only for defence but for many everyday tasks. In such circumstances the people would have tried to sink their differences in the common interest in survival.

By 1930 conditions had changed. The population, now increasing more rapidly than ever, had reached the 500 mark, a figure far exceeding that for any Gawa' village of the past. Even with stone tools the working gangs had never been so large. Steel, however, had been introduced, and although collaboration went on as before, the various jobs could be completed with less effort. The tendency therefore was towards smaller rather than larger groups. Each person looked for help mainly to those with whom he had the closest ties, the descendants of the early migrants or of the later refugees, depending on where he himself stood. In the process of recrystallization Lutu and Awasa emerged once more as self-sufficient and self-contained units.

Doubtless had there been no Europeans in control a split would have occurred, and the disgruntled elements would have gone off to start yet another settlement. The Awasa, as the minority—though by a small margin only—might have been expected to make the shift. The hill site that their grandfathers abandoned would not have been attractive as it lacked direct access to the sea, a serious disadvantage now that they had become fisher-folk, and presumably they would have looked elsewhere. There was always a risk in taking action of this kind, as we have seen, though they would probably have been strong enough to maintain possession of some favourable spot by force of arms.

No such move was made, mainly because of the land policy adopted by the Administration. Till recently the rights as exercised during the period when the Government was being established were alone recognized, and if, when a dispute arose, one of the communities could prove that it was in occupation then, its claim was always confirmed. From this decision there was no appeal. The other party, forbidden to have recourse to weapons, was obliged to withdraw. The Awasa were therefore faced with but two possibilities, to remain where they were or to retire to their hill. They chose the former for the reason indicated—as fishermen they preferred to live on the beach.

Relations between the factions grew steadily worse, and at length, in 1945, when the people were preparing to come out of the bush clearing and rebuild on the shore, the officer then in charge of the district advised separation. The Lutu descendants, he suggested, might keep to the north of Schneider Point, the Awasa descendants to the south. He probably lacked legal authority to compel obedience, though he appointed two sets of Government representatives, one to look after what was in future to be called Busama-Lutu, the other to look after Busama-Awasa. His counsel prevailed except that the boundary was fixed about a hundred yards south-ward of the Point. The earlier settlement had been on this side, and a few Lutu householders were not only sentimentally attached to the area where their ancestors had lived but also unwilling to be cut off from their coconut groves. Subsequently each section of the village erected its own school, and soon afterwards the different sets of senior men began holding separate meetings when policy matters, minor civil disputes, or petty offences had to be considered. Busama has thus become two distinct communities.

This compromise solution of the problem cannot be regarded as wholly satisfactory. True, the place has been cut in half, but the division is only an imaginary line that everyone crosses over and over again as he goes about his ordinary work. With casual encounters so frequent, conflicts are inevitable, and the arguments and quarrels will continue. The members of the Awasa group cause most of the trouble, perhaps because there are fewer of them, perhaps because long wandering has made them more aggressive.

It would seem that the Gawa' type of structure ceases to be satisfactory once the threat of warfare is removed and the population comes to exceed about 300. Nobody can now force the Awasa to leave—where, indeed, could they be sent without infringing the land rights of other communities? —and the only hope for the future is the adoption of some economic project that will demand the services of more than 600 for its fulfilment. But if this is achieved the structure will no longer be the same.

LEADING VILLAGERS

Several names will appear in the following pages over and over again. These belong to my closest friends and the other persons who helped me most with my work. I have not been back since 1950, but two or three still write to me.

First there is Nga'gili', in his mid-thirties when we met in 1944. After I had treated for snakebite a youth whom he regards as a nephew he began addressing me as 'elder brother'. The lad in question, Gi'lahi, was at the time nineteen, and soon he also regarded me as a kinsman. I became his 'maternal uncle', he my 'uterine nephew'. Nga'gili' was already married to

Nga'angkangwi, and later Gi'lahi took Dabungyam to wife. Dabungyam's father, Nga'sele', proved to have a keen interest in the past and was ever ready to talk about it.

Ahipum, six or seven years older than Nga'gili', was the centre of a second nucleus. He and his children visited me constantly, and I was a frequent guest of his wife Mu'alimawi.

Other men I shall be quoting include the Government representative Gwaleyam, the Mission teacher Ida', and Gi'lahi's cousin Sali.

2

Kin and Community

THE Busama often say that they live and work together because they are related, and certainly each one of them can trace some sort of tie with all his neighbours. Yet a person's kinsfolk are never confined to his place of residence, and he generally recognizes upwards of a score in several other settlements. Indeed, it might be argued that the members of the community are related because they live and work together. If a stranger wishes to be admitted he must first find a sponsor who is prepared to accept him as the equivalent of a brother. The rest of the villagers, should they approve, then work out their relationships accordingly.

To the native in the traditional setting there are but two kinds of people, kinsfolk (*nga'leng*) and strangers (*laudung*). With the former he co-operates, with the latter he has no close contact, except perhaps that of enemies. During his period of European employment he may refer to some of his fellow labourers from distant areas, men whom formerly he would never have met, by the pidgin-English terms meaning 'friend' or 'acquaintance', but on his return home such expressions drop out of his vocabulary. Once again all his companions are relatives. Even trading with other villages is based on kinship. The exchanges of goods take place as free gifts between pairs of men who regard each other by courtesy as *nga'leng*. They inherit their partnerships from the father or an uncle and when visiting not only offer presents but also provide mutual hospitality and protection.

It follows that if people who have collaborated cease doing so for some reason, they tend to ignore the kinship connection between them. Numbers of Busama-Lutu and Busama-Awasa, because of the present ill-feeling, deny that they are cousins despite the evidence of the pedigrees that they themselves supply. They shrugged their shoulders at me, saying, 'Never mind your papers: we are now *laudung*.' Similarly, if a person can manage without the help of the marginal kin of his parents he dismisses them as strangers.[1]

[1] Cf. the situation among the Tikopia and the African Nuer and Tonga. In Tikopia 'the survival of kinship bonds is dependent upon active social contact between the persons concerned. Tikopia is too small a community for kinship ties to be entirely lost. . . . Here there are no strangers; there are merely peripheral kinsfolk' (R. Firth, 1936, p. 266). To a Nuer native 'ultimately and potentially everybody is kin, or can be made to appear so if circumstances demand. This is understandable in a society where kinship values are the only guide to interpersonal relations. When

GRADES OF KINSHIP

Relationships are so often a topic of conversation that nearly every adult can without difficulty name all eight of his or her great-grandparents and list those of their descendants who survived to produce children. Many of the men are able to go a generation further back still, and my 'nephew' Gi'lahi when only about twenty-two named eleven of his great-great-grandparents and the descendants of the whole sixteen. Marriage between distant cousins of certain types is permitted, and in a set of genealogies of this kind several persons crop up more than once. On the other hand, a few of those regarded as relatives may not appear. When I asked how they fitted into the scheme the answer sometimes was that they were related to So-and-so, a known kinsman of the speaker, and that therefore all must be descended from the same remote forbear. But frequently I received a detailed exposition; though, considering that in every case the common ancestor turned out to be a great-great-great-grandfather, the accuracy of the accounts is questionable. Gi'lahi's reply to my enquiry about his relationship with his neighbour Taho was typical. His own mother was So-and-so, her father So-and-so, this man's father So-and-so, and that man's mother So-and-so. This woman's mother had lived a long time ago, he continued, and he was unaware of her name; but he knew that she had a sister, born of the same parents, and that this sister had had a son; the son's daughter was So-and-so, who had a son So-and-so; and this was Taho's father. On that reckoning the two were fourth cousins, as I had learned to expect that they would be.

The Busama divide their cognates into two categories according to genea-logical propinquity. They define 'near cognates' as a person's grandparents, his grandparents' children and grandchildren, his parents' grandchildren, and his own grandchildren (that is to say, his paternal and maternal grand-parents, his parents, his uncles and aunts on both sides, his brothers and sisters, his first cousins, his children, his nephews and nieces, and his grand-children). There is no word in the language to describe them as a whole, but he can refer to himself and any one or more of them as 'one blood' (*da-tigeng*: *da* = 'blood', *tigeng* = 'one'). The corresponding expression for him-self and any one or more of his remaining cognates is best translated as 'one stem' (*hu-tigeng*: *hu* = 'stem of a plant', 'trunk of a tree', 'foundation', 'cause'). Other people employ the terms in similar fashion. They say that a set of brothers, for instance, or a man and his nephews, are *da-tigeng* and that a pair of distant cousins, or a man and his great-nephews, are *hu-tigeng*.

No two persons, however many *da-tigeng* cognates they may share at the

a man has constant intercourse with another it is . . . necessary that each be in some category of kinship in respect of the other so that each may have a rough-and-ready guide to the kind of behaviour expected of him and which he may expect from the other' (E. E. Evans-Pritchard, 1951, p. 176). The basic Tonga formulation is: 'those who help one another in a particular fashion are relatives, and those who do not so help one another are to be considered unrelated' (E. Colson, 1958, p. 20).

beginning of their lives, finish up in their declining years with quite the same full set. Even brothers and sisters then differ with respect to their grandchildren. The situation can be envisaged as a series of intersecting circles each with a single individual at its centre.

All cognates and affines are expected to be mutually loyal and helpful. If somebody is engaged in a major undertaking that demands many workers over a period of weeks, every one of them is present for a part of the time. But the obligations of *da-tigeng* cognates alone are absolutely binding, and they trust each other almost implicitly. A man guilty of constant misbehaviour may find in the end that he has tried the patience of his near cognates beyond endurance, but in ordinary circumstances he knows that he can rely on their sympathy and support. If he is ill, they will nurse him; if wild pigs have destroyed a ripening crop, they will offer him taro to tide him over till another garden is ready for harvesting; if he is short of money, they will give him as much as they can afford (a returned labourer divides part of his wages among his near cognates); if he wants a special tool that is hard to come by, and none of them has one, they will borrow to see that he is supplied; if he requires the services of a specialist craftsman, the near cognate with the expert knowledge will carry out the job for nothing; when the time comes for him to marry, those who are senior to him will find him a spouse; and if he has been wronged, they will stand by him and give weight to his accusations.

In olden days *da-tigeng* cognates meant even more to one another. First, because of the poor tools, a man needed help for the simplest tasks. Then a youth on reaching marriageable age looked to his senior close relatives not only to secure him a wife but also to furnish the bulk of the dogs' teeth and foodstuffs that made up the bride price. A girl depended equally on her senior *da-tigeng* relatives to find her a husband, and in her case they received the biggest share of the payments. The *da-tigeng* cognates also played a more active part in the settlement of grievances. Personal retaliation without weapons was customary, and the injured man and his near kinsfolk went to the house of the wrongdoer to demand satisfaction. Finally, the *da-tigeng* cognates had the responsibility for organizing vengeance against outsiders. The natives attributed most of their misfortunes to magic, and when somebody died as a result of what we would accept as illness or misadventure, it was the task of the near relatives to engage a specialist magician to identify the foreign sorcerer. Once this information was available they called a public meeting to discuss how he should be killed. Usually they argued in favour of spearing him, but the more cautious village seniors, fearful of the vendetta that might follow, sometimes counselled them instead to take the safer course of performing counter sorcery. If, nevertheless, a raid was approved, all the dead man's cognates and affines (excluding only those who were also related to the sorcerer) had to join in the expedition.[1]

[1] M. Gluckman, 1954, pp. 74, 75, pointed out that in Africa membership of the

THE HOUSEHOLD

This group consists of the people who live together under one roof. A man, his wife, and his young children form the core, bu: there may be additional residents. Most frequently we find the unmarried or recently married sons of the man's sisters. Others likely to be included are the unmarried sons or daughters of his deceased brothers, one or both of his aged parents, one or both of his aged parents-in-law, and his unmarried sisters or sisters-in-law. The youths and elderly men go off at night to sleep in a club house but are always regarded as belonging to the household.

The more important a man is in village affairs the larger his household will be. The most numerous during my visits was that of Ahipum. In 1948 it was made up of himself, his wife, their eight children, his sister's son, his mother-in-law, his wife's orphaned niece, a son of one of his wife's sisters and this man's spouse, and an ex-indentured labourer from Madang, 150 miles to the north-west, who many years ago had elected to make Busama his home. He had worked on the same plantation as one of Ahipum's mother's brothers, and at the end of their term of indenture this man had persuaded him to migrate. On arrival in Busama the sponsor had treated him as a brother and found him a wife, who subsequently died. Ahipum has always regarded him as a maternal uncle.

The household carries out the jobs necessary for the satisfaction of day-to-day needs. In gardening, for example, although the preliminary clearing, and the fencing later, require extensive co-operation, the actual cultivation—the planting, weeding, and harvesting—are household matters. In fishing also the males of the household often act together. If on a particular occasion they have not done so, each makes a separate contribution to the family larder. The women prepare the meals, which are mostly eaten by the group in company, though sometimes the men have their platters of food brought across to one of the club houses.

Personal property, even if individually owned, is in the main a household concern. As a rule the head consults his wife and elder sons before killing his pigs or selling them, and returned labourers regularly hand him some of their earnings to buy tools and clothing for all. Once purchased, the various items are allocated to particular members, but a good deal of borrowing takes place among them.

Legal responsibility within the household rests with the head. He sues for damages in the informal village court on behalf of dependants who have been injured or insulted and is in turn sued on account of their misconduct. At such times he can rely on the support of all the *da-tigeng* cognates of the person directly concerned.

blood-revenge group seldom coincided with the local group. In Melanesia, though there were exceptions, generally blood revenge was carried out jointly by the members of the dead man's local group and his kinsfolk living elsewhere.

PROPERTY

A Busama male must share everything that he himself received from his predecessors with the sons of his sisters but can if he likes bequeath the goods he has obtained through his own efforts to his sons. Today rights to land alone are transmitted in the female line, and it is with these, and the groups through which they are exercised, that I shall be mainly concerned. The heirloom chattels of the past need not delay us, but a word or two may be said about magical and religious rituals, also regarded as property and in earlier times handed on according to the same principles.[1]

Some of the ceremonies were concerned with such routine activities as agriculture, fishing, hunting, and ministering to the sick. The details of the different performances varied, but probably most men learned from their maternal uncles how to enlist supernatural aid to promote the growth of a crop, to safeguard a palmgrove or garden from thieves and insect pests, to bring a good haul of fish, and to relieve pain and illness. Those who did not know what to do sought the services of someone more knowledgeable than themselves. They paid him no fee if he was a *da-tigeng* cognate but offered him a few dogs' teeth or a little food if he was not.

Other rituals, designed to benefit the community, were carried out by specialists. There was a priest to make the sacrifices whereby the goodwill of the spirits might be secured, a war magician to bring victory to the warriors, and a weather magician to protect those engaged in overseas voyages. The war and weather magicians had a further duty: the former organized and led the raiding parties, the latter the trading expeditions. Succession to all three offices, depending as it did on matrilineal inheritance, was itself matrilineal.

Land is considered to be of three main types. Two of these are common property and can be dismissed in a few words. First there is the area on which the houses stand. Anyone who was born a member of the community, or has been accepted into it, has the right to build his dwelling where he likes so long as he does not cause inconvenience to others. He is expected to keep clear of the public pathways and the springs, and if he wants to be near the beach it is felt that he ought to take care not to block the breeze from the buildings that are already occupied. He may also be asked to go elsewhere if he has inadvertently chosen a spot where someone's ancestors are buried. Nowadays the dead are taken to the cemetery, but in former times they were interred alongside the place where they had been living. A few villagers still feel that these old graves should be preserved from desecration, particularly by persons who are not descended from the occupants.

[1] The Busama have abandoned their traditional magico-religious system but not their belief in the efficacy of pagan rites. Many of the natives are still afraid of sorcery, and rumours sometimes circulate that a returned labourer has brought with him spells of black magic purchased from fellow workers on the plantation. I do not know whether such gossip is founded on fact but have positive evidence that young men while in employment spend money on love magic.

Each villager, too, is allowed to plant coconut palms and fruit trees on the open spaces between the houses. These come into the category of goods acquired by personal effort and on the man's death descend to his sons. Palms bear nuts for only about seventy years, and fruit trees have an even shorter life. The question of further inheritance therefore seldom arises.

The remote forest, at a distance greater than about two hours' walk, is also owned by the members of the community, and they all hunt and collect the wild products without hindrance.

The land between the village and the deep forest is different. It is divided into a series of named sections, the major rights in which are vested in matrilineal descent groups.

As we know already, the early settlers in Busama are reputed to have found the country almost unoccupied. It is said that each new arrival selected ground for himself and his heirs and that within a generation nothing within reasonable distance was left unclaimed. The estimate of needs was always generous, and the average estate would have supported more than a dozen large families. It consisted of strips of lowland near the coast for planting coconuts; patches of sago swamp; tracts in the near valleys and on the surrounding slopes for cultivating taro, bananas, and green vegetables; and bush as a source of timber for houses and canoes. The first owner, as he had taken the areas by his own efforts and not received them from his forbears, was able to leave them to his sons. The latter, however, being inheritors, were obliged to share them with their uterine nephews and thus became the founders of a matrilineal lineage (matrilineal lineages if they were the offspring of different mothers). Such a group nowadays includes about six householders of mature years, together with a few young people, all of whom trace their descent in the female line through five generations from a single ancestor or a set of full brothers, allegedly the offspring of the original founder.

THE LINEAGE

The men of the group control the ground acquired by the founder (or founders if there were two sons or more). The most senior has sufficient authority by virtue of his kinship status to take charge on the rare occasions when a leader is necessary, and it is his responsibility also to see that agreement is reached concerning particular demands, as, for example, if two households are simultaneously looking for a suitable patch for a coconut grove. Subject to this restriction, the lineage members are free to go where they please. Further, each one can invite any of his cognates from outside, or any of his affines, to make gardens with him. The visitors would have to leave if a member disapproved of their presence, but such objection is unlikely. Their use of a few plots is purely temporary, and after the harvest the rights revert back to the lineage.

The story of the founding of the various settlements suggests that in the past people left their lineage territory either because the pressure of population had become too great or because they feared the consequences after a *da-tigeng* cognate had committed a serious offence. Apparently such persons, once firmly established elsewhere, abandoned their interests in the land they had previously cultivated. Today there are no fresh areas to be taken up, and a man retains the rights that he acquired at birth. A labourer may spend a decade in European employment and return home assured of his rightful place; and the sons of a woman who has married into another settlement, should they wish to join her brothers, can depend on being received on the same footing as the other nephews.

The problem of the voluntary alienation of land has so far not arisen. The Government has laws to regulate the sale or lease of areas to Europeans, but it is certain that nobody from outside the lineage would interfere if a white man sought to acquire a block for a plantation or some other purpose.

Till now all that has happened is that occasionally lineages have admitted a native foreigner and let him share their rights. A stranger who seeks entry into the community, as was explained, must find a sponsor who will treat him as a brother. The members of the sponsor's lineage then signify their acceptance of the newcomer by working out their appropriate relationship to him. Yet he is never completely incorporated into the group and cannot hope to assume the rôle of leader or act as an intermediary for other outsiders. His kinsfolk-by-adoption also expect that he will use discretion when issuing invitations to other people.

Investigation of the three cases that have occurred during the last twenty years revealed that none of the sponsors had sought permission beforehand for his action. Each one had assumed, rightly as things turned out, that his own willingness to bring a new brother into his family was a sufficient recommendation. At the same time, the members of the lineage insist that they could have vetoed the arrangement had they felt unhappy about it.

There is no word in the native language for the lineage, and enquiries have to be phrased in some such terms as, 'Who makes gardens here without any risk of being expelled?' Possibly the lack is to be explained by the fact that the members never become visible as a separate entity. Unlike lineage mates in many societies, they do not form a political faction, a blood-revenge group, or a group that arranges the marriages. They are united solely by their joint concern with certain areas of land, and even in agriculture they do not work alone. When new gardens are planned they first decide which section is to be cleared, and each then asks some of his other relatives whether they wish to come. On the day appointed for the job to begin the nucleus of half a dozen expands to as many as fifteen or perhaps even twenty.

RELATIONS WITH THE FATHER'S LINEAGE

It will now be clear why so many households include some of the man's youthful uterine nephews. These boys have rights in the same areas of land,

and he likes to have them as companions from adolescence onwards. They also are aware of the advantages of working at his side and thereby learning how to make the best use of the different sections. Some lads prefer to remain for the time being in their father's household, but after marriage over half the young men build their dwelling alongside that of a maternal uncle. Those who stay on, rather more than a quarter, are mostly youngest sons of large families. If two or three brothers have moved across to uncles it is felt that the last-born has a heavy responsibility to his parents in their declining years. Another common explanation is that the uncles all died prematurely; or perhaps the only one to survive is notoriously bad-tempered. The choice of residence, however, does not lie exclusively be-tween the father and the maternal uncles. As I have mentioned, people can live where they like. Roughly one-eighth select a site near the house of the father-in-law, brother-in-law, or some distant cognate of whom they have become specially fond.

Moving from the parental home does not mean a loosening of the tie with the father. The natives are always stressing the strength of filial affection. To ram the point home, my 'brother' Nga'gili' held two fingers of his left hand close together and said, 'There, that is sister's son and mother's brother.' Then, bringing up his right hand, he entwined the first and second fingers and added, 'But that is the son and his father.' Other people assured me that the uncle has to make a deliberate effort to win the boys over. This aim was more readily achieved in the past. The old initiation ceremonies had the effect of separating the initiand from his father and making him realize that he had obligations to a wide circle of kinsfolk.

Paternal devotion is equally deep. The accepted explanation for the divided inheritance is the love of fathers for their children. People say that once everything had to be passed on to the nephews, but the men went to such lengths to divert personal property to their sons that eventually the rule was changed by general agreement. This event is supposed to have taken place in ancient times, possibly during the period when only Bukawa' was settled.

The theory of conception provides a further indication of the attachment. Many matrilineal societies exaggerate the rôle of the mother, but the Busama, despite their matrilineages, practically ignore her. The womb, they say, is 'just a container where seed planted by the man can begin to grow'. They also deny that she supplies the embryo with nourishment, citing the cessation of her menses as proof. Menstruation is looked upon as the outward sign that a woman is capable of conceiving, and it is ex-plained that the flow stops of its own accord after pregnancy has occurred. And without blood, people ask, how can the foetus be fed?

The average villager has half his gardens with his lineage mates on the land over which he and they exercise the principal rights, but the strength of the bond with the father ensures that some of the remainder will be with the members of the father's group. I took a representative sample of men whose father was still living and investigated the twelve gardens that each had made most recently (this meant a study over a period of approximately two years). In nearly every case six of the twelve gardens were located on the man's own lineage lands, two on his father's lineage lands, and four on the lineage lands of various of his other cognates and affines. The link with the members of the father's group loses some of its force after his death, and the figure then drops to slightly over one in the twelve.

Even a son who chooses to build his house close to his father's does not cultivate exclusively with the father's lineage members. As a rule, for every six gardens that the son makes with these people, he has two with his own lineage members. The number with the remaining cognates and the affines stays relatively constant at about four in twelve.

Such a son acts with his father's group as a privilege and not as a right and has no prospect of being absorbed into it. His position is similar to that of a sponsored stranger in that he is allowed to make gardens on the lineage lands but would be unacceptable either as a leader or as a sponsor for someone else.[1]

In theory the members of the father's lineage are entitled to protest against his favouring a son at their expense; in practice they never so much as criticize him behind his back. His sister's sons could hardly complain openly as they and the son have to treat one another with the utmost courtesy; but the rest explain that there is land to spare and all relatives are welcome to the temporary use of some of it. The members of the son's own lineage may occasionally murmur among themselves but are too sensitive to air their grievance in public. They feel that they would look silly if they demanded his continued presence, especially when they can easily obtain all the help they need for clearing and fencing.

Villagers not directly concerned refrain from interfering, but some of the older men express misgivings lest the practice of remaining with the father should increase. I have referred to the initiation ceremonies, when the youths were, in the social sense, weaned from their parents. The seniors feel that the loss of discipline consequent on the disappearance of the pagan rites may lead to a lowering of standards. At present such anxiety is probably misplaced, though it might well be justified if another type of agriculture were to be attempted. Inevitably new perennial crops like rubber and cocoa cause social dislocation in a community having a system of matrilineal inheritance.[2] The men plant the trees on the land of their descent group but want to transmit it to their sons. The Busama have had

---

[1] In Hogbin, 1951, p. 108, in a section with the title 'Irregular Descent', which I now realize to have been misleading, I stated that 'the only limitation on a man's participation in the rights of his father's group is that he can never become the head and superintend the work'. When I wrote this passage I was unaware of the additional handicap. The references in that book to the son's being 'incorporated' into his father's lineage are also to be discounted. He is merged to the extent here indicated and no further.   [2] See Hogbin, 1958, pp. 146–9.

some experience of the problem. We saw that the coconut palms a man grows on his lineage ground are inherited according to patrilineal principles. But a coconut grove covers a small area, is productive for a comparatively short time, and in this part of New Guinea does not yield a cash return. The difficulties would be more serious with plantations run on commercial lines.

WOMEN'S RIGHTS

Women, because they are the media through which their brothers' land rights descend, can legitimately be regarded as members of the same lineage. They also have rights of their own, though these depend solely on family relationships. A wife is entitled to expect that her husband will put sufficient plots at her disposal for the support of themselves and their children. But her brothers retain an interest in her welfare and, in addition, are vitally concerned about her sons. Accordingly, these brothers from time to time invite her husband to make a garden with them, and on other occasions, even if he has taken no part in the clearing, they may give her a small strip to plant. If she is widowed, or her husband has become an invalid, though the prime responsibility for her care now rests with his brothers and, as soon as they are old enough, her sons, her brothers offer still more help.

A woman owns little personal property—generally not more than a few shillings in cash, clothing, and the household utensils actually in use (clay pots and wooden bowls held for export belong to the husband). On her death the daughters divide the goods equally.

LAND RIGHTS AND IMMIGRATION

The admission of a male stranger has already been discussed. He secures a sponsor and, despite certain disadvantages, is then allowed to cultivate lineage land. If his sponsor arranges a marriage for him with a local woman, as is customary, the difficulties disappear in the next generation. His sons become full members of the lineage of their maternal uncles.

The position of the sons of a local man who has taken a foreign wife is less fortunate. Such lads have nobody in the village from whom land rights can be legally acquired. One solution is for them to depart at the age of puberty or thereabouts to the place whence their mother came. They can then link up with her brothers, though at the price of daily contact with the patrilateral kin. If instead they decide to stay they are sure of the privilege of being allowed to cultivate with the father. Their heirs in turn have the same sort of second-class citizenship. The handicap is so far recognized that nowadays the people often quote it as a reason for discouraging unions with women from elsewhere. Earlier a foreign marriage must often have been a useful method of guaranteeing outside aid in time of war; but once fighting ceased the need for allies disappeared. I have discovered no lineage with attached members of the third generation, and it may be assumed that eventually the genealogies are altered, perhaps unconsciously, to permit the full absorption of the alien bride's daughters' daughters' sons.

CONTRACTION AND EXPANSION OF LINEAGES

Two further questions remain: what happens when a lineage dies out; and when it increases to an unwieldy size? For neither is there a set answer.

Natives if asked about lineages disappearing at first deny the possibility. When pressed they agree that such a judgment is perhaps too sweeping; but they mostly add that never in their experience has such a thing occurred. I was obliged to suggest that they give me their ideas about a likely solution for the problem. The consensus of opinion was that today the sons of the last members to die would make a claim to the vacant sections and eventually bequeath them to their sons, who would thus become the founders of another lineage. Some people thought that in the past the same procedure would have been followed, but others believed that in those days the traditional headman would have had sufficient prestige to intervene. They felt that he might have chosen to hold the land in trust until such time as a stranger appeared to replace the extinct group. In those days such a man would have been an asset to the fighting forces of the village.

Formerly when a lineage became unduly large it seems that some of the members sought out territory that was either virtually unoccupied or ill defended, established a settlement there, carved the land into sections, and passed them on to their sons, who founded more lineages. Often a migrant maintained contact with the people who had stayed behind, but as he and his heirs no longer made gardens with them, the old land rights lapsed. In time the names must also have disappeared from the lineage genealogies. The process of group formation can be described as 'division with a remainder'.[1] Individuals split off from the unit into which they were born and became responsible for the formation at one remove of new units. The original unit went on, and the others preserved no special links with it or with one another.[2]

This prompts a query as to the trustworthiness of genealogies as a measure of the period during which a group has been in existence. Nowhere are they remembered for this purpose: they are valued as a quasi-legal charter for certain social relationships. So far anthropological analysis has been confined to communities in which each lineage is a segment of

[1] To be distinguished from 'segmentation' ('the process by which any social group becomes subdivided internally while retaining its own unity and cohesion') and from 'fission' ('the process by which a group divides into two or more distinct groups, so that the original group disappears as a social entity'). The definitions are from J. A. Barnes, 1954, p. 57.

[2] In some parts of Melanesia a 'mother-daughter' relationship is kept up between the old group and the new groups. These latter may also be in a 'sister' relationship with one another. (See H. I. Hogbin and C. H. Wedgwood, 1952-4, pp. 70, 71.)

another of a higher order. Here the genealogies are primarily a basis for the relations between the groups of the hierarchy, and we can say definitely that as a time scale they are unreliable. The people have been observed stretching, telescoping, and otherwise adjusting them so that groups at the same level of segmentation remain constant in depth.[1] Every horizontal series of lineages fits into a lineage above, and the formal pyramidal structure is preserved.

Busama lineages, however, are unsegmented, and the genealogies are concerned with the relations not between groups but between the individual members. If it is of no social significance whether a lineage is five generations deep or ten, there is no reason for deliberate alteration, and we might have expected that the lineages in Lutu, reputedly an earlier settlement, would be deeper by at least a couple of generations. In fact they go back the same distance. On the other hand, the earliest Lutu ancestors recorded are not thought of as being the sons of Bukawa' migrants; moreover, the Lutu lineages tend to be larger than those of Busama. It thus seems that the names of remote forbears are forgotten rather than wilfully suppressed. Unfortunately I have never had the opportunity for visiting the north side of the Huon Gulf and so cannot give the depth of the Bukawa' lineages.

Today the establishment of further villages is impossible. This is in some ways unfortunate, as we have seen, for Busama is already too big for the comfort of the inhabitants. Yet they suffer no material hardship. The ancestors over-estimated their needs, and as a result everyone still exercises rights over areas more than sufficient for the maintenance of his family. Now that raiding has ceased he can also, with safety if not convenience, cultivate sections at a greater distance from home. I suspect, too, that the disappearance of the pagan ceremonies and their accompanying feasts, when much food rotted before it could be eaten, has been responsible for a shrinkage in the size of the gardens. Perhaps in the future, as further expansion takes place, the lineages will break into smaller units, but there is at present no evidence of a general tendency towards fission.

An incident that occurred in 1949 should be mentioned here, though it was unusual and cannot be regarded as a pointer. The Busama, who have more land than the residents of many other villages, regard the inner valley of the Buang River as theirs. The area is a very long way from the settlement and in 1945 had been covered with heavy jungle growth. I did not inspect it closely then but was assured that there were lineage sections as in the other valleys. Four years later one of the Gaidemoe communities requested permission to cultivate a portion. The Busama seniors held a meeting to consider the proposal, and in the discussion the fact emerged that such an interval had elapsed since gardens had been made along the Buang that literally not one person could recall the boundaries. Eventually, after much argument, the people decided to allocate a site to the Gaidemoe,

[1] See M. Fortes, 1953, pp. 27, 28. Cf. R. F. Salisbury, 1956a.

Part of the beach at Busama. Looking northwards towards Schneider Point

2

(*a*) Preparing the evening meal

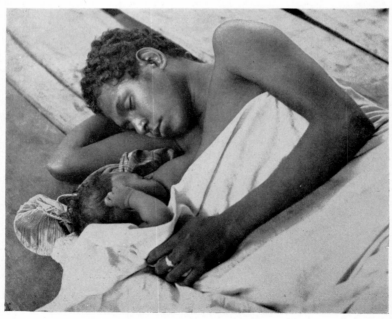

(*b*) A mother and her infant son

with limits clearly fixed, and throw the remainder open to the first-comers from among themselves. The soil, untilled for possibly two generations or more, proved to be excellent, and within a couple of months each house-holder had chosen several sections, for himself and his sons in the first instance (sometimes for himself, his sons, his brothers, and their sons) but ultimately for his daughters' sons. He established his claim by cutting down a few saplings, often without the immediate intention of planting. Invari-ably there was an obvious landmark in the vicinity, such as a tributary stream, a bend in the river, or a tall ficus tree. By January 1950 a strip several hundred yards wide and a mile deep had been taken up. The action may lead to smaller lineages nesting inside the present groups, but the valley is so far that probably the natives will again leave it until the recent allocation has been forgotten.

THE LINEAGE AND THE PAGAN RELIGIOUS SYSTEM

Every set of sections cultivated by a lineage includes a spot that is unusual on account of its gloom, chill atmosphere, or danger—a cave with a fern-covered entrance, a waterfall drenched with cold spray, a lonely pool where a stray crocodile might be lurking, or a steep precipice. Formerly each of these places was considered to be the abode of a colony of beings that we may refer to as the spirits of the land.

Normally invisible, land spirits occasionally took the form of a snake, lizard, or eel but were then easily recognizable by their varied colouring. Their breath was of the same hues and was from time to time to be seen in the sky as a rainbow. Unseasonable tempests were attributed to them, and they were supposed to be capable of causing disease and madness. Their attitude to women was unpredictable, and when offended they caused difficulties during childbirth.

Dangerous as these spirits were believed to be, it was thought that the colony dwelling at each sacred place had made a pact with the claimant of the associated areas to leave him, his heirs, and their guests unmolested provided these people took special precautions in their relations with women. Accordingly, the members of the lineage felled the timber and planted crops on the land over which they exercised rights convinced that they would enjoy protection. The only exception was when one of them had recently indulged in sexual intercourse. The spirits regarded a man with even the faint smell of a woman lingering about him as offensive, and a husband who had slept with his wife during the previous night therefore refrained from taking part in agriculture. (Women visited the gardens almost every day to gather food but incurred no penalties for having slept with the husband the night before.)

Persons who were neither lineage members nor invited guests, on the other hand, imagined that trespass would be fraught with peril. As out-siders, they were ignored in the pact and could expect no favours. Rem-nants of the fear are apparent to this day. Many people assume that the

C

village idiot, who lost his wits after a severe illness in 1938, owes his
condition to his having cut bamboo for a fishing rod in the vicinity of a
haunted forest pool in the section of another lineage.

A person who suspected that he might have aroused the wrath of the
spirits offered them a sacrifice. Generally he waited until he became ill,
and if he then recalled visiting a place where he had no business to be he
sent a message to the leader of the lineage. He begged the man's pardon and
handed him a few valuables with the request that these be taken to the
sacred spot. The leader accepted the apology and hung the goods on a
convenient tree for a few days. In that period the spirits took their essence,
and he then handed them back. Forgiveness was now assured, and a patient
who failed to recover concluded that his sickness had some other cause,
perhaps sorcery.

Storms were usual during July and August, but if there was bad weather
at any other time the people blamed the land spirits. When heavy seas day
after day made fishing impossible, or when flood rains threatened the crops,
it often happened that a leader who was especially partial to sea food, or
one who had found that the gardens of his lineage mates were in grave
danger, would try the effect of a sacrifice of pork. He killed a pig, carved it
ceremonially, and carried a plate of the meat to the sacred place. The rest
he gave to his followers and other kinsfolk. These occasional tempests
seldom lasted more than a week, and his action always appeared to have
achieved its object.

The natives also venerated the land spirits as the source of much of their
magic. They supposed that the beings had taught the spells to the ancestor
with whom the agreement was made. The formulae were a valuable part
of his fortune, and he transmitted them to his heirs along with his land
rights. As a mark of appreciation the lineage adopted the name of one of
the spirits as its battle cry and ceremonial greeting to kinsfolk from other
villages. The word was felt to have a peculiar appropriateness for rallying
purposes, but there was no thought of the call bringing supernatural aid
in time of danger. A warrior surrounded by the spears of enemies was
fortified by a reminder of the spirits of the land he cultivated and what
they had done for his ancestors.

The tie with the land spirits lasted for ever, and the souls of persons
whom they had protected in life were believed to take up residence with
them after death. The sacred places were thus doubly hallowed. The souls,
nevertheless, were clearly differentiated from the other spirits. Their supernatural power was as extensive but was exercised in another way. Ancestral
spirits never became incarnate as reptiles, and far from inconveniencing
mortals with wind and rain, they preferred to help them with large hauls
of fish and increased herds of pigs. A man who had had a good catch therefore repaid his lineage forbears with a sacrifice. Certainly the souls, like the
land spirits, sometimes inflicted the living with disease, but here again
there was a difference. They were concerned on such occasions with punish-

ing not trespass, which left them unmoved, but such breaches of custom as neglect of kinship obligations and the wilful setting aside of marriage rules; further, they ignored the actions of strangers and struck only at their descendants in the female line, the persons who normally were immune from the anger of the land spirits. Usually the offer of a pig was sufficient to appease their ill temper and secure a renewal of goodwill.

THE CLUB GROUP

New clubs have occasionally come into being, but the majority of the fourteen in Busama have a long history behind them. Till recently they also bore the traditional names said to have been derived from Bukawa'. The term *lum* is applied both to the building itself and to the collection of people, from sixteen to twenty male adults, who regularly congregate there.

Membership is determined by propinquity, geographical this time, not genealogical. A man uses the club nearest his dwelling and accordingly belongs with those who do likewise. But although he is permitted to live anywhere, personal considerations affect his choice. He may select a site alongside the house of a mother's brother, his father, a distant cognate, or an affine. Each club group is therefore made up of people related to one another in all sorts of ways. The bulk of them, nevertheless, are connected through females.

The most respected man in the club, though he receives no title, is looked up to as the head. His precise kinship relationship to his followers is not considered to be significant—the main factor is his natural gift for leadership.

People spend most of their spare time in their own club but often dally for an hour or two in some of the others. Indeed, male contemporaries, unless they are *da-tigeng* kin (brothers or first cousins), never enter one another's dwellings without an invitation and hence are obliged to transact nearly all their business in the club. A person who belongs to the same club as his maternal uncles is likely to visit that of his father frequently, whereas if he belongs to the same club as his father he is likely to be found quite often in that of his uncles. Some men even assert that they have two clubs, though the statement is inaccurate, and always their prime allegiance is to one.[1]

Women never set foot in a club house, and it is said that had they done so in pagan times they would have been killed as punishment for desecrating the sacred objects stored there. Yet they are included in the group. The men explain that 'a woman is part of the club to which she brings food and firewood'. This means that she is counted in the club group of her father or guardian before marriage and in that of her husband afterwards.

The club group, like the lineage, forms the nuclear body for certain types of heavy work, such as housebuilding and canoe construction, tasks

[1] Once it may have been correct. Before the introduction of proper bedding and mosquito nets a man could spend the night on a mat anywhere.

that occupy more time and call for more labourers than either clearing the
ground for new gardens or erecting the fences around them to keep out the
wild pigs.

A contrast with Africa should be especially noted.[1] The Busama club
group—and here there is another parallel with the Busama lineage—has
no political functions whatsoever. The members discuss village affairs
casually among themselves but never thrash things out in order to present
a united front. If the head makes a statement in support of some cause he
speaks as a private individual, not as the representative of a body of people.

THE CLUB GROUP AND THE PAGAN RELIGIOUS SYSTEM

Each club possessed two bullroarers as symbols of certain monsters that
were the object of a men's cult. One, considered to be male, gave out a low
booming note and the second, a female, a sound of higher pitch. The
surfaces of both were engraved with designs of mythological significance.
They were preserved in a carved bowl on a special shelf and when removed
for a ceremony were reverently painted with ochre and decorated with
coloured leaves and feathers.

The village priest summoned the monsters from their lair underground
on such occasions as the initiation of the youths to manhood. The clubmen
then carried their bullroarers to the bush nearby and twirled them on the
end of a long string. The noise signified that the supernatural beings were
waiting to devour any lad offered to them. Later, after a period for diges-
tion, he would be voided as an adult. The headmen also ordered the bullroarers to be produced some time before the bigger pagan feasts as a
warning that the pigs, coconuts, and bananas must not be touched. Again,
if the leader of some neighbouring community was ill or had died the
villagers took their bullroarers thither. They said that the monsters were
mourning because the man's kinsfolk had failed to take good care of him.

On certain occasions the bullroarers themselves were of special significance. A headman wishing to communicate officially with another village
entrusted one of them to his messenger. The object, because of its mystic
associations, gave the man immunity from attack, for to kill or wound him
would have been sacrilege. If two settlements agreed to make an alliance
they exchanged bullroarers to cement the relationship. Any subsequent
treachery was thought to bring down supernatural penalties.

AGE AND SEX GROUPING

Contemporaries, although not marked off formally into an age set, share
many interests and in consequence often forgather. The young children
are occupied with playtime gangs, the older children with schooling, the
youths with European employment, the recently-married men with problems arising out of the establishment of a new household, and the mature
men with weighty discussions on general village affairs. Probably school-

[1] Cf. M. Fortes and E. E. Evans-Pritchard, 1940, pp. 6, 7, 13, 14.

days and the fellowship of the labour compound provide the strongest links, and an enquiry as to why two men only distantly related to one another have chosen to garden or fish side by side nearly always brings forth the reply that they had been classmates or wage-earning companions. Conversely, near kinsmen who are less often associated than is proper gloss over their temperamental incompatibility and offer as an excuse that they were in different classes or had different employers.

The senior men of the community (*nga'-atu*, literally 'big men') are still influential. In the New Guinea of today this is the exception. Everywhere in earlier times the members of the older generation exercised authority by virtue of their ownership of the bulk of the wealth, their familiarity with the accumulated wisdom of the past, and their knowledge of the pagan ritual on which well-being was believed to depend. In the average modern village, however, the young men alone bring in the most prized valuable, money, and it is they also who have the experience, limited though this may be, of the world of the Europeans. Further, by accepting Christianity they have acquired the means of achieving their own salvation. As a rule therefore conflicts between old and young are a commonplace. In Busama such struggles rarely occur. The Mission may have unwittingly deprived the seniors of one weapon, but they retain the rest. Lae is so handy that they can not only become financially independent by selling produce in the market or taking casual employment but also learn something at first hand about Western industrial civilization.

In Busama, too, the social distinction between the sexes is less rigid than in some societies. In the central highlands, for instance, and likewise in parts of the Sepik district of western New Guinea, males and females are respectively in a state of mastery and subordination: in Busama they are in balanced opposition. The women attend all the important gatherings even if they sit by themselves and refrain from contributing to the discussions, and they always make the most of the occasion when a baby is born. At such times housewives carrying vessels of broth and hot water brush the men aside, saying derisively to one another as they do so that, of course, had God seen fit to make husbands share the pangs of childbirth the village would long ago have ceased to exist.

In the economic sphere each sex has separate tasks to perform. There is no longer a religious taboo on the one doing work ordinarily allocated to the other, but the emergency seldom arises, for if a man is ill his wife can depend on receiving help from his or her brothers, and if a woman is ill her husband expects aid from his or her sisters. Women's jobs are chiefly centred on the hearth. They look after the dwelling, take care of the young children, and cook the everyday meals. Men's jobs, on the other hand, take them far afield. They fish, hunt, trade, and collect bush timber for the houses and canoes. Both are concerned with agriculture, but the really arduous part—the clearing, fencing, and digging—always falls to the men, while the women do the planting, weeding, and harvesting. Because the house is the scene of so much of the women's life they always entertain female guests there: men prefer to take their guests to the club.

Probably the only serious disadvantage a woman suffers is that in the legal sense she is a minor. She cannot sue or be sued except through her male guardian, exercise major rights over important property, or hold any office.

Mention has been made of the old initiation ceremonies. The question to be decided is whether the youths were introduced primarily into an age group or primarily into a sex group. The rites ceased nearly forty years before my arrival, and only two elderly villagers, both of them now dead, had passed through. The account I collected was therefore so fragmentary that I cannot give a positive answer. My impression is that a dual purpose was aimed at but with slightly greater emphasis on age. This conclusion is backed up by negative evidence from Wogeo, in the Sepik district, where the sexual side receives the stress. The Wogeo men when initiating a youth concentrate on hoaxing the women and refrain from inflicting hardships upon him; yet they take sticks and stones to the female half of the population when the women are initiating a girl after her first menstruation. The behaviour of the Busama was the direct opposite. They ignored the women's reactions and the initiation of girls and devoted their energy to making the youths suffer.

My reconstruction of Busama initiation will be found elsewhere,[1] and I shall restrict myself here to a brief summary. A boy was supposed to go through when he reached the threshold of manhood, at about the age of eighteen. So much food had to be collected, however, that the ceremonies could only be held at intervals of a decade. A number of youths were admitted together, and while some were only fifteen, others were twenty-four. Each one accepted the offer of some young kinsman who had been initiated on the previous occasion to act as his companion and supporter. When the day came this man carried the lad to a hut that had been specially prepared in the bush. Throughout their journey the elders belaboured them with firebrands, sticks tipped with obsidian, and nettles. They arrived covered with blood and were received by a pair of guardians. A period of seclusion followed, during which the boys had to undergo a series of trials. They were beaten, starved, deprived of sleep, partially suffocated, and almost roasted. Water was forbidden, and if thirsty they had to chew sugar-cane. Only the coarsest foods were allowed, and even these were left raw. All the time the guardians gave them instructions about kinship responsibilities and duties to their seniors. At length, after some months, the priest summoned the supernatural monsters from underground while the other men sounded the bullroarers. The guardians now taught their charges how to incise the penis in order to eliminate the contamination resulting from association with the other sex. Subsequently this operation had to be performed regularly. A series of great feasts then took place, and

[1] Hogbin, 1951, pp. 216–21.

the initiands emerged richly decorated. The bond with the companion lasted for life. He was closer than an elder brother, and his demands took precedence over all others.

In some parts of Melanesia native history is kept alive by the residents of daughter villages sending their youths for initiation to the parent settlement. In Busama this was not the practice, and the local elders never despatched lads to Lutu or Bukawa'.

MELANESIAN SOCIAL STRUCTURE

In this section I propose to consider Busama structure comparatively. I shall confine myself to Melanesia but ignore the larger tribal societies of the central New Guinea highlands. Elsewhere the communities are all on the familiar minute scale.[1]

Throughout Melanesia cognates have mutual obligations, and everywhere the natives depend on their kinsfolk from both the father's side and the mother's side, though generally for different things. Yet in many places the social structure is based on unilineal descent. The commonest group is then not the lineage (still less the lineage segmented at four or five levels, as in parts of Africa[2]) but the clan, which may be either simple in form or divided into a single set of sub-clans.[3] Doubtless the reason is that the members of a tiny population take genealogical ties for granted and regulate their behaviour towards one another by reference to generation and order of birth.

A system of unilineal descent creates a bias. Where the male line is stressed not only is the person's own patrilineal clan, sub-clan, or lineage of the greatest significance to him, but he also tends to collaborate more often with the members of his mother's patrilineal clan, sub-clan, or lineage than with the rest of his cognates. Correspondingly, where the female line is stressed his own matrilineal clan, sub-clan, or lineage comes first, but usually the members of his father's matrilineal clan, sub-clan, or lineage count for more than his other cognates.

Land use, residence, and marriage (the last in a proscriptive sense) are all bound up with group membership. Rights to territory are exercised jointly, and a man has a claim on certain areas by virtue of his having been born into the unit with which they are traditionally associated. Frequently he and his fellows, for reasons of sentiment as well as convenience, live close by in a separate settlement or a separate ward within a settlement. Clans and lineages are exogamous, nevertheless, and wives must be obtained

---

[1] For a fuller treatment see Hogbin and Wedgwood, 1952–54.

[2] In the western Pacific polysegmentary lineages occur solely in the more densely settled parts of the New Guinea highlands; and even there they are not universal.

[3] A clan resembles a lineage except that the members cannot supply detailed information, real or imaginary, to support the contention that they are descended in one line from a common ancestor or ancestress. Often the founder is thought to have been a mythological figure.

from outside. In patrilineal communities the woman usually joins her
husband and his male patrilineal relatives, a form of residence known
as patri-virilocal; in matrilineal communities she usually joins her husband
and his male matrilineal relatives, a form of residence known as avunculo-
virilocal.[1]

Two main types of unilineal structure can be distinguished. In the first
each community is built up on a single clan, sub-clan, or lineage localized
in a separate settlement. If descent is patrilineal the males continue living
where they were born and the wives come in from other places. The natives
of the Orokaiva culture area of eastern New Guinea provide examples.[2]
But if descent is matrilineal both males and females have at some time to
move. In the Trobriand Islands children are reared in the village of the
father's matrilineal sub-clan but have land rights only in the village of their
mother's brothers' sub-clan. The sons go to the maternal uncles at puberty
and remain for the rest of their lives: the daughters go to the husband at
marriage.[3] In all systems of this kind, patrilineal or matrilineal, the people
of each community are necessarily united by a multiplicity of cognatic and
affinal ties to the residents of many other places. We can speak of the
individuals as having a broad social horizon.

In the second type of unilineal structure the communities consist of not
one but several patrilineal or matrilineal localized clans. Intra-community
marriage is accordingly possible and may be preferred. If so the wife when
she leaves her parents and enters her husband's household simply crosses
from one part of the settlement to another. The composition of the society
remains relatively constant, the links with outsiders are reduced to the
minimum, and the individuals tend to have a restricted social horizon. In
such cases the solidarity of the village is most marked; and so also is the
hostility towards other villages. The patrilineal Ngarawapum of the middle
Markham Valley are an appropriate illustration.[4]

In a variant of this type of structure the communities are made up of
several matrilineal sub-clans forming localized segments of dispersed clans.
A preponderance of intracommunity marriages would lead to settlement
isolation were it not for the wider clan organization, which is readily avail-

---

[1] A few communities are exceptional. In parts of matrilineal New Ireland the
husband has to join his wife's female matrilineal kinsfolk (matri-uxorilocal residence); and in matrilineal Dobu and some of the adjoining islands couples spend
alternate years with the man's and the woman's matrilineal kinsfolk (bilocal
residence).

These descriptive terms for residence patterns were first set out in Hogbin and
Wedgwood, op. cit., p. 250. They differ from those suggested by G. P. Murdock,
1949. It should be noted that Murdock applies 'bilocal' to a system that gives a
couple the choice of living with the man's or the woman's relatives. If I had thought
a descriptive term were necessary for this type of residence I would have used
'utrolocal' (cf. J. A. Barnes, 1960, p. 852).

[2] F. E. Williams, 1930, p. 102.

[3] B. Malinowski, 1929, pp. 6–10, 53, 54.

[4] K. E. Read, 1946, pp. 98–118; and 1950, pp. 185–223.

able to facilitate outside relationships as soon as the need arises. Thus the people are assured of hospitality from fellow clansmen when travelling away from home. The natives of the north coast of Guadalcanal fit into such a pattern. The same five matrilineal clans are respectively represented in every village by at least one sub-clan. The social horizon could be described as of intermediate range.[1]

Other Melanesian peoples have a structural system variously described as 'non-unilineal' (the term I prefer), 'bilateral', and 'cognatic'. The essential feature is the absence of clans, lineages, or any other group based on one line of descent. The men are free to choose where they will live, though usually within certain fixed limits, and marriage is permitted between every type of cousin beyond a determined range.

I stress the fact that the definition of a non-unilineal system refers only to the lack of patrilineal or matrilineal groupings. A society may have a non-unilineal structure and still recognize one or other line of descent for a particular purpose, perhaps the inheritance of personal property or the succession to titles.[2]

The details will emerge more clearly from a description. I shall take the To'ambaita of Malaita.[3]

The To'ambaita country is divided into districts or neighbourhoods capable of supporting up to about 200 natives. Inside the district boundaries a grove of trees is set apart as sacred, and here the bodies of dead residents are interred and their spirits worshipped with sacrifices. Each man has the right to erect a dwelling and cultivate the soil in any district where he has an ancestor buried—an ancestor in the male line, the female line, or a line traced through males and females indifferently. Youths and girls from the same district, provided they are not first cousins, are permitted to marry; but it seldom happens that a boy can find a partner of the right age from the few households round about. Husbands and wives mostly come therefore from different places. Social horizons are hence fairly broad, and the ordinary individual not only has relatives scattered over the countryside but is also at liberty to live near any of them and make his gardens alongside theirs. He may move after a quarrel or a series of misfortunes or if he develops an intimate bond with some remote cousin; but more often than not he stays in the settlement where he was brought up. It follows that usually the district group has a solid core of men related through males. These are given an inclusive name but are not entitled to any special privileges. The members of the local unit form a distinct community and work together under the direction of a headman. Yet each person can appeal to his other relatives if he requires help for some onerous task. The distant ties are reaffirmed when offerings are made to the ancestors. A

[1] Hogbin, 1934, pp. 237, 238.
[2] English society has a non-unilineal structure although a legitimate child takes the surname of his father and most hereditary titles descend in the male line.
[3] Hogbin, 1939a, pp. 25–9.

headman initiates the rite by announcing that he is about to honour those of his forefathers whose remains lie within the sacred grove of his district. The other descendants of these same ancestors, by whatever line of descent, are then free to come along with gifts. Later they all dance together and partake of a feast. Persons who live far away and for this or any other reason consistently fail to put in an appearance signify by their absence that they have relinquished their rights in the district lands. They soon cease to be regarded as relatives and ultimately are classed as strangers.

The To'ambaita depart in but one respect from the principle that all lines of descent are equal—personal property, including magical knowledge, passes from father to sons, or, if the man is childless, to the brothers' sons. The movables are not of much lasting value. The household goods have to be smashed; the weapons buried with the corpse; many of the trees cut down; and the pigs, garden produce, and a quantity of the ceremonial currency distributed at the funeral feast. The magic, on the other hand, is a permanent acquisition; moreover, some of the spells are tied up with leadership in such specialized activities as warfare. Accordingly, succession to a few minor offices follows the male line.

Clearly the Busama structure has features that are unusual. In some respects it resembles the Ngarawapum type: there is a set of discrete unilineal groups, generally husband and wife come from inside the settlement, and social horizons are restricted. Yet the villagers have less unilineal bias than might have been expected with such a system. Indeed, there is a similarity with the To'ambaita type of structure in that the clubs are non-unilineal groups. Then although each person collaborates in agriculture most often with the members of his own and his father's matrilineages, he recognizes that his heaviest obligations are to his *da-tigeng* cognates, a category that includes all his immediate kinsfolk irrespective of their lineage affiliations.

UNILINEAL AND NON-UNILINEAL SYSTEMS

Radcliffe-Brown stated that a majority of societies have built their structure on unilineal descent because clans and lineages possess the advantage of facilitating both the formulation of jural rights so as to avoid conflicts and also the preservation of the continuity of the structure that defines such rights.[1] Murdock quoted this view with approval and went on to say that a state of chaos may develop if the only structural group is the bilateral kindred. 'One kindred cannot . . . take blood vengeance against another if the two happen to have members in common. Moreover, a kindred cannot hold land or other property, not only because it is not a group except from the point of view of a particular individual, but also because it has no continuity over time. . . . A particular disadvantage of the kindred appears in the instance in which an individual belongs to the kindreds of two other

[1] A. R. Radcliffe-Brown, 1952, pp. 46, 47 (reprinted from *Iowa Law Review*, Vol. XX).

persons and thereby becomes involved in conflicting or incompatible obligations. If they get into serious difficulties with one another . . . he may be required to avenge the one and yet defend the other. If they become estranged, both are likely to turn to him for support and to subject him to emotional conflict and strain.'[1]

Despite Radcliffe-Brown's assurance, it is problematical whether on the final reckoning societies with unilineal descent groups will be found to predominate. Anthropologically speaking the greater part of Melanesia, for instance, is *terra incognita*. But even if this guess proves correct it is still true that millions of people (including Europeans in the Old World, the Americas, and Australia) manage satisfactorily with non-unilineal systems.

Murdock was on firmer ground when he spoke of the bilateral kindred, though he apparently failed to realize that there is no necessary connection between an absence of clans and lineages and a condition of affairs in which all a person's cognatic ties have equal value for the same things. A To'ambaita native may be a potential member of several district groups, but at any given moment he belongs to one only. Further, in spite of the element of choice, these groups are eternal in just the same way that clans and lineages are eternal. It could also be argued that divided loyalties, far from having a disruptive influence, actually help to preserve peace and harmony. A man torn between the claims of two disputing kinsmen is likely to plead with them to compose their differences as speedily as possible and without bloodshed. If, nevertheless, he takes a definite stand at the side of one, then certainly among the To'ambaita—and possibly elsewhere—he can avail himself of a rite that expiates the offence of violating his responsibilities to the other. (Usually in such circumstances the geographical rather than the genealogical factors triumph.) Finally, from personal experience in both places, I must insist that the non-unilineal To'ambaita communities work no less smoothly than the unilineal communities of Guadalcanal a few miles away.

More recently Goodenough tried to find a connection between structure and demography.[2] Unilineal groups are likely to be associated with sparse population and non-unilineal with dense population, he said. Clans and lineages fluctuate in size and within a generation can halve or double. A diminishing unit may own far more ground than is needful, and simultaneously another that is expanding may not have enough to go round. Such anomalies, and the quarrels that result from them, are avoided,

[1] G. P. Murdock, 1949, p. 61.

[2] W. H. Goodenough, 1955, pp. 71–82. In 1962, when this book was already in the press, Goodenough went further and offered 'environmental instability and recurring disaster' (for example, volcanic eruptions and epidemic diseases) as probable reasons for the development of non-unilineal groupings resembling the Busama club (W. H. Goodenough, 1962, pp. 5–12). The paper makes a useful distinction between non-unilineal structures where group membership depends upon descent and those where it is determined by contemporary relationships, but the explanation suggested for the structures of this latter type is to me reminiscent of Kipling's Just-so stories.

Goodenough maintained, if rights come down in many lines and a man is permitted to pick his group according to the amount of land available.

Records of rainfall and soil composition are so scanty that it is seldom possible to say with confidence that any particular Melanesian island, or part of an island, is under- or over-populated. But even if more of this sort of information were obtainable, the hypothesis, in its present form, would hardly be capable of proof. Native attitudes must always be of greater significance than the casual judgments of an outside observer, no matter how disinterested. If prestige depends on food supply, as is universal in Melanesia, a man may be prepared to fight for extra plots when those he already cultivates could maintain a bigger household. Again, because clearing virgin forest is hard work, the natives often confine their gardening to the strips covered with lighter secondary growth. Hence land may appear to be plentiful when the villagers feel that it is scarce.

Goodenough also exaggerated the eagerness to seek logical solutions for the problems arising out of maladjusted institutions.[1] Most peoples resort to makeshifts. In Africa we know that genealogies and segmentary structures are revised to allow for demographic changes.[2] In Melanesia the upward and downward trends of unilineal groups are counteracted by couples with several children being encouraged to send some of them for adoption; or the parents may be allowed to beg the loan of plots from cognates or affines who have too much.[3] From nowhere is there any real evidence of a sudden switch from a unilineal to a non-unilineal system; and the To'ambaita, who are free to move to any of a dozen or more districts, seldom bother to make a change.[4]

Discussion of a statement by Fortes is relevant here. Unilineal descent groups, he asserted, are most in evidence 'in the middle range of relatively homogeneous pre-capitalist economies in which there is some slight technological sophistication and value is attached to rights in durable property'; they are not found 'among peoples who live in small [bands],

---

[1] Cf. S. F. Nadel, 1952, p. 29. 'Witchcraft beliefs enable a society to go on functioning in a given manner, fraught with conflicts and contradictions which the society is powerless to resolve; the witchcraft beliefs thus absolve the society from a task apparently too difficult for it, namely some radical readjustment.'

[2] L. Bohannan, 1952, pp. 301–15; and P. Bohannan, 1954, pp. 2–16.

[3] M. Mead, 1935, p. 17; Hogbin, 1935, pp. 208–15, 1936, pp. 17–38, and 1939b, pp. 142–8.

[4] One of the few regions of which it can definitely be stated, on objective grounds, that the land is barely adequate to feed the inhabitants is that occupied by the patrilineal Mae Enga of western central New Guinea. M. J. Meggitt, *The Lineage System of the Mae Enga*, to be published soon by Oliver and Boyd, gives statistical evidence that the Enga men living away from their lineage mates and lineage territory with other cognates or affines are at a severe disadvantage. They marry late, have few wives, and never attain prominence as leaders. His theory, argued from facts such as these, is almost the direct opposite of Goodenough's. Provided a tradition of unilineal descent groups already exists, he says, then, as the population increases, so the lineage becomes more and more concentrated and exclusive.

depend on rudimentary technology, and have little durable property'.[1] The assumption here is that material riches alone are of sociological significance and that spiritual riches can be ignored. This is unwarranted. The Australian aborigines have tiny groupings and in the economic sense are miserably poor; but to them religious rituals are of enormous importance. The secrets, moreover, are often tied up with a system of unilineal cult lodges.[2]

Fortes admitted that other factors besides economic institutions might have a bearing on structural forms, and he cited a couple of examples of African tribes at the same level of subsistence with different kinds of groupings. Had he looked at Melanesia he would have found many such. Living standards, except in the interior of some of the larger islands, do not vary much, yet societies with patrilineal groups, societies with matrilineal groups, and societies with non-unilineal systems are distributed seemingly at random.

As a conclusion I would like to quote the statement made in another context by Radcliffe-Brown. In reply to why some communities stress patrilineal descent and others matrilineal descent, he said, 'My opinion is that our knowledge and understanding are not sufficient to deal with this problem in any satisfactory manner.'[3] So far as Melanesia is concerned this applies also to unilineal and non-unilineal structures.

[1] M. Fortes, 1953, p. 24.
[2] Cf. A. I. Richards, 1950, p. 222. The Bemba, she said, have plenty of land but an undeveloped material culture, no cattle, and no money. 'There is *thus* practically no inheritable wealth . . . ' (italics mine).
[3] A. R. Radcliffe-Brown, 1952, p. 48.

3

Kinship Terms

WHEN we speak of 'a kinship system' we mean social relations between persons expressed in the context of genealogical and affinal connections. Each term in the system is a symbol of a particular set of obligations, and to say that two individuals call each other 'brother', for example, or 'cousin', is a shorthand way of indicating that they have certain specific reciprocal duties and claims.

Morgan, the pioneer of kinship study, distinguished systems that merge lineal and collateral relatives from those that keep them apart. The former he called 'classificatory', the latter 'descriptive'.[1] The Busama have a classificatory system closely resembling that of the people Morgan investigated, the Iroquois Indians of North America. The father and his brothers are in the same category, the mother and her sisters, and the brothers and sisters and the father's brothers' children and mother's sisters' children; but there is a separate term for the father's sisters and mother's brothers and also for the father's sisters' children and mother's brothers' children.

Malinowski, writing half a century after Morgan, argued that the various classificatory usages could be fully explained as extensions of the relationships of the members of the simple family. Why if this were so there should be such an extreme variety of classificatory kinship systems throughout the world remains obscure. Yet despite the fact that most anthropologists now reject Malinowski's hypothesis, it provides a convenient framework for presenting kinship material.[2] Accordingly, in this account I shall work outwards from the family through the near cognates to the distant cognates, through the *da-tigeng* to the *hu-tigeng*.

Before I begin the main task one or two general remarks are necessary. First, it should be noted that some of the Busama terms are employed only for addressing a kinsman directly. English provides an approximate equi-

---

[1] See L. A. White, 1958, pp. 378–85.

A. R. Radcliffe-Brown, 1950, p. 10, asserted that some systems, such as our own, are neither classificatory nor descriptive and belong to a third type.

[2] M. Fortes, 1958, pp. 157–88, pointed out that Malinowski continually proclaimed that kinship terminologies are just metaphors and homonyms. This is not so, Fortes maintained: they are indicators of social relations and modes of grouping and arranging persons. Such relations and groupings are present in the social structure along with family relations. They have the effect of binding the family into the total jural and political order.

valent with 'mum', 'mummie', 'dad', 'daddie'. One of our children might say, 'Mum, give us something to eat', but he would probably tell his play-mates, 'I have asked my mother for something for us to eat.' The Busama mother is addressed as *nang* or *dinangwi* ('mum', 'mummie') or occasionally as *dinang*; she is always spoken of as *dinang* ('*Nang*, give us something to eat'; 'I have asked *dinang* for something for us to eat').

A second kind of term is used both for address and reference. *Wa'*, 'mother's brother', is an example.

A third kind is reserved almost exclusively for reference. Where no additional term of address is available the persons concerned normally speak to each other by name. A man calls his male sibling 'brother' only when he has a special reason for emphasizing their relationship, as, for example, if he is greeting him after returning from a journey or giving him an oblique reminder of neglected responsibilities.

With a few exceptions the terms incorporate the possessive pronoun, and *dinang*, for instance, is 'my mother', *wa'* 'my mother's brother'. The form with the third personal pronoun is used when the abstract relationship is to be indicated. 'Mother' is *dinda* ('his mother', 'her mother') and 'mother's brother' *walangga'*.[1]

Finally, although many terms consist of a stem with variants of the affix *nga'*, 'male', and *awi*, 'female', the stem cannot stand by itself. *Abung-nga'* is 'my grandfather' and *abung-wi* 'my grandmother', but *abung* for 'my grandparent' would be a false form.

THE FAMILY

Parents and Children

Usually a person speaks to his parents by the kinship terms but may refer to them either by the terms or by name. *Danda*, 'father', and *dinda*, 'mother' (*damang* = 'my father', *dinang* = 'my mother'), are used for both address and reference, *damangwi* and *dinangwi* or *nang* ('my dad', 'my mum') for address only.[2] Children are spoken to by the words for 'son' and 'daughter'. These latter vary with the age of the offspring: *bali* is applied to a boy up to the age of about puberty, *latu* to a youth, *bawi* to a girl up to the age of about puberty, *latuwi* to an adolescent girl, and so on.

The parents are together responsible for the child's nourishment, edu-cation, and discipline. The mother provides sustenance during the period of infancy, and at a later stage she has to give instruction in women's work

---

[1] See A. Capell, 1949, pp. 169–89.

[2] The *wi* suffix of *damangwi* and *dinangwi*, literally 'my female father' and 'my female mother', apparently implies familiarity and affection. Other examples of this usage do not occur, and informants were at a loss for an explanation of it here. 'My female father' may sound ridiculous, but the expression is no more absurd than 'little dad', the literal meaning of 'daddie'.

Damangwi and *dinangwi* have no other forms (one cannot say 'his dad'). The third personal form of *nang* is *na*.

to the daughter while the father teaches the son the occupations proper to males.

The father, as head of the household, controls the wealth but uses it to provide clothing, tools, utensils, and extra foodstuffs for the family. Until the children acquire livestock of their own after marriage he also furnishes pigs when they are implicated in feasts. He represents them in civil disputes, pays compensation for their misdemeanours, and collects any compensation due to them.

The mother is in theory subject to her husband but in fact has sole charge of the commisariat. She harvests the crops and, as the family cook, apportions the meals and in-between snacks.

Children treat their parents with loving respect. Undoubtedly the nutritional bond is the chief factor in building up the attachment, and it is generally acknowledged that, 'because of the milk', the feelings for the mother are even stronger than those for the father. The young people's help soon becomes an economic advantage, and ultimately the position of dependence is reversed, with the sons and daughters providing for their now aged father and mother.

Brothers and Sisters

Brothers and sisters address one another by name and keep the terms for reference; but they apply them in an un-English way. The Busama language, following the usual Oceanic practice, has a term for elder sibling of the same sex as the speaker, one for younger sibling of the same sex, and a pair of alternatives for sibling of the opposite sex. The affixes *nga'* and *awi* are added to the stems *duwa* and *lasi*, respectively elder and younger sibling of the speaker's sex, and to *dawa* and *hu'*, sibling of the other sex. A man accordingly speaks of his elder brother as *nga'duwa*, his younger brother as *lasi*, and his sister as *awidawa* or *hu'wi*; and a woman of her elder sister as *duwawi*, her younger sister as *lasiwi*, and her brother as *nga'dawa* or *hungga'* (if a man is speaking *lasing* = 'my younger brother'; if a woman is speaking *duwangwi* = 'my elder sister', *lasingwi* = 'my younger sister', and *hungnga'* = 'my brother': the other terms do not incorporate the possessive). *Awidawa* and *hu'wi*, and *nga'dawa* and *hungga'*, are interchangeable except on the very rare occasions that a person is addressed by a kinship term instead of by name. *Awidawa* and *nga'dawa* are then preferred.

Brothers are held together by their common background and common interests. They grow up in the same household, learn the various technical processes and accepted standards side by side, and are co-inheritors of the personal property of the father and the land rights of the matrilineage. As adults they depend on one another for help and moral support. They share many of their tasks, and a popular saying has it that one should never engage in any discussion, no matter how trivial, with a single individual without being prepared to out-talk his brothers.

(a) Gi'lahi

(b) Carrying the baby

(*a*) Agi'wi minding her young sister at the edge of the garden

(*b*) Playing at housebuilding

The separate terms for older and younger brothers reflect a distinction in status. The seniors have a certain amount of authority and act as guardians for the juniors, who in turn treat them with a slight degree of deference. The former act as leaders and initiate and direct the joint undertakings.

The firstborn is the most important, and his marriage is celebrated with the greatest ceremony. To some extent he takes the father's place and is always the principal heir to the goods transmitted in the male line. He can if he wishes claim the largest share, but instead he generally acts as trustee and keeps the property intact. He also has some control over his brothers' possessions and if one of them is holding a feast advises the rest on how much they should contribute. They are not bound to accept his decision but almost invariably do so. He rebukes them if they openly disagree with one another but is always ready to defend them should an outsider accuse them of wrongdoing. They speak for themselves at the meeting called to investigate the charge and look to him for aid in picking out the weak points in the plaintiff's case or, if they are guilty, in minimizing the offence.

Sisters stand in much the same kind of relationship and are equally ready to help one another. Here also the seniors have authority over the juniors, who are expected to be submissive. At the same time, the women of the family are never as firmly united as the men. Much of their work is focused on the hearth and demands little co-operation—they do not normally need help to keep the house clean, fetch wood and water, or prepare ordinary meals. The communal activities, such as certain tasks in agriculture, are organized by the menfolk, each of whom wishes his wife to accompany him. Again, joint ownership of the women's property left by the mother is out of the question. Clothing, bags, baskets, and utensils wear out quickly and within a year or two are forgotten. The eldest daughter takes the best and distributes what is left. Finally, women seldom address public gatherings. If caught up in legal proceedings they are defended not by an older sister but by the husband and the brothers.

Sisters maintain contact by regular visiting and in emergencies are always quickly on the spot. Consequently a sick woman is not harassed by worries about her family. She takes to her bed secure in the knowledge that other people will nurse her sympathetically and feed the husband and children. During pregnancy also, and after the infant is born, the sisters relieve her of many household responsibilities.

The terms *awidawa*, a man's sister, and *nga'dawa*, a woman's brother, are said to be derived from *dawa*, the net for catching bandicoots. The animals, once inside, are held fast; and, the natives add, so are brothers and sisters. The bond acquires some of its strength from the customs relating to the inheritance of land. The man's interests are concentrated on his sisters' sons, who share his rights.

The brother is always prepared to support his sister. He makes a home for her if the parents die during her girlhood, and later, even when her

D

husband is fully capable of attending to her needs, he occasionally puts gardens at her disposal and presents her with small gifts of money and clothing. He also comes to the rescue if she is badly off as a result of the husband's dying, falling seriously ill, or undertaking employment away from the village. Further, he allows her to take temporary refuge with him after domestic disputes.

The sister returns her brother's kindness with services when extra help is needed. She is a frequent visitor at his house and constantly gives his family food. Yet she seldom stays as long as the wife's sisters. The dwelling is less the province of the man than of the woman, who naturally gives a warmer reception to her own relatives than to those of her husband. At the same time, the man's sisters always remain during illness. If he is the patient they act as nurses, leaving the wife free to carry on with her work, and if she falls sick they do the household chores while her sisters minister to her needs. Sisters-in-law also give valuable aid during the woman's pregnancies and after the babies have been born.

OTHER DA-TIGENG COGNATES

Kinship Terms

Grandparents and grandchildren address one another by name and reserve the terms for reference. The root is *pu*, and *pungga'* is used for 'grandfather', 'grandson', and *puwi* for 'grandmother', 'granddaughter' (*abungnga'*, *abungwi* = 'my grandfather', etc.).

A person addresses and refers to his paternal uncles by a single set of terms, though he may also refer to them by name; they address their nephews and nieces by name. The uncle terms are the same as those for 'father' with the addition of the suffixes *ka* and *saung*. The former appears only in this context and is said to mean 'great' (the usual adjective is *atu*); the latter is the normal word for 'little', 'small'. The father's elder brothers are *damba-ka*, his younger brothers *damba-saung* (*damang-ka* = 'my father's elder brother', *damang-saung* = 'my father's younger brother'). The suffix is omitted only if the real father is dead and the man is acting *in loco parentis*. The uncles refer to their nephews and nieces by the ordinary words for 'son' and 'daughter' (*bali*, *bawi*, etc.).

The father's elder brothers' wives have the courtesy title of *dinda-ka* or *na-ka*, 'great mother', his younger brothers' wives that of *dinda-saung* or *na-saung*, 'little mother'. They refer to their husband's nephews and nieces by the terms that he uses.

Maternal uncles are addressed with equal frequency by name or by the kinship term *walangga'*, which is also used when referring to them (*wa'* = 'my mother's brother'); and they address the sister's children either by name or by the kinship terms *nisip*, 'sister's son', and *nisipawi*, 'sister's daughter' (*nga'sip*, *awisip*, 'my sister's son', 'my sister's daughter'—man speaking).

The mother's brother's wife is referred to as *walawi*, which is also the word for 'father's sister' (*wa'wi* = 'my mother's brother's wife', 'my father's sister'). This may be a courtesy title, but if, as can happen, a brother and a sister have married a sister and a brother, she actually is the father's sister.

Paternal aunts are addressed by name or by the term *walawi*, which is also used when referring to them, and they address the brothers' children either by name or by the terms *nisip* or *nisipawi* (*nga'sip*, *awisip*, 'my brother's son', 'my brother's daughter'—woman speaking). The father's sisters' husbands, even if they are not mother's brothers already, have the title of *walangga'*.

Maternal aunts are addressed and referred to by a single set of terms; they address their nephews and nieces by name. The mother's older sisters are *dinda-ka* or *na-ka*, 'great mother', her younger sisters *dinda-saung* or *na-saung*, 'little mother' (*dinang-ka*, *nang-ka* = 'my mother's older sister', *dinang-saung*, *nang-saung* = 'my mother's younger sister'). These women refer to their sister's children by the words for 'son' and 'daughter', *bali*, *bawi*, etc. The sisters' husbands have the courtesy title *danda-ka* or *danda-saung* and refer to their wife's nephews and nieces by the same terms as she does.

The cousins are divided into two sets, the first, known as 'parallel cousins', consisting of the children of the father's brothers and mother's sisters, and the second, the 'cross cousins', of the children of the father's sisters and mother's brothers.

Parallel cousins refer to one another by the same terms as siblings. A male speaks of his father's elder brothers' sons and his mother's elder sisters' sons, no matter what their real age, as *nga'duwa* ('elder brother') and of his father's younger brothers' sons and his mother's younger sisters' sons, again no matter what their real age, as *lasi* ('younger brother'); and a female of her father's elder brothers' daughters and her mother's elder sisters' daughters as *awiduwa* ('elder sister') and of her father's younger brothers' daughters and her mother's younger sisters' daughters as *lasiwi* ('younger sister'). He calls the daughters of all his father's brothers and mother's sisters *awidawa* or *hu'wi*; and she calls the sons of all her father's brothers and mother's sisters *nga'dawa* or *hungga'*.

Cross cousins employ special terms for address and reference. Nowadays they sometimes speak to one another by the name given at baptism but are careful to avoid mentioning the traditional native name in one another's presence. The word for 'male cross cousin' is *tengga'* and for 'female cross cousin' *tiwi* (*tengnga'* = 'my male cross cousin', *tengwi* = 'my female cross cousin').

Kinship Behaviour

The grandparents, uncles, and aunts share the responsibilities of the parents. They invite the children home, set them at ease with food, and later help with their training and discipline. Should the father and mother die the obligation to care for the orphans rests upon them all, and the

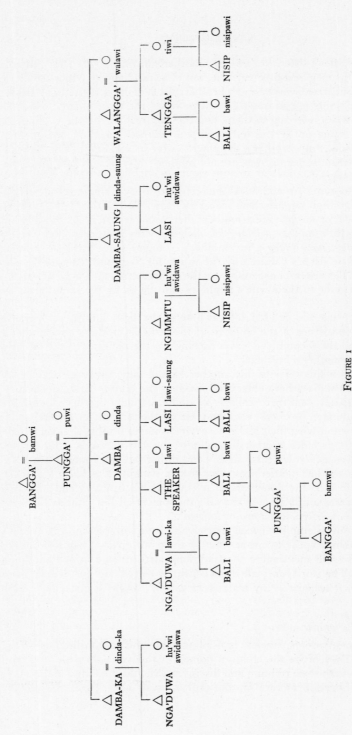

FIGURE 1

Kinship terms used by a male for relatives on the father's side.

△ represents a male; ○ represents a female; and the sign = indicates marriage. Terms for males are in capitals, for females in lower case.

decision about which one shall take them into his or her household is determined by the circumstances of the case. An uncle or aunt without a family is always eager to act, but if everybody already has offspring the younger boys usually go to the father's eldest brother, the older boys to a mother's brother, and the girls to the mother's eldest sister.

Yet despite a fundamental similarity of behaviour, there are certain differences. The grandparents are by far the most demonstrative and indulgent. They allow the children to have their own way and often laugh tolerantly when an uncle or an aunt would be inclined to scold. Then as a rule the maternal uncles display a keener interest than the paternal uncles. The boys share their land, and they are anxious to have them close by as often as possible; in fact the youngsters are explicitly told that the mother's brothers come next in importance after the parents. The significance attached to the relationship is indicated by the derivation of the term *nisip*. It is said to come from *sip*, the name of the timber from which people cut plugs to mend a leaking canoe. The implication is that the uterine nephews will 'prevent their mother's brothers from sinking in old age'. The maternal aunts are also likely to be warmer and more affectionate than the paternal aunts. The former make visits oftener and remain for a longer time.

The uncles-in-law (father's sisters' husbands and mother's sisters' husbands) and aunts-in-law (father's brothers' wives and mother's brothers' wives) share the duties of their spouse and endeavour to make the children welcome, though those who are unconnected by close cognatic ties on their own account are seldom markedly sympathetic. The wife of a maternal uncle, if she is a distant cognate or a stranger, may be jealous on her children's behalf at the favours showered on the nephews and nieces. Her husband then administers a stock rebuke: 'My sisters' sons are my testes. They are vital to me, and I refuse to cut them off.'

Children, drawn initially by the food and kindness, hold their grandparents, uncles, and aunts in high regard. But, unless they have been orphaned, they do not spend as much time with them as with the parents and so fail to develop the same depth of feeling. They obey orders, however, and repay the attentions with economic assistance.

Boys revere their maternal uncles most, a fact that the kinship term again brings out. The word *wa'* (*walangga'*) is also the name of a strong creeper that serves for tying up bundles. 'The *wa'* relationship remains fast like the *wa'* liana,' the natives explain. The paternal uncles come next, and after them the aunts. Not much extra deference is shown to those who are senior to the parents, and the adjectives 'big' and 'little', apart from the formal symmetry they give to the kinship system, have no practical significance. The grandparents are treated with almost the same freedom as contemporaries. The children love them dearly and are obviously happy in their company.

Parallel cousins act in a brotherly or sisterly manner and support one another. On the father's side the distinction between senior and junior (respectively, the father's older brothers' sons and the father's younger brothers' sons) is not important. On the mother's side this is only true as long as the cousins are still young. Later, when they are old enough to make gardens, they exercise their rights to the same areas of land, and now those who are senior begin to have authority. Ultimately leadership of the lineage passes to them in order not of age but of seniority.

Additional requirements, over and above being brotherly or sisterly, are demanded of cross cousins. They are said to be taboo (*dabung* is the Busama form of this common Oceanic expression) or set apart (*tasingtu*) and to have 'a bitter touch' (*kisi maki*). They must behave with restraint and avoid

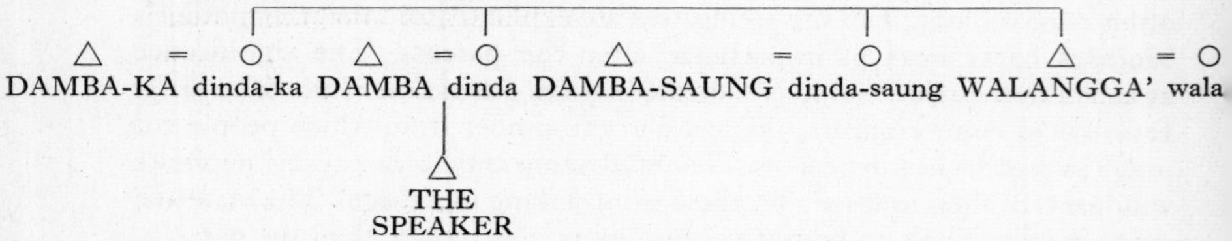

DAMBA-KA dinda-ka DAMBA dinda DAMBA-SAUNG dinda-saung WALANGGA' wala

THE
SPEAKER

FIGURE 2

Kinship terms used by a male for relatives on the mother's side

quarrelling and take care not to come into physical contact, handle one another's belongings, sit on one another's bedding, eat from the same dish, share cigarettes or a lime pot, undress or bathe in one another's presence, or mention any word connected with excreta or sex. If the distinction between patrilateral and matrilateral cross cousins can be made—obviously it cannot if a brother and sister have married a sister and brother—the prime obligation to take the appropriate precautions rests on the former. They are described as being 'like the younger brothers', whereas the matrilateral cross cousins are 'like the elder brothers'. If someone offers a bowl of food or suggests a bathing party the brother's children take the initiative and decline, leaving the sister's children free to accept.

HU-TIGENG COGNATES

The only remaining kinsfolk for whom special terms exist are the great-grandparents and the great-grandchildren. No-one today has great-grandparents living, but it is sometimes necessary to refer to them. The root is *ba*, and *bangga'* = 'great-grandfather', 'great-grandson', and *bamwi* = 'great-grandmother', 'great-granddaughter' (*abangnga'*, *abangwi* = 'my great-grandfather', etc.).

These and the other terms of reference are used for all the remoter kinsfolk, the *hu-tigeng*, the persons with distant ancestors in common. Such relatives may address one another by name, but if a speaker wishes for some reason to stress the link the appropriate term is there ready to hand.

The terms for great-grandparents, *bangga'* and *bamwi*, are applied to the cognates of that and previous generations. The great-grandchildren and the cognates of that and subsequent generations are called by the same terms.

The terms for grandparents, *pungga'* and *puwi*, are applied to the cognates of that generation. The grandchildren and the cognates of that generation are called by the same terms.

The terms for father's elder and younger brothers, *damba-ka* and *damba-saung*, are applied respectively to the father's senior and junior male relatives of his generation. *Damba-ka* and *damba-saung* are also applied respectively to the father's male matrilateral and male patrilateral cross cousins.

The terms for mother's elder and younger sisters, *dinda-ka* and *dinda-saung*, are applied respectively to the mother's senior and junior female relatives of her generation. *Dinda-ka* and *dinda-saung* are also applied respectively to the mother's female patrilateral and female matrilateral cross cousins.

The wives of all cognates called *damba-ka* and *damba-saung*, if not already cognates in their own right, are regarded by courtesy as *dinda-ka* and *dinda-saung* respectively; and the husbands of all cognates called *dinda-ka* and *dinda-saung*, if not already cognates in their own right, are regarded by courtesy as *damba-ka* and *damba-saung* respectively.

The term for the mother's brothers, *walangga'*, is applied to the mother's male relatives of her generation.

The term for the father's sisters, *walawi*, is applied to the father's female relatives of his generation.

The wives of all cognates called *walangga'*, even if not already father's sisters, are regarded as *walawi*; and the husbands of all cognates called *walawi*, even if not already mother's brothers, are regarded as *walangga'*.

The terms for elder siblings of one's own sex, *nga'duwa* and *duwawi*, are applied to the children of the appropriate sex of the persons called 'father's elder brother' (*damba-ka*) or 'mother's elder sister' (*dinda-ka*), and the terms for younger siblings of one's own sex, *lasi* and *lasiwi*, are applied to the children of the appropriate sex of the persons called 'father's younger brother' (*damba-saung*) or 'mother's younger sister' (*dinda-saung*). The terms for siblings of the opposite sex, *awidawa* and *hu'wi*, and *nga'dawa* and *hungga'*, are applied to the children of the appropriate sex of all the persons called 'father's elder (or younger) brother' or 'mother's elder (or younger) sister'.

The terms for cross cousins, *tengga'* and *tiwi*, are applied to the children of the persons called 'father's sister' (*walawi*) or 'mother's brother' (*walangga'*).

The cross-cousin terms have additional applications. The conventional greeting to a remote kinsman, if he (or she) is a contemporary, is '*Tengnga*' (or *tengwi*), whence have you come?' The proper answer in '*Tengnga*' (or *tengwi*), where are you going?', and a man who gives an account of his movements is regarded in the same light as one who, among ourselves, tells

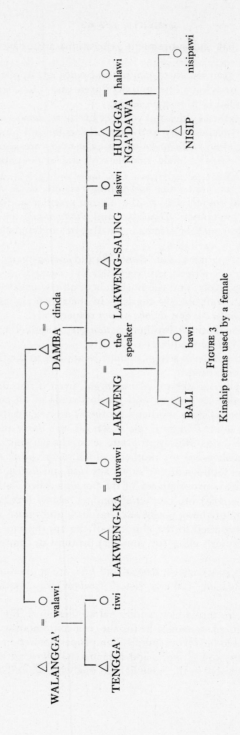

FIGURE 3
Kinship terms used by a female

of his latest ailments when asked 'How do you do?' Simple requests to a companion, no matter what his (or her) relationship, are also preceded by the word *tengnga'* (or *tengwi*), and all day long people may be heard saying, '*Tengnga'*, pass me a match' or '*Tengnga'*, have you an areca nut to spare?' In most Melanesian societies the word for 'brother' (or 'sister') is in these circumstances employed. The Busama are aware that they are exceptional and explain that in their view the sibling terms would imply too much intimacy. They add that brothers sometimes refuse whereas cross cousins never do.[1]

The terms for sons and daughters, *bali, bawi,* etc., are applied by a man to the children of the males whom he calls 'elder (or younger) brother' or 'male cross cousin' and by a woman to the children of the females whom she calls 'elder (or younger) sister' or 'female cross cousin'.

The terms a man uses for his sisters' children, and a woman for her brothers' children, *nisip* and *nisipawi*, are applied by him to the children of the women whom he calls 'sister' or 'female cross cousin' and by her to the children of the men whom she calls 'brother' or 'male cross cousin'.

Thus each person refers to his *hu-tigeng* cognates by one or other of the terms for *da-tigeng* kinsmen. By this means he draws the wider community in towards the family circle.[2]

Distant cognates who are frequently together, either from personal choice or because by accident they happen to be neighbours, take care to conduct themselves like near cognates of their respective categories; but those with fewer contacts, though aware of their exact status, are usually satisfied with diffused goodwill and generalized loyalty. They do not go out of their way to co-operate but are ready to help one another in times of need, as, for example, if some major undertaking is afoot or a serious calamity has occurred.

In many families the father and mother share certain relatives, and the children in consequence can choose some of their kinship ties. A particular individual may perhaps be in the category of the father's brothers and also that of the mother's brothers. Indeed, because of other marriages besides that of the parents, it is frequently possible to refer to a kinsman by three or four different terms. One householder could with perfect propriety call a neighbour 'father's elder brother', 'mother's brother', 'cross cousin', 'grandfather', and 'son'. In such circumstances the most suitable word is chosen. These two men were on good terms, and, as they were contemporaries, they decided to be cross cousins.

The different genealogical paths provide a way out when two fairly close

[1] In folk tales characters who share danger or adventure are always cross cousins.
[2] Cf. E. E. Evans-Pritchard, 1951, p. 175: 'All members of a man's community, whether it be large or small, can thus be addressed by one of the family relationship terms. We do not, I think, understand this convention so well by regarding it [as Malinowski did] as an extension of family terms and sentiments from members of the family to kin as when we regard it as the verbal telescoping of kin into the circle of family reference. . . .'

relatives are the wrong age for their kinship status—a classificatory 'younger brother', for instance, who is old enough to be his 'elder brother's' father. They deliberately abandon the direct route in favour of one that gives a more seemly result.

OTHER RELATIONSHIPS

Each child is called after a relative from a senior generation, and if the person is still alive he drops the ordinary term and instead uses the reciprocal *waka* (*wakang* = 'my namesake'). The new tie replaces the old, and the adult is more attentive than his kinship status would warrant and the youngster more devoted.

An institution in some ways resembling blood-brotherhood, except that the parties were already related, was in former times also of some importance. The word is *nengga'* (*nengnga'* = 'my blood-brother'), the kinship term for the wife's sister's husband. A youth and the supporter who went through the initiation ordeals with him, and a warrior and anyone from his own side whom he saved in battle by personal intervention, were *nengga'*. They are described as having been 'the same as brothers, children of one father and one mother'.

CONSISTENCY WITHIN THE SYSTEM

Leaving namesakes and these pseudo brothers aside as special cases, we can say that the Busama separate their cognates into ten categories. They have terms for the great-grandparents and great-grandchildren (with sex affixes), for the grandparents and grandchildren (with sex affixes), for the father and his brothers (with seniority affixes), for the mother and her sisters (with seniority affixes), for the father's sisters and mother's brothers (with sex affixes), for the siblings and parallel cousins of the same sex (with sex and seniority affixes), for the siblings and parallel cousins of the opposite sex (with sex affixes), for the cross cousins (with sex affixes), for the children and the children of siblings and cousins of the same sex (with sex affixes), and for the children of siblings and cousins of the opposite sex (with sex affixes). The sex of every relative is given, and in several instances the terms also indicate the sex of the speaker, the sex of the linking person, the differences of generation, and the differences of seniority within the generation.[1]

The system is internally consistent and, within certain limits, reflects social reality. Speaking broadly, kinsfolk referred to by a single term are

[1] A. L. Kroeber, 1909, pp. 77–84, set out the social facts that a kinship terminology may recognize. Apart from those mentioned above, the list included differences between lineal and collateral kin and between degrees of collaterality, differences between cognatic and affinal kin, and whether the linking kinsman is alive or dead. F. G. Lounsbery, 1956, pp. 168, 169, added type of cognate (agnatic or non-agnatic, uterine or non-uterine). G. P. Murdock, 1949, pp. 101–6, referred to the following criteria: generation, sex of the relative, affinity, collaterality, bifurcation (whether the linking relative is a male or a female), polarity (whether the terms are

treated alike and those referred to by separate terms are treated differently. One or two obvious anomalies are not of great significance and, moreover, are easily capable of explanation. The distinction between the mother's older and younger sisters, in itself pointless, is rendered necessary by the useful division of the matrilateral parallel cousins into senior and junior. The marking off of the father's older and younger brothers, and of the senior and junior patrilateral parallel cousins, suggesting as it does patrilineal groupings with the senior male as leader, is also pointless. But the demands of symmetry require that discrimination on the mother's side should be mirrored by similar discrimination on the father's side.

As Nadel remarked, however, classificatory systems cannot possibly be consistent in all respects.[1] Once that of Busama is examined without reference to its own self-imposed logic other discrepancies become apparent, notably (a) the failure to recognize the considerable differences between the intensity of the obligations of *da-tigeng* and *hu-tigeng* kin and (b) the presence of matrilineages. I know of no system in Melanesia that keeps lineal and immediate collateral relatives apart from the rest of the collaterals, and even a correlation between kinship terms and descent groups is rare. The Busama nomenclature, generally spoken of as the Iroquois type, after Morgan's Indians, is not only the commonest in the islands but is also associated with every kind of structure—patrilineal, matrilineal and non-unilineal.[2] In the context of one sort of consistency, that linked with the

reciprocal), relative age, the speaker's sex, and decedence (whether the linking relative is alive or dead).

In the first ascending generation the Busama make no terminological distinction between cognatic and affinal kin (uncles and aunts' husbands; and aunts and uncles' wives). The other affines, and the terms applied to them, will be discussed in a later chapter.

[1] S. F. Nadel, 1951, p. 264: 'A classificatory kinship terminology may operate consistently (or not) with the criterion of generation differences and consistently ignore sex differences; it may even consistently operate with the same principle of word formation, expressing all generation differences by means of the attributes "great", "small", and so forth. These two consistencies, one obtaining between the symbol system and the set of things symbolized, and the other within the symbol system, mostly diverge at some point. Thus a classificatory terminology operating consistently with the generation principle will often express distinctions which are not practically important or leave unexpressed differences which are so important. This merely indicates something that common sense also tells us, namely, that consistency cannot be made to prevail all round.'

[2] Patrilineal societies in Melanesia with an Iroquois terminology include the Abelam, Banaro, Epi, Kiwai, Orokaiva, Tanna, and Wanimo (G. P. Murdock, 1949, p. 237). Matrilineal societies include New Ireland (H. Powdermaker, 1933, pp. 44–50) and Santa Cruz (W. H. R. Rivers, 1914, Vol. I, pp. 217–23); and non-unilineal societies the To'ambaita of Malaita (Hogbin, 1939a, p. 41).

Some writers (e.g. G. P. Murdock, op. cit.) have reserved the term 'Iroquois' for societies with matrilineal groups (the Iroquois themselves were matrilineal) and substituted 'Dakota' where the groups are patrilineal. Making such a distinction when the terminologies follow identical principles seems to be both unnecessary and confusing. If the example were to be followed a third term would have to be matrilineages, a type that distinguished between uterine and non-uterine kin would be appropriate. Although in Busama a man's mother's sisters' children and father's brothers' children are in some respects similar, he has land rights in common with the former alone. Such a terminology, known as the Choctaw or Crow type, is not often met with in Melanesia.[1] (The Omaha type, distinguishing between agnatic and non-agnatic kin and therefore in this sort of context well adapted to patrilineal communities, is equally rare.[2] The Hawaiian type, which stresses generation differences only, occurs more frequently but has as haphazard a distribution as the Iroquois. Instead of being confined to places with a non-unilineal system, as might have been expected, it turns up in conjunction with both patrilineal and matrilineal descent groups.[3])

found for the societies with non-unilineal groups (and possibly a fourth also for those with double unilineal descent).

[1] The Trobriand Islands and the Banks Islands are two examples (B. Malinowski, 1929, p. 435; and W. H. R. Rivers, op. cit., Vol. I, pp. 390, 391).

In the context of social groupings the Iroquois terminology is adapted to a division into moieties (patrilineal or matrilineal), where parallel and cross cousins are always on opposite sides. It would also suit a social system having obligatory cross-cousin marriage without acknowledged moieties.

[2] The Iatmül, Kwoma, and Arapesh, all in the Sepik-River region of New Guinea, have systems of Omaha type (G. Bateson, 1932, pp. 262–4; Whiting and Reed, 1938, pp. 200–2, 206; and Mead, 1938, p. 168).

[3] The natives of Eddystone Island (also known as Simbo, in the Solomons) and of Möwehafen (New Britain) have an Hawaiian terminology and a non-unilineal structure (Rivers, op. cit., Vol. I, p. 396; and Todd, 1934, p. 97); the Koitapu an Hawaiian terminology and patrilineages (Seligman, 1910, pp. 49, 50, 66, 67); and the natives of central Guadalcanal an Hawaiian terminology and matrilineal moieties and clans (Hogbin, 1937, pp. 64–67).

4

Birth and Early Childhood

ALL Busama men want a family, and those without children say continually how sorry they are. As is usual among primitive peoples, the natives do not know that males may be sterile, and a childless man invariably blames his wife. Undoubtedly if today further marriages were permitted he would seek a new partner. But polygamy has disappeared in the face of advancing Christianity, and divorce, also forbidden by the Lutheran missionaries, never had a place in the local tradition. 'What's the use of gardening when there's no-one to eat the taro?' my 'brother' Nga'gili' answered sadly when, early in our friendship, I enquired why was he not in the company of his kinsmen at the cultivations. 'With a barren wife, how can I hope to be remembered after I am dead? If I could take someone else, and she gave me offspring, I would clear new ground with the rest.' The wider public condemn such a man if he conducts an outside liaison, but his relatives may make excuses for him. They say sympathetically that his conduct is understandable seeing that his wife has failed to produce a baby.

The women are no less eager for children than their husbands. It is significant that, although I occasionally heard people suggesting that a single girl or a widow suspected of sexual indulgences might have chewed certain herbs as a contraceptive or abortifacient, they practically never made accusations against a wife.

Fathers, despite a partiality for their daughters, generally say they want sons first. When asked why, they quote the old adage that whereas sons remain to look after their parents girls marry into distant settlements and have children 'who return with spears'. Even if true once, today this is nonsense. Native warfare ceased at the turn of the century, and nowadays most brides and bridegrooms come from the village.

Mothers have an honest preference for sons. Their usual comment is, 'A boy makes gardens for his mother all his life; a daughter thinks of her husband.'

Admittedly sons care for their parents in old age and show them veneration; but they are rarely in the position to give them as much material assistance as daughters. Household supplies are controlled less by the husband than by the wife, who is drawn more towards her own father and mother than towards her parents-in-law. An overwhelming majority of elderly people therefore live in the house of one of their daughters.

PREGNANCY

As was mentioned, the natives grossly misunderstand the processes of
reproduction and insist that the man alone is responsible for the embryo.
Yet they deny that a child can inherit the physical features of his father.
Obvious resemblances they attribute to association. 'We grow like the
persons with whom we live,' they told me. As proof they pointed out
similarities between mother's brothers and sisters' sons. The uncles, it was
explained, could not possibly have contributed in any way to the flesh of
their nephews.

Character traits, on the other hand, are often ascribed to 'ancestral blood';
further, if a moral defect is in question the mother's side is as likely to be
held responsible as the father's. The two ne'er-do-wells of the settlement,
the brothers Biyaweng and Ki'dolo', are the sons of an improvident mother
who was left a widow while they were still small. 'They have her bad
blood,' said the villagers, 'just as, so we've been told, she had the bad blood
of her mother.' People made similar remarks when Ahipum began behaving
in a high-handed manner a few years after his appointment as a Government representative. 'We ought to have known; it's his mother's bad blood
coming out,' a friend wrote in a letter giving me recent news. Ahipum's
maternal uncle, who had held office earlier, was a notorious evil-doer.

The two theories are appealed to in such different contexts that the
inconsistency is not apparent. As far as I know nobody has tried either to
reconcile them or to discover how a mother's—or a father's—bad blood
might be transmitted.

The woman informs her husband as soon as she is sure of being pregnant. From then until the child is about a year old he has to refrain from
having sexual intercourse with her. People say that in the early stages
further seed might be injurious and that later a second conception would
necessitate weaning the infant too soon. I cannot tell whether the probi-
bition is strictly observed before delivery, but it is sometimes neglected
afterwards.

The woman's sisters and sisters-in-law take over some of the more
arduous household tasks, and the husband also helps. They fear that if in
the first few months, 'before the foetus is properly set', she were to carry a
heavy load she might miscarry. (They warn her, too, not to sleep on her
back, 'lest the seed should run to the two sides and become twins'. Multiple
births are dreaded not for religious reasons but because a pair of young
infants presents such difficulties in the home. There are today, however,
no less than six sets of twins in the village.)

Yet at a later stage grandmothers hold that activity is essential, and they
advise the woman to walk about vigorously, climb over stiles quickly, and
swim a few strokes when she is bathing. 'The child will feel too comfortable
in your womb and refuse to be born,' they tell her if she is lethargic and
lies about. I once indicated that this implied pre-natal development of

consciousness, but the old lady to whom I was speaking replied laughingly that I had better take my enquiries to someone who could still remember his feelings before birth. She then added that although too much rest can, indeed, cause prolonged labour, I must not pay serious attention to the reasons offered.

Emotional disturbances are regarded as particularly dangerous, and the relatives caution both husband and wife against quarrelling. 'Wives are often irritable on these occasions,' the mother of newly-married Sali explained to him, so he told me afterwards. 'You must put up with that and give in to her. You want to be a father, so remember and take care.' Several persons intervened when a woman about to have her fifth child was drawn into a heated argument with a neighbour. They led her away, and bystanders then castigated the opponent for lack of feeling. 'You ought to have agreed and admitted you were wrong even if you knew you weren't,' they scolded. Attendance at funerals is also potentially harmful, and for the same reason.

Morning sickness is common. The villagers believe that the berries of a wild vine, not otherwise eaten, are beneficial, and the woman's sisters and sisters-in-law gather supplies on their way from the gardens. Longings for all sorts of curious things are also usual, and many pregnant women devour such stuff as bark, ashes, soft coconut shells, and fruit normally thought to be unpalatable. People excuse these cravings with the expression 'blood is killing her' (*da' gi aing*; cf. *ndip gi aing*, 'urine is killing him (or her)', said of a person who wishes to urinate). Busama women may well suffer from calcium deficiency. No milk is available for them to drink, they do not chew betel-nut, which contains lime, and the local water is soft.

As the time for delivery approaches some couples prefer to avoid opening wooden boxes. They fear that a miscarriage might result if they were careless and let the lid fall.

The menfolk accept pregnancy as a matter of course and never make jesting remarks about a woman big with child. At the same time, they are sometimes critical when she has not been married long or her earlier infant is not yet weaned. They sniggered a good deal when Yawi conceived within a few weeks of her wedding, and several whispered to me that her husband must have been having intercourse with her beforehand. 'The largest penis couldn't inject all that seed so quickly,' one elder remarked.

BIRTH

The maternal-mortality rate is high, and the natives often say that this is the Lord's vengeance on Eve for her sin. In one version of the Garden-of-Eden story God is reported to have addressed her in the following words: 'You, Eve, listened to Satan first and persuaded Adam to join you in evil-doing. Women's punishment shall therefore be greater than men's. They shall suffer the pangs of labour, and many will die in bringing children into the world.'

First confinements give rise to a good deal of anxiety. Often the young wife is afraid and not at all convinced when her mother and mother-in-law try to calm her down by pointing out that they came through the ordeal safely. The husband, father, and brothers may also be worried, and several men said that they had offered up prayers in private for a safe delivery. The women become impatient with their questions and warn them to keep their thoughts to themselves and not harass the expectant mother still further.

As a rule the initial labour is not by our standards unduly prolonged (though it may last for several hours), and later births seldom cause any trouble. One woman recently had her third baby while at work in the garden, and Ahipum's wife, Mu'alimawi, declined help when giving birth to her seventh, eighth, and ninth children. Usually women who have difficulty during second births continue to do so afterwards.

Shortly before the delivery is expected the husband forces two of the floorboards aside and digs a hole in the ground below ready for the blood and placenta. He then retires to the beach or club, where generally his father-in-law, brothers-in-law, and one or two close associates join him. Though plied with food, he seldom has any wish to eat. Sali was unable to keep still or give his attention to anything for more than a few minutes, and he sat, stood, and walked about for the whole of the night. A group of us tried to distract his thoughts with conversation, but his mind was elsewhere, and we had to repeat all our questions several times. 'No, no food—it would stick in my throat,' he answered when we urged him to share our meal. Not until a messenger came at sunrise with word that he was the father of a healthy daughter and that his wife, though worn out, was well, did he compose himself. He then lay down and was soon fast asleep.

The woman's mother if alive is always present to act as midwife at the early confinements. Their mutual affection is especially evident at such times, and it is said that young wives who are orphans always feel miserable at the lack of maternal support. One or two aunts may also help, but the husband's mother and aunts remain outside on the verandah until after the delivery. Relatives-by-marriage have to observe a number of taboos and must never see one another's naked bodies.

I have not witnessed a birth, and my account is necessarily second hand.

The midwives take off the parturient woman's calico dress, an expensive item, and replace it with a grass skirt. Afterwards one of them kindles a fire to provide warmth and better illumination. They then make the woman lie down, and they take turns massaging her back and abdomen with a steady downwards pressure. The pain is now excruciating, but she accepts it with resignation. A dozen or more births have at different times taken place in houses close to my own, but, apart from the unaccustomed movement, I have heard no sound till the thin wail of the infant broke the silence.

For the actual delivery the woman crouches near the hole in the floor with her knees bent. One of the midwives supports her back, and a second continues the frontal massage till the child's head appears, when she holds her hands ready. If the placenta comes out immediately afterwards the cord is cut with a razor blade so as to leave several inches. The mother preserves the end and, after it has dried and fallen off, buries it underneath a taro shoot in the garden. She chooses a healthy plant and good soil, for the later growth of a large corm is looked upon as a happy omen. For a day or two the baby's navel is smeared with a mixture of ashes and saliva.

The woman's mother now bathes both her and the infant with warm water, and the mother-in-law, who can at last enter the house, sends word to the father. The aunts meantime push the placenta through the floor, fill in the hole below, and clean the house. This is the women's great occasion, and they make a good deal of unnecessary fuss as they hurry to and fro with their dishes of water. The men, apart from the husband and immediate relatives, do their best to pretend that they are not interested. 'All this nonsense over a baby,' they grumble.

If the placenta is retained, as sometimes happens, the midwives leave the child and go on with their massage. They do not cut the cord until sure that their efforts are in vain. They then tie the protruding end to a stick and rush the mother by canoe to hospital.

The death of a woman in childbirth creates problems for the widower. Normally he would not have handled his offspring for some weeks; but he now has to accept full care of it. He abandons all other work and takes it round the village and gardens to women who are giving suck to an infant of their own. The prime obligation to supply milk rests on his sisters and the sisters of his dead wife, but they may have none to give; and at best they do not have enough. He therefore casts shame aside and approaches all, irrespective of relationship ties or lack of them. Two fathers during the last few years have successfully reared an orphan by these means. A third child, a baby named Tumala, was still more unfortunate in that his father also was dead. His paternal grandmother took charge of him with passionate devotion, and later, when he no longer needed the breast, her elder son accepted him as his. This man, Balimboa, and his wife Awimasu are childless, and they now lavish as much care on the boy as though she had borne it (see below, pp. 117-19).

The father is also called upon to share the nursing when his wife gives birth to twins.

Midwives lay the newborn infant on a piece of blanket covered with clean calico, but as soon as the mother is strong enough she cuddles it against her body in the crook of her arm. For the first couple of days she allows it to be moved for bathing and feeding only. In the beginning, before her own milk becomes available, it sucks from the breast of one of her relatives.

The husband does not ordinarily come near for the first twenty-four hours. He may look in for a few minutes if the child is his first, but the

E

midwives show no consideration and brusquely order him to go away. They tell him everyone is busy and that, instead of making himself a nuisance, he ought to be at the sago swamps gathering shoots from the crown of a young palm so that his wife could have nourishing broth. Her brothers help him, and she always has plenty.

Men are supposed to be too clumsy and unskilled to minister to a tiny infant, and, except in the circumstances described, the father does not touch his young offspring. After about two weeks the women may give it to him for a few minutes, but six months elapse before he holds it for any length of time.

No formal notification of the other relatives is required. Most of them live in the village and come to hear the news through the channels of daily gossip. Today the birth is also unmarked by any form of public celebration.

The midwives watch the mother's progress and usually between the sixth and the twelfth day give approval for her to go outside. Her sisters and sisters-in-law first prepare her a meal of freshwater fish steamed without salt, and she is then free to sit in the shade under the trees. The child occupies the whole of her attention for some weeks longer, and during this period the relatives cheerfully provide food, firewood, and water for the household.

The parents always name the firstborn, generally after one of their deceased forbears, perhaps a grandfather, grandmother, great-uncle, or great-aunt. But in later births relatives take the initiative. The second and third children are left for the living grandparents and the parents' brothers and sisters. One or other of these approaches the couple in about the sixth month of the woman's pregnancy and says that, if the baby is of the right sex, he or she wants it as a namesake. A distant kinsman can only step in after the third birth. If his tie is very remote he offers a pig as a present, and the father signifies approval by accepting it. Later the parents make a counter gift of pots, mats, and string bags. Many persons have two or more namesakes.

Over half the names are those of places, which are themselves often called after a stream or spring. The word for 'water', and also for 'river', 'creek', 'lagoon', and 'spring', is *bu*, which is therefore a common prefix. Buasi', Bumbu, and Buaki are examples. Other names were apparently given in the first place in fun—Nga'gili' ('man at the end of the line'), Nga'lai ('fighting man'), Nga'yaba ('foreigner'), Hagalu' ('sore feet'), and Gi'lahi' ('warrior from Lahi'). Many men's names have the prefix *nga'*, almost all women's names *awi* or *wi*, used either as a prefix or a suffix; and for some names there are masculine and feminine forms (e.g. Makisa, Makisa'wi).

Christian names, which are bestowed along with the native name, though baptism does not take place till later, are either taken directly from biblical characters (e.g. Aaron and Elijah, pronounced and spelt 'Along' and 'Ilia') or else made up after the fashion of seventeenth-century England (e.g.

Dabung-yam, 'Good-holy-things', and Yaing-nga-yam, 'Good-tidings'). Some persons are regularly called by their native name, some by their Christian name, and some by both.

The number of names is restricted, and many are shared by four or five persons. The adjectives *angkwa*, 'senior', and *waku*, 'junior', do not always prevent confusion, and some such phrase as 'son of So-and-so' or 'from Such-and-such a place' may have to be added.

INFANCY

At first the mother keeps the baby constantly in her arms or nestled alongside her on the floor. She pushes it away only if it begins to soil her, and then with such a gentle movement that it seems to suffer no sense of shock —certainly I have never heard a very young infant scream in fright.

The natives are alive to the need for cleanliness, and although napkins are unknown, they place a few soft leaves or some rag handy for wiping purposes. The mother also gives the infant a daily warm bath. The few who have had close contacts with Europeans seat the child in an enamel basin, but the majority hold it firmly on their knee and rub it with water taken from a dish alongside. All regard soap as essential no matter how short money may be. (In 1950, when the minimum wage for a labourer was 15s per month, common yellow soap cost 3s 3d a bar.)

By the end of a month the infant is strong enough to be placed in an ordinary string carrying bag. The mother slings this from her head as though she had a load of firewood, except that she may hold it in front of herself instead of hanging it at the back, the normal position. She now has both hands free and can resume light tasks around the house.

Babies who dislike the bag and cry when put into it have to be left on a blanket in a corner or else borne about on the hip or in a sling. But the bulk of them soon get used to it, and it then becomes a sort of cradle. The mother hangs it on a rope from a hook in the rafters so that it is only a few inches off the floor, or on hot days she may suspend it outside from a bough or a post. The baby lies contented for several hours at a time, but should it become restless anyone who is close by tries to pacify it by tapping gently on the bottom of the bag and crooning.

No young child is ever left to cry, and the mother drops what she is doing and takes it to her breast at once. She fondles it tenderly, strokes it, and gazes at it lovingly as it sucks its fill. If it is still unhappy she concludes that it must be ill. I often found that women who had brought their babies for medicine were incapable of giving any details of what was wrong. 'No, he hasn't a fever, and he doesn't cough,' they would say. 'But there must be something the matter because he has been crying for a long time.'

For the first year milk is the chief form of nourishment. The woman's sisters and sisters-in-law, if their breasts are full, are happy to suckle the infant occasionally, but in the early stages she politely declines their offers. She regulates her own diet but cannot be certain whether these other people have been careful of their food. The presence of salt is believed to be dangerous, a view confirmed by physiologists. The deciding factor is that native infants never drink water until they are big enough to hold the heavy coconut or bamboo containers for themselves. This means that they would only be able to digest salt by absorbing the water from their tissues. The nursing mother takes the precaution of cooking her meals separately in order to avoid seasoning and fish caught in the sea.

Practical measures of child care are supplemented by many of the old magical observances. Thus the father also abstains from eating salt-water fish, though for a shorter period, and the mother makes certain that the child's excrement is completely destroyed by fire. If she were to throw it into the sea with the household rubbish the precious life might 'ebb like the tide'. The persistence of such beliefs may be attributable to the high infant-mortality rate. A survey carried out in 1949 in the Sepik Administrative District revealed that in one area, out of every 1,000 babies born, 500 died before the end of the first year (the corresponding figure for the city of Melbourne was 18).[1] The number for Busama is lower than this but still far too high. Malaria, hookworm, framboesia, dysentery, and other diseases are endemic, and all exact a heavy toll.

Other magical taboos are supposed to have more particular effects. Even when the father is allowed salt-water fish he does not eat those with large scales—they might give the child a skin disease—nor those with protruding eyes—they might cause it to develop a squint. Parents also guard their fire lest anyone should take a live coal to light a cigarette. Neglect of this precaution would cause the child to have an outbreak of scabies.

At last the needs of the family force the mother to give some thought to the gardens, and in the fourth or fifth month, depending on the attentiveness of her relatives, she takes up ordinary work once more. In the beginning she carries the baby along in its bag, which she hangs in a convenient spot not far away. She glances over every few minutes to see that all is well and if she has to suckle the child seats herself under the trees, for the moment completely absorbed. On the homeward journey she carries the food and firewood in a bag on her back and the infant in a bag in front with a cloth over it as a protection from the sun.

The child grows heavier with the passing weeks, and most women soon prefer to leave it at home with a grandmother or some sensible older girl, possibly an unmarried sister or sister-in-law. If no relative is available two neighbours may come to an arrangement to relieve one another on alternate days. Failing this, a young girl has to be set to watch under supervision. Agi'wi when not yet eight used to sit in a rough shelter trying to keep her infant sister Nga'angkangwi amused while the mother, a little harassed, gave half her energies to the work in hand and half to the two children.[2]

---

[1] J. K. Murray, 1950, p. 89.
[2] Although the Mission established a school in the village so long ago, few adults are aware of their age. Recently numbers of parents have begun noting down the

At first the mother limits her visits to the gardens to three or four hours, but after a month or two, if the nurse has no trouble, she gradually extends the time. She clearly derives pleasure from the renewed physical contact with the child and spends many minutes nuzzling it and blowing on it gently.

By now the infant can be given other foods. Taro comes first, towards the end of the second month. The mother or the nurse chews a few ounces thoroughly and warms the pappy mass in a leaf over the fire before pushing it into the baby's mouth a little at a time. The child may turn its head away, but she breaks down its resistance by gentle persuasion. Bananas, roasted and then crushed, come next, in the third or fourth month. These are followed by occasional spoonfuls of coconut fluid, and later still, in the fifth or sixth month, freshwater fish and prawns are suitable. By this time, or shortly afterwards, the salt precautions do not have to be observed quite so strictly, and the mother no longer minds if her sisters or sisters-in-law suckle the child.

The father makes his first real acquaintance with the infant at about six months. If he is by nature fond of children, or if this is his firstborn, he may hold it earlier, but the women are so doubtful of his skill that generally he waits. If, on the other hand, he already has a family, he may postpone his attentions for some time longer. He takes the child during the late after-noon when his day's work is done and carries it about on his hip, thus relieving his wife while she is busy cooking. Fathers are no less tender than mothers, and they also croon, nuzzle, and stroke.

The next stage, when the baby begins to crawl, is perhaps the most troublesome, and parents often have nightmares about possible disasters. 'Yes, a crawling infant is a great worry,' one mother sighed. 'It goes from one corner of the house to the other without understanding peril.' People speak of four special dangers, the verandah, the fire, hot water, and knives. The front of most houses is protected by railings and a gate, but the children often fall, and I was several times called upon to treat bruises, gashes, cuts, and burns. Not long ago a toddler pulled a pot of boiling water over himself.

The nurse does not prevent all movement, as is the custom in some parts of New Guinea where the houses are also raised up on piles,[1] but hauls her charge back each time it appears to be in jeopardy, repeating endlessly as she does so, 'No, no, not there.' Some mothers are, I fancy, relieved when at last an accident occurs. 'There, he's learned what happens when he puts his hand in the flames,' Mu'alimawi muttered as she comforted her youngest son. 'You won't ever do it again, will you?'

The sight of a child of any age handling a great bush knife with an eighteen-inch blade would horrify European parents, but the natives show

date of birth of their children, and I have used this information in the following pages except for the youngsters whom I had known all their lives.

[1] Cf. Hogbin, 1943, p. 301.

alarm only during the first two or three years. At this stage they snatch the implement away and offer something else as a distraction. They also ask visitors to leave their tools on a shelf outside. Older children of three and four run about freely knife in hand. They show remarkable dexterity in flinging it aside when they become unsteady in their balance, and I had only one patient, a little girl of about six, with a very bad cut. A brother two years her junior had slashed her.

The child's first attempt at walking is an event. From now on everyone encourages it to persevere, and while persons sitting at a distance beckon it across, those nearby hold out a finger or a stick as a support. They reward success with smiles and ignore failures. But a toddler who has hurt himself is sure of being comforted. Generally somebody says that the ground is at fault. 'Naughty, naughty earth for tripping our little boy's feet', he exclaims. Or he may try to make the child forget his bruises by pointing out an imaginary dog or iguana.

As the infant becomes more independent, so the mother increases the length of her absences, and by the time that it is able to walk about with reasonable assurance and to some extent feed itself, at the age of from eighteen to twenty months, she often spends a full day in the gardens from eight o'clock till fairly late in the afternoon. She does not now offer it the breast but waits for a demand—if it insists on being fed at once, she complies; if not, she goes on with her work. Her change of attitude seems to be the result of social pressure, for she is eager as ever to give it suck, and if no-one else is present she nuzzles and croons with all the old absorbed attention. But the other women discourage such indulgence and warn her that her husband may become jealous. Sometimes the men are, indeed, impatient and pointedly ask when will dinner be ready.

Grandmothers if available continue to act as nurses, but younger women who serve in this capacity can now expect occasional relief, perhaps on one or two days each week. A mother never asks boys to help, and they do not volunteer, but she is glad to accept assistance from girls of seven or eight. 'It's good to have Lutuwi in the village looking after the baby,' her aunt remarked to me while gardening. 'But I must go home soon. No, it's not the child's milk I'm thinking of—it's just that I can't trust Lutuwi for too long. She's still small herself, and I'm afraid of her joining in some game and forgetting.' Yet most of the little girls are thoroughly conscientious. Agi'wi, at this period scarcely ten years old, when left to look after her two sisters, then a month or so over four and a month or so under two, used to carry the baby on her hip for an hour at a time and do her best to keep the other child in sight. A neighbour's wife had agreed to come over if necessary, but whole mornings passed without her intervening.

Both the parents neglect their work if the child falls ill. Mu'alimawi sat at home nursing little Kamaya for five days when he developed an abscess on his leg. She had guests from Bukawa' at the time, but her obligation to provide hospitality carried less weight than her anxiety over the boy's health. Ahipum was forced to send word to relatives, who came to the rescue with supplies of cooked food. He took no part in the nursing, for this is women's work, and was somewhat at a loss to occupy his mind. Later he admitted having invented various errands, 'I couldn't sit still and watch the boy suffer,' he told me.

There is a saying that the more sickly an infant is, and in consequence the more the parents have to tend it, the greater their attachment becomes. This is borne out by numerous examples, of whom the deaf mute Gagala is the most conspicuous. His infirmity dates from an early illness, and ever since he has been the favoured member of the family.

Deliberate weaning is seldom necessary. By the end of the second year the child eats everything except pork and certain kinds of fish and now asks for the breast only when he is miserable, on account perhaps of some injury or slight. The mother, urged on by the other women, makes good-natured fun of the request but for another month or two is prepared to acquiesce.

Stronger measures are as a rule required only when a fresh pregnancy has occurred. Births are supposed to be properly spaced, and people condemn as heartless women who conceive too early. Yet intervals of eighteen months are fairly common. The mother then smears her nipples with ginger and the juice of bitter herbs and forces herself to laugh at the child's discomfiture. 'There, I told you it would be nasty,' I heard one woman remark to her small son. 'You're big and strong now and can eat bananas and fish. They're enough. They taste good, too; not like milk. Milk! Certainly not! It's for infants in arms, that's all.' The boy, though too small to understand what the words meant, realized that he had done something wrong and ran crying to his grandmother, who reproved the mother for her cruelty. 'I know, I know; but what else can I do?' was the answer.

The older child is seldom seriously jealous of the new arrival. His emotional link with the mother persists, but it has already been perceptibly loosened, and she is no longer the sole focus of his attention. His outbursts of temper against the infant who has displaced him are therefore attributable in the main to an immediate cause and not to general ill-will. The behaviour of Kamaya, Ahipum's sixth child, was typical. He ordinarily showed great kindness to his brother Sa'gab and often babbled playfully alongside the string-bag cradle. Then one day when he had a cold his mother refused to put the baby from her knee and nurse him instead. 'Go to your grandmother,' she told him. 'Can't you see that I have to hold Sa'gab?' 'Send Sa'gab away,' Kamaya stormed. 'Give him to someone else. I don't want him here. I hate him.' Yet the following morning I discovered him trying to share his piece of taro. The case of Buaki was similar. His mother said that the only time he resented his brother was when she had declined to find him something to eat until after the latter had sucked his fill.

Parents expect that a two-year-old child will have his bowels and bladder under control, at least during the daytime. Training begins much earlier, in about the third month, when the mother makes a practice of holding the infant out as soon as it wakes in the early morning. She grunts and strains to indicate what is wanted but is still extraordinarily gentle. Later she comes to recognize the signs and takes appropriate action. Once the child can toddle she tells it to go outside or ask one of the elders to carry it to the latrine, and she may now scold it for making a mess. The men, more sensitive about such matters than the women, are profoundly irritated if a youngster defecates in their presence. 'Excreta, bad, stinking, disgusting,' one father told his son in my hearing. 'Tell me before, and I'll take you to the bush.' Another man was so annoyed by a three-year-old approaching a group of visitors with a dirty behind that he first hit the child and then sought out the mother to upbraid her for permitting such an outrage. 'Your child is big enough to know how to wipe himself with a twig,' he told her. 'You have shamed us all.'

Latrines are a fairly recent innovation, and, though few will admit using the brushwood behind the village, a person who passes that way runs a risk of soiling his feet. Thus hookworm and dysentery are universal. Yet the need for protecting the water supply is accepted, and people avoid the banks of all streams, including those at a distance from the settlement. Any adult will punish a child who neglects this precaution.

The people are not prudish, and the phrase 'Urine is killing him' (*ndip gi aing*) is frequently heard in mixed company provided relatives to whom respect is due are not present. 'Excrement is killing him' (*ta' gi aing*) is considered to be slightly improper, and outside the family circle a euphemism is usual.

Children begin bathing in the sea at about two-and-a-half and are soon as much at home in the water as on land. Taho and Nga'tigeng, sons of a couple of my nearest neighbours, seemed to be unaware of the difference between the two elements. I watched them one afternoon when their respective ages were three years and three months and two years and eleven months. They ran along the beach, paddled for a time, returned to the shore to roll in the sand, then tried diving, went swimming once more, and finally clambered over the rocks out of sight. Neither they themselves nor the nearest adults fifty yards away showed any sign of fear.

The grown-ups consider swimming lessons unnecessary, and apparently small children master the art by imitating those slightly older than themselves. It is looked upon as a 'natural' accomplishment like walking, which everyone acquires as soon as he reaches a certain age. (The hill country inland has no large rivers where the inhabitants can learn to swim, and they sometimes drown in the flooded estuaries when visiting the Government station on the coast). Parents therefore do not keep a watch so long as another youngster is present. Their faith is fully justified, and only two accidents, neither of them fatal, have occurred during the past two decades.

In 1947 a child of two years and seven months waded out of his depth and was in difficulties till a companion rescued him, and shortly afterwards another child had to be brought up from the bottom. 'The sea has its dangers,' Ahipum grudgingly admitted, 'but they aren't serious like the perils of the house.'

The child no longer has a warm bath, but the elders are fastidious and insist on his washing off any excess of dirt before he goes to bed at night. On wet days, when the water may feel chilly, they send him to a stream or to the beach at least once. If he resists they may take him out by force and give him a good ducking, followed by a brisk rub with sand.

Few Busama children are precocious talkers, but parents always identify the earliest babbling noises, which have no linguistic significance, as *tata*, the babyish form of the word *i*, 'fish'. 'Asking for fish already!' the mother exclaims proudly. She looks upon this and the first teeth as landmarks and is careful to inform the relatives. These latter are under no obligation to make the child a gift, but those who are closely attached to the parents almost always bring along a few prawns and freshwater fish.

The first proper words are *bu*, *na*, and *ma*. *Bu*, actually 'water', is used instead of *su* for 'mother's milk' and 'breast' (the *s* sound is said to be too difficult as yet), and *na* and *ma* are respectively the shortened form of *dinang*, 'my mother', and *damang*, 'my father'. The mother murmurs *bu* and *na* as she suckles the infant, who eventually begins to imitate her. For a short time it applies *na* to everyone, but the father soon teaches it to say *ma*. Then for a time all females are *na* and all males *ma*.

Deliberate language instruction is otherwise spasmodic. Adults only occasionally play a speech game in which they pick up various objects and ask the child to repeat the name, and they are inclined to leave grammatical mistakes uncorrected for years. Amusing errors, however, give rise to general laughter, and the villagers tell of them from house to house.

KINSHIP BEHAVIOUR

The various female relatives take an early interest in the child. The grandmothers and their sisters handle it before even the mother does, and later on, when she resumes her normal work, one or other of them may look after it for hours at a time. Usually she is too old to give it milk, but she prepares mush for it to eat and fondles and strokes it as tenderly as if it were her own.

The aunts are also anxious to help, but most of them have family responsibilities and can spare a short period only now and again. They then nurse the infant on their lap, cuddle it, and, after the salt taboo has been relaxed, offer it their breasts to suck. Subsequently, when it has learned to walk, they take it to their houses, give it delicacies, and try to make it feel at home. They introduce it also to their sons and daughters and urge them to keep it entertained.

The male relatives now join in and behave with equal cordiality. They bring the child to their dwellings and tell their wives to give it perhaps a ripe banana or a plate of vegetable broth.

The youngster returns such kindness with abiding trust. By the time it is ready for weaning it wanders confidently from one kinsman to another babbling away without a trace of fear.

The natives often refer to the place of food in establishing these early kinship ties. The Mission teacher Ida', pointing to his young daughter, remarked that she had already divided the village into houses where she received something to eat and those where she did not. 'That's how children learn about kin,' he said. 'They feel comfortable with someone who gives them meals and finds out afterwards about the relationship.'

The reactions of the boys and girls where I was a frequent guest provided ample confirmation. I used to take them biscuits and sweets and before long found they were visiting me regularly. One day while passing the back of a dwelling I overheard Kamundong, at that time four years old, explaining to a companion that he was going to find Obin (the name by which I was known). 'I'm hungry,' he said. 'Obin will offer me a biscuit: he always does: he's my uncle.' 'There was no need for us to tell the boy you're his uncle,' his father replied when I described the incident. 'You give him food just like my brothers do, and, of course, he calls you "uncle" too. So do the other boys who come here. They say to their mothers that they're off to see their uncle Obin-*ankwa*.'

A minor panic occurred when little Taho failed to inform his mother where he was going. She and his grandmother searched for him in vain and became seriously alarmed. 'I thought you were drowned,' she exclaimed when at last she saw him. 'Silly mother,' he replied. 'I am all right with uncle.'

But Taho in good health was a different being from Taho ill with malaria, and he now resisted my coaxing and refused to leave his parents' side. 'All children are the same,' said his mother. 'They want the father and mother at a time like this. The other relatives won't do.'

The children fail to recognize the true meaning of kinship for another year or two. They gradually restrict the babyish words for 'father' and 'mother', *ma* and *na*, at first applied to everyone, to the persons who go out of their way to be kind irrespective of their status. The next step, the adoption of the proper forms, takes several months longer. *Ma* becomes *damang* and *na* either *dinang* or *nang*, but both are still used for all the kindred. Not until the fifth year are the different words for 'grandparent', 'uncle', and 'aunt' employed correctly. At three Taho called me *ma*, six months or so later I was *damang*, and six months later again I became *damang-ka*, 'my father's elder brother'. He made a further change when he was between five and six. He continued to use *damang-ka* for his father's real elder brother but preferred names for the men classed with him, including myself.

ORPHANS

Uncles and aunts who are without offspring and unlikely because of age or infirmity to have a family in the future are eager to accept the care of any child whose parents have died. Indeed, if two aunts or uncles are childless they may struggle with one another for the custody of the orphan.

The issue is not so simple when the relatives already possess sons or daughters. One of them may be especially fond of children, for instance, or more than usually devoted to the dead couple, or eager to enlarge his household in order to have an extra helper at a later date. If these conditions do not apply, then, as has been indicated, a girl generally goes to one of her maternal aunts, a small boy to his father's eldest brother, an older lad to a mother's brother.

The youngster who becomes a member of a household hitherto childless is sure of a good home. The couple are pleased to have someone with them at last and behave exactly like real parents. Thus they take it for granted that he will inherit their personal possessions. He responds as a true son would and calls them *damang* and *dinang*, terms that are socially appropriate but formally incorrect. Yet his general kinship status is unchanged, and land rights come to him through his dead mother, not his foster mother.

Nga'gili' and his barren wife Nga'angkangwi took in the four-year-old Ho'nung in 1948 and have ever since cherished him dearly. An observer unaware of the facts would assume that they were an ordinary family, for the boy also is as loving as well could be. Yet a few years earlier Nga'angkangwi, at that time about thirty-two or thirty-three, had refused to accept the care of two recently-orphaned nephews-in-law. The neighbours said pityingly that they supposed she thought she still had a chance of conceiving and hesitated to admit her disability.

Not all orphans are as fortunate as Ho'nung. No native would be deliberately unkind to a young child or allow him to starve, but couples with offspring of their own to consider do not always welcome a small nephew as a permanent member of their family group. They may have been agreeable to him previously as an occasional guest, but caring for him all the time is a different matter.

Children who have lost one parent only may find themselves in a similar plight when the surviving parent remarries. The mother's second husband, or the father's second wife, tends to regard true sons and daughters as of greater importance than step-sons and step-daughters.

The natives maintain that orphans reared by childless couples grow into pleasanter youths and girls than those reared by couples with children. I cannot say whether this is universally true, but it is a fact that Ho'nung and one or two like him have more balance and self-assurance than some of those who have been brought up in larger households. These latter tend to be timid and retiring or quarrelsome and over bold.

AFTER THE THIRD YEAR

People often say that the intellect no less than the body requires time to grow. 'Infants cannot walk at once,' they explain, 'and it would be foolish to expect understanding from a child.' This attitude is well illustrated by an answer to my question why small girls and boys own no property. 'They can't use it yet. We give them something as soon as they know what it's for, clothing first, gardens next, pigs not till they've settled down in marriage.'

On another occasion an elder expressed disapproval when one of my friends attributed adult sentiments to his small son. Such talk, said the senior, was sheer rubbish. Dahungmboa, the friend, was presenting me with some bananas and had brought the child along. 'Hagalu' here has been pestering me all day to give you these,' he explained. 'He saw you hadn't any hanging on the verandah when we passed this morning and thought you might be hungry.' The remark was obviously intended as a joke— Hagalu' was another of my 'nephews'—but I made a point of thanking the boy for his solicitude and then gave him some biscuits. 'Dahungmboa, what are you talking about?' the elder asked. 'Hagalu' concerned that Obin might be hungry! Don't be silly. He can't think at all yet.'

The men also say that young children are too immature to listen with profit to serious discussions. 'Nothing for little ears here, so stay where you are,' they call out when assembling in the afternoons under the trees above the beach to talk over their problems. A rumour of adultery was once being debated, and, following on a brusque order that a boy of four must leave, someone remarked that he might cause embarrassment by repeating the conversation. 'A good thing if he did,' another man interjected. 'The wrongdoers would then know what we each of us think of them.' 'Dale' doesn't mean that,' a companion whispered in my ear. 'We sent the boy away because he's still without sense.'

A youngster is sometimes to be seen at the more formal gatherings after darkness has fallen, but only because the mother, who is expected to be present herself, has no alternative to dragging him thither. As a rule he is by this time too sleepy to pay much attention, but if not the seniors refuse to allow him to refer afterwards to the subject under discussion. They also prohibit games leading to an imitation of the meeting, and I have several times seen men belabouring troops of small boys who were mimicking the speakers of the night before. 'Making fun of something important!' an old man yelled to them one day. 'Stop it, I say; you know you can't understand.'

This treatment of the four- to six-year-olds is in marked contrast to what happens in Wogeo, an island off the New Guinea coast further to the west. The educational technique there is to assume that even the smallest children are miniature adults. The father allocates property to his sons almost from their birth and pretends when giving presents to a relative that he has yielded to their solicitations. He also tells them when they are naughty that unless they mend their manners no girl will want them for a husband.[1]

Yet Busama parents take great trouble to prevent young children from fighting or interfering with other people's property; and they are most insistent on their showing respect for relatives and sharing any food with playmates. The training is more by compulsion than precept, and at this stage they prefer to administer a hasty slap rather than explain the offence. They drag quarrelling youngsters apart, and I have often listened to such threats as, 'I'll give you a clout if you don't put that bag down at once: it's Igapowi's, not yours', 'You'll have a smack if you go on sitting there when your uncle Nga'sele' has asked you to fetch him a firestick: do as he says', and 'I'll take my stick to you if you don't give Kamaya half that banana.'

Early childhood, nevertheless, is a time of almost uninterrupted enjoyment. Busama is a paradise for the young. The climate is so warm that clothing is unnecessary and bathing a joy, and there are shelving beaches, clean white sands, lapping waves, long coral reefs, clear freshwater streams, dozens of waterfalls, thick forests, rocks and hills for scrambles, trees for climbing, and lianas for use as swings; moreover, the village is so big that a dozen or more playmates are always within easy reach.

Play groups at first include both sexes, and children in consequence are fully aware of the appearance of the external genitalia. The parents hand out cast-off strips of calico, but these are not cut to fit and fall to the ground within a few minutes. The laughing attempts of bystanders to induce a sense of shame are never successful, and the boys proudly point to the penis as proof that they are male (*nga'*), while the girls maintain that they will one day have breasts and are female (*awi*). The difference is so far of little importance, and all run, clamber, and swim together with the same facility and venturesome spirit. Further, they make no discrimination when pretending to carry out adult tasks. Boys as well as girls play at cooking, normally women's work, and girls as well as boys play at fishing, men's work.

Perhaps the most striking feature of the various activities of the children is the absence of any form of competition. These natives have not a single game for young or old in which an individual or a side can be declared the winner. Two persons may struggle in fun, but no wrestling matches are organized, no races, no tugs-of-war. Even football, introduced twenty or thirty years ago, does not here require the selection of teams, and the players kick the ball about aimlessly from one part of the village to another and back again. Collections of special kinds of objects also make little appeal. It is true that such items as stamps and cards are not easily obtainable, but coloured shells and birds' eggs abound.

Favourite pastimes of the small fry include string figures, blowing pea-like seeds through a tube, hopscotch, skipping, diving, bowling hoops of cane, ninepins with conical shells as pins and immature coconuts as balls,

[1] Hogbin, 1946, pp. 275-96.

and imitations of grown-up pursuits, including cooking, canoeing, and housebuilding. Such very young children do not concentrate for long and frequently change the game. On one occasion half a dozen five-year-olds began putting up a house. They had brought the poles from the bush, and the frame was nearly completed when one lad tripped and pulled down a couple of the uprights as he fell. A girl standing nearby kicked him in the abdomen as he lay prone and called him a clumsy fool. This precipitated a fight, and a grandmother had to restore order. She gave everyone a banana and sent them all off to the water, where they remained for half an hour. Four of the party then returned, bringing three new companions. Some of them set to work on the poles while others collected a broken clay pot, abandoned by some housewife, and played at boiling stones for a meal. Shortly afterwards a lizard came too near, and the boys chased and killed it. They dubbed this 'a pig for the feast' and began cutting it up for distribution. They had removed three of the legs when some other children arrived and suggested that the body should be buried. A man had died a few days before, and the ritual must have been fresh in their minds. All now joined in the funeral, with much realistic wailing and embracing the 'corpse' before the interment in a hole in the sand. The group then split up. One half took a log, which they said was their canoe, and the other party went crab hunting.

Awareness of some of the social implications of sex begins to dawn somewhere about the latter end of the seventh year. Boys and girls still play together for some time longer but now keep to their separate spheres. Gaya's parents live near one of the springs from which drinking water is drawn, and when I knew him first he used to set off with a bottle every time the game related to household concerns. Then suddenly he refused. I heard him telling a girl cousin slightly younger than himself that this was her business. 'A man carrying water!' he laughed scornfully. 'My father doesn't go to the spring: that's mother's job.' The change in Tawasiwi was equally sudden. One week she was romping with some boy companions and the next sending them off to catch a pig 'while we women tidy the house and go on with our mat making'.

From this moment onwards the little girls are more careful with their garments, and many of them like to sling a string bag from their head. This has become a sort of badge, and the females generally are seldom without it. They even wear it to church and say that although there is nothing to be carried they would feel too uncomfortable to leave it at home. Children's bags are at first only a few inches square, but the mother increases the size as they grow taller.

The boys have nothing comparable to wear or carry and perhaps for that reason do not as yet identify themselves so closely with their fathers. They run about naked for a year or two longer.

The next step is separate sex groupings. Parents say that they would object to continued intermingling, but the main impulse seems to come from the boys, who now refuse to allow the girls to accompany them. Yet they are moderately polite and do not call their sisters names or try to bully them.

The older boys play many of the earlier games but with more imagination. They pretend to be policemen, for instance, and attempt to arrest passers-by with the aid of their pea-shooters. Again, instead of using any rough piece of wood as a canoe, they try first to cut it into shape and attach an outrigger. Their efforts are usually crude but display some slight appreciation of form. They also make models of cars and trucks, and one day a group of seven-year-olds, after a visit with their parents to Lae, rigged several abandoned petrol drums in trees to serve as street lamps. They intended to light a fire in each of them but found that the suspending rope burned through as soon as the blaze gave effective illumination. Other popular pastimes are spearing fish and shooting birds and bandicoots with arrows. The boys themselves cook the catch and eat it as a snack with pawpaws or mangoes.

The girls also continue playing as before but favour the quieter games, such as hopscotch, ninepins, and skipping.

Parents maintain that daughters are 'soft'. Girls, they say, cry easily and are more amenable than their brothers. I observed no difference in the amount of whimpering, but it is a fact that little girls begin carrying out odd jobs earlier than the boys. The explanation may lie in their more yielding nature, but probably the demands of the mother are of greater significance. Household chores crowd upon the women at certain periods of the day, notably during the early morning and evening, and it is convenient for them to have someone to look after the baby for a few minutes, fill the water containers, clean the dirty utensils, watch the saucepans, or tend the fire. They summon a girl rather than a boy because domestic tasks are looked upon as her concern. As a rule, too, she is playing close at hand, whereas he is scampering about half a mile away. Men's work is in the main heavier and necessitates a long journey first. The father would thus find children an encumbrance, and he consequently postpones calling on his sons until they are bigger.

Little girls have no interest at all in dolls or similar toys—they have real infants to mind, real meals to prepare, and real fires to stoke. They have no proper playthings of their own and quickly abandoned those I distributed among them.

5

Later Childhood and Adolescence

At last the time comes when the children have to enter the world of the grown-ups. It is characteristic that the natives should see the change in terms of food. People say that at first a child receives his supplies as though by magic—he asks for something, and there it is in his hand. But as soon as he is grown in understanding he is fit to be taught that meals must be earned by toil. I judged that the turning point was reached at approximately the seventh birthday—perhaps a little earlier for girls and a little later for boys.

The most striking change for the boy is that he is turned out of the house at night to sleep in one of the clubs. This practice has been carried over from pagan times, when the growing male was supposed to need protection from the contaminating influences of women. Christianity ignores most of the sexual distinctions that the old religion served to reinforce, but the elders still insist on the move. They justify themselves by saying that the club is 'a kind of school' where the lad makes closer contacts with the wider circle of kinsfolk and learns how to behave by 'chewing betel-nut and smoking with the seniors and listening to their talk'. (The boy has his first betel-nut at about seven, his first cigarette at about fifteen; girls neither chew nor smoke.)

In the beginning the lad usually goes to his father's club. An older brother or a cousin sleeps at his side for a night or two, but the new arrangement is seldom a severe wrench. The club buildings are scattered through the village, and the family residence is never more than a few minutes' walk away. Sometimes an only son is reluctant to leave his mother, and the men have then to intervene and shame him into going.

The maternal uncles also hasten to offer the boy the freedom of their club. They explain his ties with the land and tell him that he will do well to spend his evenings hearing something about the location of the allotments, the boundary marks, the types of soil, and so forth. Before long many youngsters spend half their nights with the father and the paternal kinsmen and the other half with the maternal kinsmen.

The aims of the traditional system of education are set out in one of the books published by the Mission for native reading. Various natives compiled this particular volume, which deals with features of the old culture regarded as worthy of preservation. Lads should be obedient and industrious, one passage runs, listen carefully when spoken to, carry messages, refrain from eating the choicest foods, distribute their fish, and look after any guest. They will thus enhance the good name of the village and in time win themselves a bride. But if instead they are disobedient and lazy, pay no heed to orders, stay away when work is to be done, give fish only to their mother, eat greedily, and neglect visitors, then the reputation of the village suffers; further, nobody will want them for a son-in-law, and they will have to remain bachelors.

The model girl follows her mother to work, plants taro, brings back heavy loads of firewood, and minds the babies while the women cook. She takes over if someone is ill and remembers to feed the family pigs and to bring wood and water to her father's club house. The elders regard her with favour and are eager to accept her as a bride for a young dependant. The bad girl, on the contrary, goes unwed. No-one wants to have a wife who is always tired or refuses to help with the garden and in the house.

SCHOOLING

Another landmark of the eighth year is the entry into the village school. The establishment is supervised by the Mission, which also provides training for the native teachers, but is largely controlled by the people themselves. Classes are held every morning, and the course lasts for four years. No further educational opportunities are available for girls, but the boys pass on for two years more in the Area boarding school at Mala'lo. The best pupils are then free to enter a Government high school or one of the Mission colleges.

Instruction has a strong religious bias but is not restricted to the inculcation of Christian principles and biblical knowledge. Village schools teach reading, writing, arithmetic, geography, elementary hygiene, and pidgin-English. The main language used is Yabim, into which the complete New Testament, stories from the Old Testament, many hymns, and two or three other books have been translated. This dialect is closely related to Gawa', and the Busama scarcely consider it a foreign tongue. The children are fully literate by the end of their fourth year.

The same subjects are taught in the Area school but at a higher standard. Recently English has been introduced but so far without conspicuous success. The natives grasp pidgin readily, but the structure of standard English is so different, and the spelling so illogical, that many years will be required for its mastery.

TECHNICAL TRAINING

A boy acquires many of the techniques by direct imitation. He goes out with his elders in a canoe, for example, and after a few minutes' observation begins flicking his paddle through the water in the same rhythm as the rest of the crew. He watches a few times while the others rig the sails, but this task also presents few difficulties. Again, once he has seen the hooks baited

F

and the lines cast he can do his share of fishing. The art of steering follows, and within a couple of months his father trusts him to bring a small craft from place to place by himself. Guiding it in heavy weather demands accurate timing to breast the waves, but ultimately he also achieves this skill.

Gardening is mastered in much the same manner. The men find the child useful from the start when they collect the dried rubbish for burning, and they also send him to gather the vines that serve as lashings for the fences. At first he finds the digging stick a trifle heavy, and for a year or two he has to be content with planting the suckers in holes that someone else has made for him.

But fishing, navigation, and horticulture also demand a certain amount of background knowledge. The adults have to explain such basic matters as the seasonal changes of the prevailing winds, the weather signs, the reefs where the fish are to be found, the types of taro best suited to the different soils, the kinds of areas to be cultivated in the rainy months and during the drier periods of the year, and so on. The accepted practice is to let the child take the initiative rather than force the educational pace. 'The boy's judgment grows till at length he wants to know,' said Ahipum. 'Then, when he enquires, we give him the answers.' 'Why can't we plant our yams with the taro along the Buang River?' young Taho demanded. 'This is the ground for yams here; they wouldn't grow in the Buang clay,' his father replied. 'Feel this with your fingers. Light and crumbly, isn't it? Well, that's what yams like.'

Similarly, the seniors wait until the child begins to display an active interest before telling him the land tenure system. Then they talk about the different localities, explain how the ground is divided into strips, and list the persons associated with each one. I found that boys of about ten could always tell me the whereabouts of the territories cultivated by their closer relatives. One day when I was out walking with young Alum he pointed out that his maternal kinsmen regularly cleared the bush on one side and his paternal kinsmen that on the other. 'My mother's brothers go over there to the left, and my father and his brothers to the right. My mother's brothers and I have the same land, but I can go with father too. They can't, not unless he asks them; and he can't go with them unless they ask him.'

The daily journey to the cultivations serves as an occasion for imparting information about the flora of the country. The natives make some use of almost every tree or plant and therefore have a practical interest in their forest surroundings. Two kinds of trees can be cut into canoe dugouts, three into outrigger floats, two into house posts, one into wall boards, and so forth. Various shrubs and herbs are also of value—they furnish food-stuffs and flavourings and material for canoe lashings, string bags, fish-lines, dyes, and medicinal potions.

Eating is not allowed in school, and as workers do not carry luncheon packages the children must soon control their appetite and partake of proper meals with the rest of the family. The parents always insist on good manners, and the boys and girls have to learn to face the other diners, break the food into small pieces, hold the relish in one hand and the taro in the other, eat at moderate speed, and avoid belching loudly or smacking the lips.

One job in particular, gathering green drinking coconuts, is always assigned to schoolboys. Indeed, the men and the lads over the age of fourteen are unwilling to climb any kind of tree if a younger person is handy. Boys begin by choosing easy palms with a sloping trunk and eventually graduate to those that stand up straight. First they fasten loops of rope or tough creeper around the wrists and ankles; and they then ascend, holding a knife between the teeth, by gripping the trunk and thrusting upwards with the feet. They hack the nuts off, husk them, and carry them home slung on a pole.

Thus a youngster of nine or ten is already a part of the social system. The grown-ups still permit him a good deal of time for play and do not expect him to make a daily appearance after school or to put forward the same effort as themselves; but he has a more-or-less regular place in the fishing team, and the value of his help in cultivation is so far recognized that the seniors set aside plots on his behalf. The labour organization is scarcely affected, but he can if he wishes say that the produce is his.

Groups of young brothers and cousins now make gardens by themselves in the valleys close to the settlement. They take taro suckers from their own plots and beg banana cuttings and pineapple tops from relatives. The yield is usually poor, partly on account of the over-worked soil, partly because the flimsy fences offer little hindrance to the domestic pigs. But the parents and uncles, who look upon the enterprise as excellent training, encourage the boys to persist and are proud of their achievements.

The girls do not have to adjust themselves to the same extent as their brothers. Their course has already been set, and, though they attend school, there is no women's club to which they can be sent. They keep on with the old tasks, but the mother expects them to display greater perseverance.

The first job the little girl does by herself is to prepare the vegetables. The mother shows her how to remove the tough stalks and fibres from the green leaves and how to peel the taro corms without undue waste. By the time she is about nine she can also lay and make the fire. This is not easy, for the conical cooking pots readily fall over. She scoops out a shallow depression in the ground and then builds up a triangular framework of sticks around it. Next she scatters dry leaves in the centre, takes live coals from another fireplace in a pair of bamboo tongs or a loop of long Cordyline leaves, and throws them on the top. Then as soon as the wood is thoroughly alight she fixes the pot in position with the base resting in the depression. A lining of banana leaves goes in first to prevent the food from sticking to the sides, then the liquid, and finally the vegetables. In the beginning an older woman has to pour in the water. Some of it comes from the sea, some from the spring, and the proportions vary according to the recipe to be followed. The children soon know what is required and at the age of about eleven can in an emergency cook the family meal alone.

Like her brother, the girl also visits the gardens after school to assist in burning the rubbish, planting the suckers, weeding, and harvesting; and, like him, she soon has plots allocated to her.

Girls readily fall into such routine tasks as sweeping and mat making and need guidance only when they wish to net string bags. Most of them take the initiative, as in the case of the boys, and ask to be taught. As the craft is new to the village, not all the women can do it, so many children have to seek instruction from an aunt or some more distant relative.

MORAL TRAINING

The notion of 'conscience', an inner guiding voice giving approval or con-demnation, is foreign to traditional Busama thought, and the early mission-aries had to find other expressions to convey the meaning. The nearest local concept is that of *maya*, described as the discomfort a person feels when he has been found out in some unworthy act. I shall translate the word as 'shame'.

Normally a person who has made a moral decision when asked for his reason answers that he would have felt shame had he acted in any other way. He then goes on to explain that the other villagers would have made unpleasant remarks about him and that he would have been embarrassed. Nga'gili' said that, anxious though he was to raise a family, he 'would have been ashamed' to divorce his barren wife; Ahipum that, much as he detested Abong, he 'would have been ashamed' to stay away from the funeral of the man's infant daughter; Buasi' that, despite his poverty, he 'would have been ashamed' to ignore his kinship obligations by failing to offer compensation for a theft committed by a nephew; and Mabiyeng that he 'would have been ashamed' to have gone on with urgent garden work while his near neighbour and kinsman Gwaleyam needed help to repair his house.

Parents inculcate a sense of guilt by reiterating such phrases as, 'Have you no shame?' 'What, would you swallow your shame?' and 'Go, hang your head in shame.' The slaps of earlier days are still in order, but the children have now to listen, in addition, to a long lecture.

'Aren't you ashamed of what you've done?' Gili'wi once asked her seven-year-old daughter Agi'wi when she suspected her of stealing some bananas from the next house. 'Go, hang your head in shame and sit by yourself. You'll get a name for being a thief, my girl; that's what's going to happen to you. People will say, "Look, here's Agi'wi: lock up the boxes: she takes everything she sees." ' At this point the child sneaked outside, but Gili'wi, busy with the baby, did not notice and continued. 'Stealing isn't our fashion—your father doesn't steal, and I don't steal—and now we have a daughter like you! Haven't I told you not to touch what doesn't belong to you? Alas, alas! I think you've thrown shame overboard. The idea of having a thief for a daughter, a girl who forgets shame and takes bananas from another house!' I then broke in to say that Agi'wi had left. 'Naughty child,' was the response. 'I'll teach her to be ashamed in time: by and by she'll know.'

These homilies always make much of the results of bad conduct, such as unpopularity and loss of reputation. 'You know what it means to be called a thief,' Ahipum reminded his eldest son, then aged eleven. 'People will talk about you and sneer. They'll point you out to strangers, and you'll have to hang your head in shame. If you talk to them they'll put their hands on their belongings and walk away. You'll be alone, disliked, and ashamed.'

The father of another lad of the same age told him that he would have to leave the village unless he mended his ways. 'You'll be turned out of the place,' the man scolded. 'We Busama haven't boxes with keys to lock up everything, and the people will say that they can't let a thief remain. We'd be afraid that you'd go on helping yourself. You'll end up in court and be sent to gaol; that's what'll happen.'

Ahipum also reprimanded his daughter Igapowi in similar terms when she wished to play instead of minding one of her young brothers. 'You may have no shame now in disobeying your mother, but just you wait,' he told her. 'Who's going to be ashamed later when Obin here writes a book about us?—you are. He'll put a photograph in it and say underneath, "This is lazy disobedient Igapowi who spends all day playing. Other girls help their mothers, but not Igapowi." Where will you hide your head when you see that?'

Yet although the adults so often call the child's attention to the shame that he himself ought to feel, they are unwilling to add to the embarrassment of others. The girl Agi'wi once complained that a neighbour, Mayeng, had been angry with her for calling his son Gwale a thief after he had beaten the boy before her eyes for stealing a piece of fish. 'Mayeng said that if I made Gwale ashamed he'd tell you, father, and that you'd give me a talking to,' she said. 'But you won't, will you? Gwale was a naughty boy, and all I did was to say he was bad.' 'Mayeng was right,' the father replied. 'You shouldn't have let Gwale see that you were there. It's enough that Mayeng reproved him without your shaming him as well.'

At times parents even go to the length of drawing their children aside and advising them to take no notice when someone has corrected a playmate. 'Call the boy over and continue the game,' they say. 'You don't want to drive his shame in deeper.'

Meanness is another subject for dissertations. The two common words are *tita'-gaming* (literally, 'his belly holds him back', 'he is constipated') and *gewe'-boa* (literally, 'head bowed down always', i.e. 'paying no attention to others'). The seniors say over and over again that people who do not share food become notorious. They remind the children that generosity is the best method of attracting helpers and to ram the point home quote the adage that the person who keeps his fish for himself has no-one later to sit with him. 'Give to your playmates,' they urge, 'and you'll have assistants in plenty.'

'That's the way to make a good name for yourself,' Mu'apu' commented, when, after long persuasion, her young son had at last divided his plate of pudding with a couple of other boys. 'Give away food, and your house will be full of people. When you want to make a garden they'll go along and cut down the forest with you.'

Yet ordinary householders cannot afford to share food all the time, and the children have to learn to temper liberality with common sense. One of the stock jokes deals with the awkwardness caused by the too-well-brought-up youngster who produces for casual guests the bunch of areca nuts that his father had carefully concealed. If such an incident occurs the boy is told either to confine his giving to his own things or to make certain that there will be plenty left. He soon comes to realize when a gesture will be inexpedient.

Food was short during the Pacific war, and most families instead of taking their meals on the verandah, the usual place, withdrew behind closed doors. Children who went outside were allowed to present portions to playmates in the accustomed manner but were later chided for their foolishness. 'You ask for more taro now when you've just given half to Buaki,' Abong's mother grumbled. 'Where shall we find more when this is finished? Tell me that.'

The parents use similar arguments against fighting. They warn that it is folly to incur the ill-will of those from whom help must eventually be sought. 'You two are *da-tigeng*,' I heard a neighbour exclaim as he dragged a young relative from a childish brawl. 'Those who are of the same blood must never fight. Haven't your father and uncles told you that? How can you work together after you've squabbled? You'll both be too angry.'

A few parents, here as elsewhere, make a habit of supporting their own offspring regardless of the rights and wrongs of the case. Inggantang once said sarcastically that his neighbours Madulu and Makisa'wi were fortunate in rearing a son who was always blameless. In his exasperation he ordered his children to tell the boy not to approach them. They obeyed at the time, but I noticed him back in an hour or two.

Many Melanesian societies recognize explicitly that, if a person is not allowed the natural expression of his anger, he must be provided with an alternative means of easing the emotional tension. The Wogeo have a proverb, 'Smash a pot if you are angry with your wife; otherwise you will be bad-tempered for a month.' These natives take the trouble after they have separated two quarrelling children to give them an axe or knife each and tell them to split a post. The Busama instead leave the youngsters to exhaust themselves with howling.

The people also deprecate lying. Mu'alimawi once discovered a broken pot pushed to the back of a shelf. She taxed young Mingkwa with hiding it, and, though at first he said 'no', he soon confessed. His untruthfulness, she told him, was worse than the loss. 'You do well to be ashamed,' she scolded. 'If you go on lying like this you'll find that no-one will believe a word you say.'

Fortitude seems to be almost the only virtue that the natives ignore. They never send a child who is afraid of the dark outside without giving giving him a torch (they multiply his fears by agreeing about the danger of treading on a snake or falling over a log), and if he dreads heights they refrain from forcing him to climb coconut palms. 'It's some people's nature,' they murmur consolingly. 'You'd better stop down below if you feel dizzy. We don't want you to fall and be killed.' The same attitude is revealed in illness. They comfort sick children with good food and advise them to lie down until the fever has subsided, never urge them to make light of the pain and carry on.

I do not wish to imply a lack of appreciation of the value of self control: the people exercise their will-power to a considerable degree in the face of physical injuries. A child who is hurt in a fall often goes on with his game after shedding the minimum of tears, and the old men say that in the past a youth passing through the initiation ordeals rarely disgraced himself by showing terror.

Adults nearly always display endurance in major crises—for example, the women in childbirth and the men during unexpected squalls at sea. Yet it is a fact that the urge to prove oneself by courting danger is conspicuously lacking in the Busama make-up. I am certain that no-one would take out his canoe if the weather signs were unfavourable, and European officers of the Administration have told me that the young men who enter the police force make poor scouts when called upon for exploratory patrols into new territory.

The Manus of the Admiralty Islands, off northern New Guinea, are in this respect the direct opposite of the Busama. They are contemptuous of danger and brave to the point of foolhardiness; and they actually boast of how often they have cheated death. It is hardly surprising that they should be the most efficient sailors in Melanesia—the *Argonaut* Trobrianders are longshoremen by comparison—and yet scornful of canoe magic; or that they should be regarded as the perfect scouts.

Thunder and lightning give rise to what is perhaps the most curious manifestation of the Busama attitude. On my earlier visits to the village I was accompanied by a personal servant who came from the Sepik district. One evening we were both entertaining friends, he in the kitchen and I in the other room, and when a storm broke we were equally astonished to find our guests, all fully-grown men, suddenly diving under tables or beds, where they remained for upwards of an hour. Certain places in New Guinea are notorious for bad storms, but Busama is not among them, and I know of only one person being killed by lightning.

The babies are indulged so much that they seldom cry; but the older children cry a great deal, perhaps because of this lack of emphasis on hardihood. They yell consistently whenever an adult interferes with them, as, for instance, by preventing them from having their own way, or giving them a light tap, or by delivering a mild rebuke. My sleep was invariably disturbed at sunrise by howling, which went on till the workers began to leave for the cultivations at about eight o'clock. Sometimes the noise came from one direction, sometimes from another, and occasionally from all at once. Several children whom I timed with my watch cried continuously for over an hour. The adults seldom take notice unless the offender begins to throw things about, when they either beat him or hold him tightly in their arms. Girls bawl lustily but are probably less inclined to violence than boys, who stamp and kick or hurl themselves down and hammer the ground with their fists in transports of fury. Yet they show little malice afterwards; and they do not sulk.

The outburst of the child Siawa was typical. He had asked his mother for something to eat but refused to fetch the water for the sago gruel that she promised to cook. 'Very well,' she told him, 'you can go without.' He marched outside and aimed billets of wood at the wall till she emerged and hit him. Then, when he had been stamping and yelling for half an hour, his father called out, 'Shut up! I can't hear what I'm saying. If you don't keep quiet I'll give you to a policeman. We don't want you here making all that fuss.' Still crying, the child now lay down in a puddle and smeared his body with mud. I photographed him sprawling there in misery while his mother stood close by roaring with laughter. 'Yes, Siawa's irritable today,' his father called out calmly.

On another occasion young Gala'pawi burst out crying when upbraided for neglecting some order. After twenty-five minutes of uproar her mother strode over and gave her a few harmless taps with a piece of folded cloth, saying as she did so that no husband would be prepared to put up with such tantrums. At this the child's howls became louder still. Ten minutes later again the mother kicked her three times, but she went on wailing for another quarter of an hour.

La'ku' made a similar show of himself after his father had refused to take him to the gardens. His mother held him for some minutes, but as he still wished to follow she had to confine him once more. Freed at length, he screamed and stormed for twenty minutes. The neighbours, smiling to themselves, watched for a short time and then went back to work.

PUNISHMENT

Discipline presents a greater problem than is usual in New Guinea. In the average village, where the population does not exceed a couple of hundred, the young offender has few companions of his own age and cannot escape the grown-ups' disapproval. They frown or give a shake of the head, and he soon minds his manners. But Busama has 600 inhabitants, and the children form a series of gangs. The natives here, as I said, are prone to lecturing and slapping; and they sometimes feel compelled to shut the youngsters up or tie them to a post.

In the early stages the parents intimidate a naughty child by hinting that a bogey man will intervene. An evil spirit may serve the purpose, or they may refer to white men or to the police. 'We'll leave you with a European,' they caution; or 'A policeman will come and take you away.' The father of my young 'nephew' Taho was taken by surprise when the boy replied that being sent to a white man would be no hardship as he had already decided to accompany me to Sydney. The bullying habits of the native police have aroused widespread distrust, and the people genuinely fear them. Young Ngada'pu was much alarmed when his father said that he intended to report the boy's repeated misconduct to the sergeant in Lae. 'You'll be locked in gaol, and you know what happens to prisoners. They're given a hiding every morning before work. No answering back then! The cane does all the talking.' I enquired what parents spoke about in earlier days before the police force was established. 'Sorcery,' Ngada'pu's father replied. 'They used to deafen me with it.'

Children are unimpressed if the father threatens to deprive them of their dinner. They know that he is unlikely to leave them hungry for long and that, in any case, they can always approach one of their aunts. Usually they sit outside and wait patiently until someone calls them back. A summons came for Moali, for instance, within half an hour. He had incurred the wrath of his father Nga'sele' for answering rudely when asked why he had stayed in the village instead of coming to the gardens. 'I was playing, of course. Where did you think I'd be?' he had said. 'Go back then,' Nga'sele' told him. 'You'd better eat the sand that grows on the beach. The food from the garden is for those who work. Off you go at once. Be off!' I was visiting the house, and after an interval both the parents, who had clearly been thinking of the child continually, said they supposed he must have something after all. Nga'sele' then delivered the usual homily. 'Taro doesn't come up like grass: it has to be cultivated by men and women. The ground must be cleared, the suckers planted, the fences put up, and the weeds removed. Not till all this is done can the supplies be harvested. People who are afraid of work don't have anything to eat. Hear what I say, my son, and follow me to the garden. Remember—no work, no food.'

Some parents adopt the practice of ignoring the child until he apologizes —they pretend that he does not exist and remain silent when he speaks— or they perhaps tie him up for half an hour. The uncles sometimes take out a rope and threaten to bind a disobedient nephew, but I am doubtful whether they would ever dare face the father's subsequent criticism. On the other hand, they may shut the boy up in the house, a method of punishment that is widely approved despite its inconvenience (there is only one room, and if the door is closed no-one can enter). People also warn of the torments of hell, though these, as matters pertaining to religion, are as a rule left to the teachers in the schools.

Parents offer a reward only if the titbit is in full view, and even then many condemn the practice as foolish indulgence. 'It's silly to give presents every time you want something done,' Ahipum chided Kaneng. 'Once you start that you'll find that the children expect too much. They'll become a nuisance by for ever asking for this and that.' Kaneng replied that he would not have thought of bribing his eldest son Lasu' but that little Busilim, to whom he had been speaking, was still very young. 'Busilim asked could he come to the garden, and, as I didn't want him, I gave him some bananas that were on the verandah and said I'd bring back more if he stayed here. He'll forget about it, and everything will be all right. I agree with you. I wouldn't have spoken like that to Lasu'. He'd have thought me a liar unless I found him some.'

The natives never compare the child with his fellows. They judge conduct on its merits, not in relation to the behaviour of other persons. It is a fact that adjectives implying degrees of comparison, common in European languages, are not found in Oceanic dialects, and that such phrases as 'This is better than that' or 'This is bigger than that' must be expressed in clumsy circumlocutions; but the lack does not prevent some of the other Melanesian peoples from using comparisons as a method of training.

The final weapon, when everything else has failed, is violence. The people quote with approval the maxim 'Spare the rod and spoil the child' —presumably it was introduced by the early missionaries—but they usually smack the youngsters with the open hand. They deliver the blow on the cheek or shoulder, taking care to avoid the ears for fear of injuring the drums, or else bend the child over and whack him on the buttocks. Too great severity is regarded with disfavour, nevertheless, and the village leaders reprove those who have been guilty of cruelty.

The educational value of a beating is widely acknowledged, and the seniors take care to remind weak parents of their duty both to the community and the child. 'Your children are a pest to us all,' a neighbour told one couple. 'This is your fault, not theirs. Don't answer that they're different, because they aren't—anyone who isn't punished will grow up badly. See that they listen to you and hit them hard when they refuse to do what you say. Don't you understand that they're a disgrace and will go on being a disgrace as they grow bigger? They'll be liars, thieves, adulterers, and good-for-nothings if you fail to beat them.'

Yet the parents take action only when the child has provoked them beyond endurance, and they never punish him in cold blood. The bystanders call out, 'Teach him, teach him', but the man dealing the blows is concerned solely with venting his anger. He might agree afterwards that he had been more distressed than his victim but would then be rationalizing his action. One afternoon when I was sitting on the beach with a group of men we heard yells coming from a house nearby, and a little later somebody asked a youth who had emerged what was the matter. 'Tigandu had been naughty, and father hit him,' the lad replied. 'The cries were loud. Did he beat him hard?' the enquirer persisted. 'Enough to relieve his temper,' was the answer.

An incident in Ahipum's house is worth quoting here. Igapowi, left to look after her brothers Mingkwa and Kamaya, had persuaded the younger boy to go inside and then slammed the door. Alone and terrified, he threw himself on the floor and in doing so upset a four-gallon drum of kerosene. Igapowi rushed to the rescue but fled on discovering that she could save only half a pint. Mingkwa in the meantime fetched their father. Too out of breath to give the whole story, he related what Kamaya had done without mentioning their sister's responsibility. Ahipum asked no questions and put the boy across his knee. When he paused Mingkwa gave a full account of the preliminaries to the disaster. 'I'll beat Igapowi till the blood runs,' Ahipum exclaimed. But when several hours later she came home he was content with scolding her. He admitted subsequently that he had been unfair but added that if Igapowi had been there he would have tied her up.

Women are as heavy-handed as men and have no hesitation about be-labouring their offspring. Early in my stay I asked one housewife was she in the habit of leaving any beatings for her husband. 'What would be the good of waiting?' she asked. 'I couldn't expect him to do anything when he came back in the evening. The children don't irritate him if he isn't here. Of course I hit them myself.'

One afternoon my neighbour Ikabob called to her daughter Anggawi to bring some firewood from the stack under the verandah. When she saw that the child was not obeying she first gave her a hard slap and then collected the fuel herself. Anggawi followed and threw a handful of sand, some of which went into the cooking pot. Then, realising the gravity of her offence, she fled into the sea. Ikabob chased her and, undeterred by splashings, seized her by the neck, pummelled her face and arms, and ducked her three times.

It is of interest that no-one should have suggested during the Pacific war, when many married men were conscripted, that the children were becoming unruly. The wives were distressed and gave good reasons why they wanted their husbands sent home (such as that new land could not be cleared, the gardens were unprotected by fences, and the houses were falling down), but they laughed at my concern for discipline. They declared that they were fully capable of inflicting punishments.

My impression is that men are more severe with the boys and women more severe with the girls. No overt tradition supports such a conclusion, and people declared that, if what I said was true, the explanation must be sought in the sexual division of labour. Undoubtedly this is in part correct, but it is not the full story. Over and over again I have watched fathers and uncles who would not have borne the misdemeanours of a son or nephew accepting those of a daughter or niece with tolerance; and, correspondingly, mothers and aunts who would not have endured bad behaviour from a daughter or niece offering an excuse when a son or nephew was the culprit. Thus Kaneng beat Busilim for losing a fishhook but two days later said nothing when Tawasiwi broke a cooking pot. On my reminding him that the vessel was the more valuable he replied that, as it was now old, he was thinking of obtaining a new one; and that, besides, Busilim, a boy, was for that reason the better able to stand punishment.

The result of such differential treatment is that girls are apt to run to the father for comfort and boys to the mother. Sometimes a family squabble follows. The parent appealed to wipes the child's nose with his or her fingers and charges the spouse with unfairness and cruelty.

KINSHIP

The grandparents, uncles, and aunts became important in the child's early life because they treated him with such kindness. At that stage he accepted their favours and was not called upon to make a return. Now in later childhood they try to make him understand that he has obligations to fulfil. They remind him of how often they have fed him and point out that in consequence they expect obedience when they ask him to run their errands or carry out odd jobs.

The parents insist that any order from a kinsman must be respected, and they invite the relative to punish negligence. 'Hit the boy, hit him,' they call out. 'Are you not his maternal uncle? Have you not stuffed him full of food since his infancy? Make him listen to you.' Yet they may feel resentful at a too literal interpretation of their remarks. Sometimes brothers quarrel over the treatment of their respective offspring, but brothers-in-law are hedged about with taboos and have to keep criticisms to themselves. Grandparents, though urged to exercise their right of correction, more often take the child's part against the father and mother.

Parents also hand the child gifts for presentation to kinsmen, generally with a brief account of the relationship. 'There, take that joint to Kaneng,' Kawe' told his son, indicating a portion of a wild pig he had caught. 'Kaneng is your father, you know—I call him "elder brother" because his father's mother and my father's mother were real sisters. He's always giving you taro, and when you were little he used to carry you about. His hands were soiled with your urine, and we must repay him now that we have meat.' On another occasion Gwaleyam asked Agi'wi to deliver a bowl of pudding to Kisi, a man whom he regards as a uterine nephew. 'Give Kisi this,' he said. 'I call his mother "sister", so he is your cross cousin. You have no brothers, but if we share with him now he'll keep you in mind and make gardens for you after I'm dead.'

The child hears kinship coupled so often with food that he becomes even more convinced that they always go together. He does not as yet take in the complicated mathematics of the more remote relationships but is well aware of the correct terms for those who entertain him regularly. Further, he understands that the bonds imply obligations on his part—that his acceptance of a meal imposes the duty of making a fair return.

Lahilu, then aged ten, once caused family discomfiture by ingenuously querying a connection with Ahi, one of his father's brothers and the laziest man in the village. 'Go, help Ahi to carry those baskets to the canoe,' his father had ordered. 'You shouldn't go on playing when you see him working so hard. He's your own small father, my younger brother, the son of the same mother.' 'How can Ahi be my small father?' Lahilu answered. 'Other men give me taro, bananas, and fish, but Ahi never offers me anything. If he doesn't feed me, why do you say I must help him?'

A child of this age feels comfortable with most of his closer relatives and stays with them happily for days at a time when the parents are called away to another settlement to transact business, take part in a ceremony, or tend an ailing kinsman. Usually, however, he prefers maternal uncles and aunts to paternal kin. The land-tenure system unites him and his mother's brothers, and his mother's sisters will have been at the house more often than his father's sisters.

Relatives not only offer food voluntarily but are also glad to supply it when the child asks. Yet boys and girls of only ten or perhaps less realize that the direct approach, even to a kinsman, is to some extent shameful. I found that my own 'nephews' as they grew older still visited me but now waited for me to make a move towards the biscuit tin. The Mission teacher Ida' told me how when a youngster he had so much disliked admitting his hunger that he was almost killed gathering coconuts in the dark. His parents were not long dead, and he had joined the household of his mother's brother. This uncle, Buasi', made him welcome, but the wife treated him badly. One day she went on a visit to another village and failed to leave him any dinner. He waited in vain for someone to take pity on him and then climbed a palm tree, from which he fell.

At about this time the children also begin assuming responsibility for their younger siblings and cousins. They take the lead in the various tasks and games and give advice on what ought to be done.

TEMPERAMENT

People say that an individual's personality is established for life by the time his childhood is drawing to an end. A boy who at that age has an equable temper can confidently be expected to develop into a good-natured man, and if, in addition, he possesses common sense he may achieve village leadership. On the other hand, lads who are quarrelsome always remain bad team mates, just as clumsy children become blundering adults.

Males generally are supposed to be like the father, females like the mother. 'There goes his father,' the bystanders often remark as some youth walks along the road. 'A man never dies while his son is alive.' Two factors are thought to operate, spontaneous copying and deliberate moulding.

The child adopts the gait, voice, gestures, turns of phrase and other mannerisms of the parent, and the parent imposes his judgments and moral standards on the child.

The similarity is often striking. Mtu' is sensible and shy like his father Andi'; Nga'balu stolid and painstaking like Kamapu'; Muengpop disgruntled and fiery like Gase'; Humawi soft-voiced, retiring, and hospitable like her mother Gingdahawi; Makisa'wi hot-tempered, mean and shrewish like Gali'mayeng—instances could be multiplied indefinitely. Brothers, and also sisters, tend to have temperaments of the same type. Awasa, Nga'sele', and Sali are all modest, quiet, witty, and beautifully mannered; Kamaya and Hagatu' both co-operative but irascible; and Apu' and Ampi mild and easy but untrustworthy.

Usually there is a convincing explanation for those who violate the rule. Nga'gili' attributes the difference of temperament between him and his brother Madulu, of whom he is the physical replica, to their having been reared by different men. Madulu is the elder by several years and came under the influence of their father, who died shortly before Nga'gili' was born. The mother and baby entered the house of the dead man's brother (see below, p. 141). Again, the incurable laziness of Ahi, who is the brother of the industrious Kamaya and Hagatu' mentioned in the previous paragraph, is said to be the result of his parents' spoiling him in childhood. He was the baby, became the favourite partly on this account and partly as a result of his delicate health, and never learned to work properly.

Of the orphans absorbed into another family, those who receive devoted care, the majority, take after the foster-father or foster-mother; those who are treated indifferently and without warmth or sympathy find models elsewhere. Dambilasi, reared as though he were an only son by Bu'da', is this man's counterpart: Haku, an extra member of the household of his uncle Mala'tu', is in temperament unlike him.

Dambilasi will probably grow up a normal citizen, but the chances are that Haku may become a social misfit. Among the adults of today who were orphaned in infancy two habitual criminals and a would-be suicide are included. The last, a young man named Tusili, is healthy, strong, well-built, and handsome both by native standards and our own; yet he is inordinately jealous of his wife. In 1950, when he was twenty-four, he objected to her going with the women to choir practice, where he alleged that she intended to flirt with other men. She insisted, and during her absence he attempted to hang himself. Cut down in time, he then tried to hack off his left hand with a large bush knife.

Poor Tusili had had a particularly unfortunate childhood. His mother had died in giving him birth, and within the next couple of years he lost first his step-mother, then his father, and finally his foster-father. By the time he was four all his close kinsfolk were dead, and from then on he passed from one distant relative to another. My 'nephew' Gi'lahi, a contemporary, described him as having no fixed place anywhere. 'He rolled about from side to side like a pebble in an empty drum. He was always secretive and always taking offence.'

Suicide occurs occasionally, though only two people have taken their own lives within the last few decades. There are also precedents for self-mutilation, and in 1944 one of the habitual criminals deliberately blew off his left hand with a grenade when rebuked severely after an episode even more disgraceful than usual. Tusili possibly expected to arouse sympathy but if so must have been disappointed. The villagers were so disgusted with him that they refused to man a canoe to take him to hospital. I was preparing to intervene when by good luck a schooner put in at the anchorage to land a native passenger.

Two other men who were left fatherless in early childhood have become social climbers. They are in this respect exceptional, but I would not describe them as misfits. They have found a place for themselves in the accepted scheme as heads of club groups.

The absence of any woman's name from the list is probably accidental. At the present time there is no female who could be described as a delinquent, and no living female has ever tried to kill herself: yet the last person to succeed in committing suicide, in 1936, was a young girl, and stories are also told of women who made a regular practice of stealing.

YOUTH

Boys after completing their course at the local school pass on for two years in the Area establishment at Mala'lo. They board there during the week but maintain close touch by means of visits on Saturdays, Sundays, and holidays. The best pupils, an average of three annually, go from Mala'lo direct to the Lae high school for further education, but the majority stay in the settlement till the age of sixteen or seventeen, when they seek paid employment with a European.

The students at the Area school are expected to go fishing regularly and to tend gardens under the supervision of a teacher. On returning home they are fully capable of carrying out ordinary village tasks. Most of them spend from six to seven hours each day working, a figure that compares favourably with the nine of the married men. Naturally their output is less than that of an adult, but their efforts are always highly valued.

The girls are equally competent and just as useful around the house and in the gardens; moreover, they work for about an hour longer. The married women with whom they labour, however, spend some ten hours of the day toiling as against the nine of the men.

Such habits of industry do not come into being spontaneously, and from time to time the elders still have to use disciplinary measures. They no longer administer slaps and must now adopt new methods. Their best weapon is a warning that they have the privilege of arranging the marriages and can always refrain from seeking a spouse for someone who has given offence. 'The idle youth is single in middle age, single when his hair turns grey,' they say. 'You choose to be lazy now; very well then; that's your business; your uncles and I will have our turn later,' one man told his son. 'Don't think we'll be in a hurry when you want to be married. No, indeed! We'll be thinking of the work you neglected.'

As a rule daughters do not need so many reminders, though occasionally the father and mother may have to point out that men may decline the offer of a girl known to be indolent.

The young people are unaware that threats of this kind can be disregarded. The seniors may honestly believe what they are saying, but when the time comes they have to take other factors into consideration, and seldom is there any possibility of delaying a marriage.

Young wrongdoers also risk the shame of a public reprimand at a village meeting. The elders do not call an assembly for the express purpose of dealing with trivial misdemeanours but often take the opportunity once major business has been concluded. They then chide any adolescent who has displeased them and urge him to do better. On such occasions they harp on the same old themes again and again. Have not the relatives supplied food?—then their kindness must be repaid. Is not the period of childhood over?—then the moment for accepting responsibility has been reached.

Generally the grandparents intervene if a parent so far forgets himself as to strike an older child. They agree that the youth or girl ought to suffer in silence but point out that he or she may resent the loss of dignity and hit back. This seldom happens, and I only once witnessed a fight between father and son, Gase' and Muengpop. The incident began when Muengpop scolded one of his sisters for bleaching her hair with peroxide. His companions, he said, were convinced that she was a harlot. Gase', overhearing, at once knocked him to the ground with a blow on the jaw. Muengpop picked himself up and retaliated, but neighbours rushed forward and dragged him away. The result was a domestic crisis. The mother sided with Muengpop and made life so uncomfortable for Gase' that he went to stay for a week or two with relatives. The villagers were of the opinion that both had behaved shockingly but that Gase' was more to blame.

THE FAMILY

Sons continue to be deeply attached to their mother and often perform little services for her without being asked, such as helping if a load is especially heavy. They may also give her the best of their fish instead of sharing it. Although they remain uncomplaining in the club for a day or two if suffering from a cold or a slight attack of malaria, they always go home when afflicted by a more serious illness. At such times they want her to soothe their pains and cook them special food.

A measure of the sons' devotion is the fact that nowadays the worst insult is telling a person he has copulated with his mother. Nobody would accept the words lightly, and on the one occasion I have known them to be used the man addressed swore that for the rest of his life he would never

(b) Her first string bag

(a) Fetching water

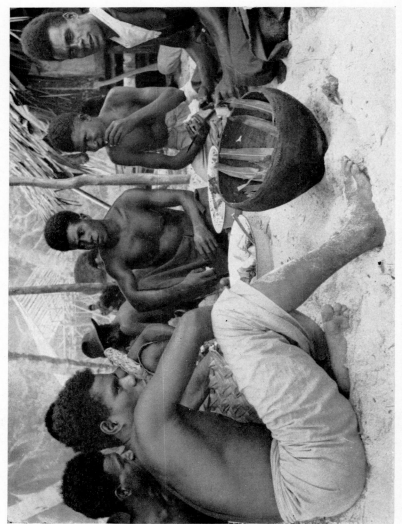

A group of men at a feast to celebrate the completion of a house frame

speak to his opponent. Four years later he was still sticking to his vow. An accusation of copulating with a sister is also a serious matter but after a sufficient interval may be forgiven without loss of face. Both expressions have been lifted from pidgin-English, apparently to fill a gap in the vernacular. In pre-European times people who had quarrelled could only call each other pigs.

The villagers always insist that no youth would hit his mother. He might if enraged aim a blow at his father, but she is in a sense sacred. 'He thinks of the breasts he has sucked and of all the early care, and his anger dies,' they assured me. Yet Malawatim, the fourteen-year-old son of Ahipum, one day attempted to hurl a block of wood at his mother. His father caught him in time, wrenched his arm behind his back, and roundly abused him. 'Evil, evil, evil, to try to hurt Mu'alimawi,' Ahipum exclaimed in some agitation. 'My son, you will come to a bad end. Tell me if she touches you, and I'll punish her. But for you to raise a hand against the woman who bore you is abominable. Go, out of my sight. Don't let me see you for the rest of the day.'

On another occasion Kamundong, a fully-grown man, threw his aged mother out of the house, injuring her arm, after she and his wife had had an argument. The incident scandalized the villagers, who immediately dismissed him from his post as teacher at the village school. 'She allowed herself to be soiled by his excrement and urine,' one man lamented, 'and now he repays her with cruelty.' Many were convinced that the death of Kamundong's small daughter a year or two later was God's judgment on his sin.

The bond with the father also remains as strong as ever. My friends continually emphasized that the now growing association with the other kinsmen, especially the maternal uncles, in no way diminishes this primary allegiance. I have already quoted several of their remarks and will add only one more—that the father is firm like the rocks or like the log to which a man clings when his canoe has foundered in a stormy sea.

Brothers mean even more to one another now than they did earlier. If two of them are at boarding school together the elder acts as guide and is a substitute for the father; and the younger cooks the food and runs the errands. Back in the village they exchange confidences, work side by side, and are ever ready with help in an argument. Later still, when they are old enough to enter employment, the junior members of the family nearly always choose as their first master the European who has already engaged an elder brother. They then lean on him for support in the difficulties of the new environment.

THE KINDRED

Boys and girls of twelve can thread their way through the *da-tigeng* kinship ties with complete assurance. 'Danto is my younger brother and does what I tell him,' the lad Gaya remarked complacently after he had sent the boy

G

to fetch coconuts for us to drink. 'His father is my father's younger brother. Old Alumba, my grandfather, is their father. They had the same mother, too, but she's dead, and I never saw her.' 'Who was she?' I enquired. 'They've told me, but I forget,' was the reply. 'It might have been Alengwi, or perhaps Wahengtuwi—they were two of the grandmothers I've heard about.' I then asked for a list of Alumba's other sons and daughters, also deceased. Gaya was aware that there had been four of them but recalled the names of two only. He enumerated their children, however, and divided them up correctly as elder and younger brothers, sisters, and cross cousins.

At this age many children can also give a few details of their *hu-tigeng* relationships. Samyam's reply to a question of mine illustrates how well the principles are applied. 'You want to know why I call Dale' "great father"? Well, he must be. Father speaks of him as "elder brother".' How could that be, I interrupted, when Samyam's father was an only son? 'Father and Dale' are not true "older brother" and "younger brother"— no, I didn't mean that they were. I suppose their fathers' fathers had the same father and mother; or perhaps their mothers' mothers were sisters. I've never heard, and you must ask someone else. All I know is that father says Dale' is his "elder brother", and if that's so, then Dale' must be my "great father".'

Once when on a visit to another village a boy from the Busama party, which I had accompanied, made what to him was the surprising discovery that he and the son of one of our hosts were related in several different ways. They were both about thirteen and had been at boarding school together, where, because their mothers were 'sisters', they had considered themselves to be 'brothers'. Now for the first time they learned that the father of one looked upon the mother of the other as a 'sister'. This new linkage made them cross cousins, and they laughingly said that they ought not to be sitting together with such little concern for the proprieties. Then one of them began wondering whether their fathers also might be connected. Off they ran to see—and discovered that the two men were 'maternal uncle' and 'uterine nephew'. 'Apilum here is my younger brother, my cross cousin, and my son,' the Busama youth shrieked across to me. 'As his elder brother I can ask him for things, as his cross cousin I can't, and if he's my child I must feed him. It's as well he lives in Buakap. We'd have to straighten it all out if we came from the same place.' A few years later I found them working together in Lae. 'We decided to stay brothers,' they explained. 'Look at us; we're not father and son, are we? And it would be silly to become cross cousins after we'd been brothers.'

The growing youth has most of his meals with his parents or a maternal uncle, but other relatives continue to offer him hospitality, and he also eats occasionally in the houses of his grandparents, paternal uncles, aunts, or more distant kin. He divides his evenings between the club houses of his father, maternal uncles and cousins.

The seniors sometimes complain of a young person's taking their benevolence too much for granted and not giving sufficient help in return. 'We're throwing our food away.' Nga'sele' grumbled. 'We grandfathers get nothing back, nothing. If we cast it into the sea, then at least the fish might come around for us to catch.'

These lamentations are in my view unreasonable. Time after time I have seen youths clearing, fencing, fishing, and building with all sorts of relatives, *da-tigeng* and *hu-tigeng*. Lahung when aged fifteen, for instance, in a period of thirty working days spent nine with his father (who had no brothers), eleven with one or other of his mother's two brothers, two with a grandfather, and six with other men: he devoted only two days to visiting distant places or lounging about. Inggantang, then sixteen, during the same month laboured with his father and father's brother for six days, with his mother's only brother for eleven days, and with distant kinsfolk for ten days: he was idle for three days. I could supplement these examples with a dozen others.

If the demands conflict, as when two men both want something done, obviously the boy has to exercise his discretion. Normally the closer relative has the better claim, but at times a more sympathetic distant kinsman is preferred.

The father and maternal uncles, whatever they may have done previously, now make a regular practice of marking out a plot for the boy each time he accompanies them in clearing new ground. The gesture is perhaps still a token, for he will soon go off to an employer, but he expects his mother and sisters to plant 'his' taro, and he speaks of 'my garden' with the proprietary air of a seasoned householder having several children. The more distant relatives do not set aside a plot when he works with them. They consider that such a proceeding would be premature. They are grateful to him, however, and show their appreciation by pressing him to stay for meals, when they assure him that after marriage they will be glad to have him cultivating their land.

The girls stay closer to home and mainly confine their help to *da-tigeng* kinsfolk. They go further afield only when the mother has offered her services as cook for a feast at which many workers have to be fed, as, for example, during the building of a new house.

THE MOTHER'S BROTHERS

This is the period when the maternal uncles make certain that their nephews fully understand the system of land tenure. 'It's my job,' one of the men told me in an aside as he paused when explaining at length the different rights. Some people assert that they give the same kind of information to their sons, but in my experience they tend to wait for questions and refrain from raising the subject spontaneously. They then lay great stress on the fact that the boys would never be turned off the ground of their paternal kinsmen.

I one day joined Kaneng and his thirteen-year-old uterine nephew while they were resting for a few minutes at the side of their garden. I made a few notes at the time and from these have reconstructed the conversation.

'This land is ours, and nobody can put us off it,' Kaneng was saying as I approached. As he spoke he took up a handful of earth and let it rest in his fingers. 'It was my mother's brothers' before me, and their mother's brothers' before that; and when your sisters marry it will go to their sons and their daughters' sons. This is mine and my brothers' and yours and your brothers'.'

'And Ahipum's and Ya'pi's and Kamaya's,' the lad interjected, naming several neighbours who were busy a short distance away.

'No, the land isn't theirs. They're here because I let them come. We're all related, all *hu-tigeng*, and I wanted them to be with us. But it isn't their land.'

'I know that father's ground isn't mine. He says, though, that I'll always be able to go there.'

'Over there you're like Ahipum, Ya'pi, and Kamaya here,' his uncle explained. 'You can have gardens—of course, your father and your cross cousin Wapa will want you to be with them. (And we'll ask them here, too.) But it is their ground, and only the taro and bananas will be yours. They'll say what must be done, just as we'll say what must be done here.'

I repeated the gist of these remarks that evening to one of my older 'nephews' and sent him off for his father's comments. 'Yes, I said you were right before I left,' the lad told me on his return. 'But father wants you to know that I can garden on his land till I die, and that my sons, and my sisters' sons, will be able to do so as well.'

Most of the youths follow their maternal uncles willingly. 'Left my father? But I haven't,' Lahilu replied to my query. 'I worked with him yesterday and shall be there again the day after tomorrow.' The knowledge that he could never be master of his father's ground also left him unmoved. 'I shall always go on working on it,' he said. 'My father and his sisters' sons will welcome me.'

People were amused when I asked them did they object to the elevation of the sisters' sons at the expense of the sons. 'You were there when I talked to my nephew and now want to know this!' Kaneng reproached me in playful tones. 'Why do you think I encouraged him? Sisters' sons make a man complete. With only sons he'd be like someone with arms and no legs. He must have both.' The simile is apt, and the villagers I knew best were pleased to have the two sets of kin close at hand. Any criticisms of the system were directed not against rights going to the nephews but against the sons' failing to receive an equal share.

Men without children find compensation in paying greater attention to the sister's children, who in return show them increased affection. As with Nga'gili', they complain about their misfortune; but they are probably under a less serious handicap than if the land was associated with a patrilineal group.

Those who have no true sisters are only at a slight disadvantage. The relationship with uterine nephews is so much less personal than with sons that heirs provided by women classified as sisters are a reasonably effective substitute.

COUSINS

Male parallel cousins build up a close fraternal intimacy. Those related through their fathers are associated as co-workers on the land of their paternal kinsmen and as either fellow members or fellow visitors in the paternal kinsmen's club; and those related through their mothers have the same matrilineal inheritance and congregate around the same maternal uncles for work during the day and for leisure in the evenings.

Male cross cousins, on the contrary, are in an unbalanced relationship. Thus although each lad must do his best to make his father's sisters' sons at home in the parental dwelling, he is under a partial obligation to them when cultivating his father's ground. Correspondingly, he is under a partial obligation to his mother's brothers' sons when he visits the uncles' dwellings but must make them welcome when they cultivate the uncles' land. There is some risk of friction, and it is for this reason that the natives use the expression 'bitter touch'. The taboos, they say, have been worked out to minimize the danger. The following statement is typical of many: 'Cross cousins who are often in one another's company must be helpful and kind like brothers. Yet they are not really brothers. They are on a bad footing, what we call a "bitter touch". You can see that there is a lot for them to disagree about. So we build a fence between them and forbid their calling each other by name, using playful speech, eating or smoking together, sitting on beds, and asking for things. We divide them to keep them united —my fingers here, my thumb there, but still my one hand—and in this way they stay brothers.' We can agree on this being the effect of the regulations, though there is no evidence that they were consciously designed for the purpose.

A further point must be mentioned. The social code is so rigid that a man who finds his son and his uterine nephew arguing, as when children they may do, is obliged to stop them at once and lecture them on the respect they owe each other. He does not pause to investigate the origin of the dispute, which in the light of the major offence is irrelevant, and so has no chance of taking sides.

Girls are more restricted in their movements and co-operate less often than boys; moreover, their rights to land are less important. Female cousins, parallel and cross, simply consider that they are 'like sisters' and help one another as often as they can.

Cousins of opposite sex behave with easy familiarity and comradeship. The girls plant taro for the boys, cook food for them, and take a genuine interest in their affairs.

6

Awakening of the Sexual Impulses

OUR growing native has now reached puberty, an event that takes place later than among ourselves, about fourteen or fifteen in the case of girls and a year or two after for boys.

The villagers have always condemned sexual relations outside marriage. When discussing the matter in the abstract, without reference to particular individuals, they lay as much blame on the boy as on the girl and insist that scandal impairs the future marriage chances of both. The teachings of the missionaries reinforced the traditional code, and today the native pastors and other Church leaders denounce the sin of pre-marital intercourse on every possible occasion. So obsessed with the subject are they that they see immorality in all forms of dancing. Recently they have even undertaken to stamp out the universal island practice of adorning the hair with flowers. 'Blossoms above are the sign of evil desires below,' they say.

In other Melanesian societies with a puritanical attitude to sex the females are expected to efface themselves; but in Busama the girls always exchange cheerful badinage with any youths whom they meet along the bush pathways. 'Where are you off to? Are you looking for husbands?' the boys call out. 'No, no, we are good daughters and await the wishes of our parents,' comes the answer. 'As for you, you must be keeping appointments with our sisters.'

Parents feel concern about the reputation of their daughter from the time she first menstruates. Formerly they would have sponsored several feasts as a celebration, but these have been abandoned on account of missionary disapproval. The mother simply summons some experienced old woman to give the girl sexual instruction. The men are ignorant of what exactly takes place and refused to make enquiries on my behalf—it was 'something for the women', they said, and must be left to them—but I gathered that in the course of a practical demonstration the teacher ruptures the girl's hymen.

From now on the mother speaks a great deal about the disgrace that would follow an intrigue. In illustration she quotes some of the better-known incidents from the past—Gwammla'wi, who took a casual lover to her bed and then discovered that the only man willing to marry her was a cripple with a withered leg; Ginggala'wi, who had to accept an elderly widower with a fully-grown family; and so on. She gives special warnings about the dangers of the late afternoon and early evening, when there is much movement about the settlement. The men are returning from work, and visits between the different households take place. Covetous youths are said to wait in the shadows at this hour ready to tempt any unwary girl to slip away while her absence will not be noticed. The best commentary is the explanation given for the name of the evening star, Kwi-ta'dung, literally, 'stepping in excrement'—polite greetings may cover up bad intentions, just as fading daylight obscures mess on the ground.

The mother also does her best to ensure that the girl is accompanied wherever she goes. If forced to leave a daughter in the village while she is herself absent she either appoints a young child to act as a spy or asks the neighbours to keep a careful lookout; and if obliged to send her to the gardens she makes certain that other families will be working nearby.

The men have an easier time looking after the youths. Employment for wages is accepted as normal routine, and few males between the ages of seventeen and twenty-two are to be found at home. But a labourer may return for a short spell between two engagements and become a source of temporary concern. All that the elders can then do is to see that he sleeps at night in a club house and caution him against entanglements. They particularly stress the stupidity of listening to a girl who makes advances. She may be inspired by genuine desire, they agree, but is more likely to be pregnant to someone who has abandoned her.

Most young people heed the advice, though even if tempted to disregard it they would find an assignation difficult. Privacy, except for married couples, is almost unheard of: the villagers walk about in company, work in company, and sit at their ease in company. The sight of a girl alone in the bush, no matter what her reasons, is in itself sufficient to set the tongues wagging. A boy wishing to have an affair is unwilling to place himself in the power of an accomplice. He feels that the value of a false alibi would be more than counterbalanced by the risk of the man's exposing him later from motives either of conscience or jealousy.

Yet the seniors constantly deplore the prevalence of moral laxity, which, they say, grows worse with the passing years. As a pointer to the changed attitude they refer to the looseness of the talk of the younger folk. In earlier days masturbation might have been practised, an old man remarked, but it would never have been openly mentioned. He had just been deeply shocked by some lads in one of the clubs arguing as to whether a little girl could possibly conceive. At first they had decided that the smallness of the vagina would prevent penetration, but one of them had then suggested in all seriousness that the problem might be overcome by the man masturbating into a tin and inserting the semen with an eye-dropper.

Views of the members of the older generation are never a satisfactory guide to the past, and these natives see it according to their mood as either too bright or too dark. Yet we must agree that some of the earlier restraints no longer operate. In former times the seducer suffered severe punishment

—the girl's relatives attacked him and drove their spears through the fleshy part of his upper arm or thigh. They were careful not to inflict a mortal wound—killing him would have brought vengeance on their heads —but his injuries were often so serious that he lay disabled for several weeks. Today he can escape at once to an employer, and the wronged family is powerless to harm him. They cannot even bring him to court unless there is evidence of rape. Increased facilities for travel enable the people to visit other places where the sexual standards are different. Many young men have experiences while in employment, and even if circumspect at home they feel little shame at escapades with outsiders.

Selep's confessions were the most romantic of those I recorded. While employed as a personal servant at the Finschhafen Mission station he had accompanied his master and mistress on a visit to the neighbouring Tami Islands. Here he had been much struck with the beauty of one of the girls, who, from her admiring glances, appeared to be equally attracted to him. The following morning, while he was minding the missionaries' baby, she asked might she take it for a few minutes. On his handing the child over he felt her palm run down his thigh. He interpreted the gesture as an invitation but was too shy and inexperienced to arrange a meeting.

Some days later, after the party had returned to Finschhafen, Selep had the pleasant surprise of seeing the girl walking up the garden path. She had come across by canoe with kinsfolk, she told him, and was now on her way to spend a few weeks with a relative who lived close by. They chatted for some time, and in the course of the talk she mentioned that the local shop had run out of needles and thread. Had he any she could borrow? He replied that if she would meet him that evening in the garden outside the dining room he would bring her some. He promised to signal when his work was nearly finished by turning the lamps up and down.

I know from long experience that at ordinary times Selep is scrupulously honest. Yet that afternoon he entered the Mission sewing room and stole half a dozen packets of needles and several reels of thread. Armed with these, he later set off for the rendezvous and spent the night with the girl.

The liaison continued until Selep's labour contract expired. The cousins who then came to fetch him home brought word that his father and uncles had chosen a bride for him and were making preparations for the wedding. He spoke to me feelingly about his dilemma. Should he abandon the Tami girl and cause her distress? Or should he take her back with him and so upset his kinsfolk? The cousins convinced him after a long argument of the wisdom of adopting the former alternative. Tami women were unfamiliar with Busama ways, and if he married this one she would soon be crying to go home. The island folk are traders, obtaining most of their food from the mainland, and she was thus so unused to garden work that his sisters would think her lazy. Coming as she did from a place where there were no land snakes, she would be terrified of the reptiles of the Busama countryside.

Gwaleyam's affairs were more casual. 'While working at a store at Salamaua I bought some magical paint from an old Kaiwa sorcerer,' he related, 'and when I rubbed it on my face no-one could resist me.' He asserted that the wives of all the married labourers made advances to him and that on one occasion he had had intercourse with a Rabaul woman as her Chinese husband slept on a verandah only ten yards away. In the end the villagers of Buakap, half way between Salamaua and Busama, discovered him in an adulterous intrigue with one of their women. The Elders of the church at Busama suspended him from membership as punishment. 'But that didn't matter much,' he went on. 'I was away from home and wouldn't have been able to attend services anyway.' He was gravely shocked, however, when I asked had he any of the wonderful cosmetic still in his possession. 'Of course I couldn't bring it here,' he protested. 'We Busama have been baptized: we are Christians.'

The older villagers disapprove of the youths having sexual relationships in foreign places but are not vehement on the subject. As yet even the devout can scarcely accept the universal brotherhood of mankind, and persons from other places, as non-relatives, are still considered to be undeserving of serious respect. The reply of a respectable Mission leader when I enquired whether a man who was a candidate for public office had an unblemished record was revealing. 'His name has never been coupled with anyone except his wife. Oh yes! I remember now. There was some trouble once, but we didn't hear much about it. You see, it happened at Wau while he was away working.'

The homosexual activities of the labour compound give rise to greater anxiety. Living conditions make these inevitable. The workers are all young, have practically no female society, and sleep in such cramped quarters that their bodies almost touch. The Busama ascribe the chief blame to natives from the Sepik district, where allegedly a young man is expected to select a youth as a sexual partner. This may be the truth, but if so these Sepik people have many willing imitators. It seems that numbers of labourers begin by playing the passive rôle and eventually with advancing age become active. The practices are freely acknowledged, and, despite the disapproval of Government and Missions, indecent dances known as Bagana frequently take place. Boys either sit on the shoulders of their lover or stand in front of him, and conventional movements inspired by those of sexual intercourse are carried out in a rhythm provided by a chorus singing bawdy songs.

Four young Busama have in recent years been charged with homosexuality while in employment. One of them was discovered after his dismissal for laziness from his post as deck hand of a schooner. His work mates protested that they had agreed to carry out his duties in consideration of his promise to provide them in rotation with sexual satisfaction. A second youth contracted anal gonorrhoea at the age of sixteen. This lad, Ki'dolo', is the only person, so far as is known, to bring overt homo-

sexuality back to the village. He offered himself for three shillings to a
returned labourer, who declined the invitation, and was then caught having
intercourse with a schoolboy. At an earlier date Biyaweng, the elder brother
of Ki'dolo', had served a term of imprisonment for seducing a fellow
worker. I have mentioned this pair of ne'er-do-wells already, and shall be
doing so again. Their mother was a thief, and they had the further misfortune of losing their father in early childhood. Biyaweng married soon
after his release from gaol and proceeded to sell his wife's favours to
policemen and others at Salamaua. He continued the practice during the
Pacific war and sent her to members of a Signals unit posted at various
places along the coast.

Two other men, also notorious bad characters, acted as procurers while
the Army was in the vicinity but have at no time hawked their wares among
their fellow villagers. Yet what occurs in Busama may take place in the
settlements nearby, and it is possible that some of the local youths have
found obliging husbands there.

VILLAGE AFFAIRS

On the rare occasion that an intrigue becomes public the people's initial
reaction is to say that the man must have been responsible. The girl also
insists that he undermined her resistance, usually with magic. But a study
of the facts reveals that often women are the tempters. 'A man is always to
blame when a girl first falls,' one villager explained, 'but some women, if
they have felt the pleasures of intercourse, are as eager to go on as any
youth. Mind, we'd be ashamed to say this in front of them, and we therefore make out that they've been seduced.'

The first incident of which I became aware concerned Kamsili and the
girl Mde'wi. Late in the afternoon, when the village was thronged with
people returning from the day's tasks, we heard sounds of blows followed
by screams coming from the house of a man named Haku. 'Get out, get
out, you swinish creatures,' he then yelled, and a moment later his wife
and daughter tumbled through the door. Wailing piteously, they fled to a
kinsman, though the older woman was limping badly and clutching her
side. Various people followed and began questioning them. It emerged that
the youngest member of the family, a girl of about six or seven, had seen
her sister Mde'wi in the bush with Kamsili. The child had told her father
the story without realizing its implications, and when he taxed Mde'wi
with it she admitted she was carrying on an affair.

That evening one of the senior men, Busilim, summoned a general
meeting. The crowd soon gathered, and he opened the proceedings by
calling mother, daughter, and lover to the front. He gave an account of the
afternoon's disturbance and asked the girl what had she to say.

The story came out bit by bit in response to Busilim's promptings.
Mde'wi began by accusing Kamsili of suggesting an assignation that
morning. She had tried to put him off and told him how wicked he was.

'Do you mean that Kamsili's intentions were evil now that you've been found out?' Busilim enquired. 'Was this the first time'? No, she admitted, there had been earlier occasions. But, of course, she had been bewitched. Kamsili had stood behind her and touched her shoulder with charmed oil, thus paralysing her will. 'I know I have done wrong,' she wailed; 'but he is the cause of it all.'

The old mother then broke into loud lamentations, calling out: 'How miserable and ashamed I am! I have cared for this good-for-nothing girl and guarded her reputation. I've kept her in my sight nearly all the time. Now this happens! Alas, alas, that she should have let my warnings pass unheeded.' Again Busilim made a terse comment: 'If she wasn't out of your sight, how did this go on occurring? You've been careless and are as much to blame as she is.'

Busilim next interrogated Kamsili. Beyond denying the use of magic, the young man said little, though later he confided to me that he had only yielded in response to Mde'wi's repeated approaches. 'I was too ashamed to say that out loud,' he added. 'But she's a bad woman, and I'm not the first who's lain with her. Her husband, if she ever gets one, will find that out.'

Haku now stepped forward and began beating his breast. 'My name is on my daughter still,' he mourned. 'This lecher came to the house and stole my little girl. Oh for the past, when I might have killed him! Now we elders have to sit by while our daughters are seduced before our eyes. Alas, my fathers, that we should have forgotten your ways!' (He was indulging in wishful thinking. As we have seen, he would have been permitted only to wound the seducer: slaying him would have been regarded as murder.)

Various leaders in turn gave the offenders a lecture on their misdeed. Were the two of them not ashamed to have violated Busama custom, God's commandments, and the Government's laws? (This is another example of self-deceit: the Administration takes no action against those guilty of pre-marital intercourse.) Evil would overtake them, and certainly God would make them suffer. Then, who would wish to marry either of them? What man would be willing to take a harlot as his wife, and what girl would accept the lover of another as a husband? Mde'wi's mother also came in for a reprimand. One speaker told her plainly that her notorious lack of care for her children was the real cause of the trouble.

The crowd at last retired, and the culprit crept away. In normal times they would have been suspended from Church membership, but the war was still in progress, and no further action was taken. Kamsili went to relatives in another village for a few months, and the girl and her mother kept to themselves. He married three years later, at approximately the normal age, but she had to wait for a year longer.

The second case arose over an attempted seduction. The youth Laugwi', aged seventeen, had crept into the house where a girl slightly younger,

Homkiwi, was sleeping with her parents. She awoke to find him fumbling with her dress and screamed for help. Her father, a man named Isom, came to the rescue and punched him about the face, but he made his escape. A public gathering took place the next day, and the elders made the usual harangues. Isom was aroused almost to frenzy by the ingenuousness of the excuse that Laugwi' offered. Homkiwi had accepted his presents, said the boy, and he therefore concluded she was willing to have him in her bed. Isom would have beaten him with his stick had relatives not intervened. Laugwi' did not go away but for many weeks was careful to keep in the background and speak only when addressed.

In a third incident two men, Magatu' and Tigandu, were carrying on with the one girl, Gaiwi. Magatu' had had a liaison with her for some time when Tigandu discovered them by accident and demanded access also as the price of his silence. From then on the intrigue became triangular until somebody saw all three in the forest together. The girl's reputation was irreparably damaged, and at the time the seniors said that no-one would be prepared to take her as his spouse (in fact she was married four years later). Magatu' appeared suitably chastened in demeanour, but Tigandu went about his affairs without any obvious show of concern. 'He's a man without shame,' was Ahipum's comment. 'He doesn't know how to hang his head, and we can do nothing with him. He's got bad blood like the rest of his kin. (You knew he was related to Biyaweng?) But he's digging his grave. He'll come to a bad end, that one.'

The most disturbing case was that of the girl Angki, her parallel first cousin Gi'sali, the married man Tangapi', and the youth Tabi'. This occurred during 1947, shortly after an administrative officer, acting without proper authority, had advised the villagers to set up a formal tribunal to deal with offences. They appointed a clerk to keep a record, and the following is a translation of a statement in his book:

'29.IX.1947. The court of Angki, with Tangapi', Gi'sali, and Tabi'. Angki said Tangapi' had intercourse with me four times. Tangapi' has a wife and children, but he committed adultery with his relative Angki. This is bad. Angki said Gi'sali had intercourse with me three times. She said Tabi' had intercourse with me once. Tabi' said, "Yes, I had intercourse with her once. It was not my wish. It was the wish of the girl and Gi'sali. The two of them had completed intercourse, and they persuaded me. I agreed and had intercourse once." Tabi' is a young boy. This is the court of the girl Angki and her "brother" Gi'sali, the married man Tangapi', and the boy Tabi'. The elders heard the court, but Gi'sali was not present in the village. The married man Tangapi' and the boy Tabi' were there with the girl Angki. The court said, "This is against the law." The court ordered Tangapi' to work on the roads for three weeks. The court ordered Tabi' to marry the girl. Tabi' refused, and his mother and her "brother" Da-hungmboa supported him.'

I was not then in New Guinea but returned two months later. The people were still most distressed at the incestuous relationship of Gi'sali and Angki and were convinced that he would never dare to come back home. By the end of 1952 their animosity had to some extent waned, but so far he had not written even to the members of his family. Tabi' soon went to Lae and sought employment with an air line, which sent him to Port Moresby, where he stayed till 1950. He then settled in Busama and within a few months married another girl. Angki remained unwed till 1952, when a widower aged about thirty-five took her as his wife.

PREGNANCY

A single girl who conceives can always depend on her mother's help in attempting to procure an abortion. Several methods are available, but it is recognized that none of them is certain. The mother may knead the girl's abdomen with a large stone, bind her tightly with a stout piece of canvas, or encourage her to jump from the lower branches of a tree. Should all these fail, she begs some skilled older women to brew an abortifacient. The draught is perhaps mildly poisonous as it is said to cause acute diarrhoea and vomiting.

If even drugs prove ineffective the mother has to inform her husband. He at once takes the matter up with the man's kinsfolk and endeavours to persuade them to agree to a match. Unless committed elsewhere they usually acquiesce, thereby preserving the reputation of both parties.

The youth Lauya', then a handsome lad of about twenty-one, found himself against his will espoused to Yansaiwi, a woman five years his senior who was disfigured by a form of incurable skin disease that caused her to smell offensively. When questioned about her pregnancy she had said that he had been her lover over a period of months. His father was dead, but the eldest brother took charge and insisted on the marriage. Lauya' protested that he had 'only been playing' and had had no serious intentions, but the brother replied that he would make no effort to secure another bride or contribute supplies for another wedding feast.

Four of the young children of today were conceived prior to their parents' marriage. They are not ostracized, and probably in time the near-scandal of their birth will be forgotten. Nobody ever refers to any member of the senior generations as having arrived too soon, though there can be little doubt that some of them did.

Usually if the young man's family does not insist on his marrying the girl he avoids unpleasantness by going away to work as an employee. No such easy expedient is open to her, and she is forced to live with her shame. The other villagers refrain from taunting her openly unless they have quarrelled with her, when for the moment they may wish to be deliberately insulting.

Eight of the present population are of illegitimate birth, three the offspring of single men and single women, three of single men and married women, and two of married men and single women. Of the first group two are from Buakap, the village four miles to the south. The mothers preferred to seek refuge with kin in Busama rather than suffer the reproaches of their nearer cousins. All the women who were single at the time of the birth subsequently married, though to widowers or men suffering from some handicap, such as physical deformity or unattractive appearance. The married women are in a slightly different category. I shall consider them later when dealing with adultery.

Two only of the bastards are still children. Both take their kinship status from their step-fathers, who treat them as though they were their true offspring. Some of the men find such behaviour surprising. 'I couldn't do it,' Nga'gili' told me. 'I wouldn't want to have someone else's child taking over trees and palms that ought properly to go to my son.'

It seems that some of the older step-fathers shared these views. Five of the adult bastards look upon their mother's husband as a true parent and expect to inherit his personal property, but the sixth, after a series of violent quarrels, now works exclusively with his maternal kinsmen. The other villagers were specific about the reason—the step-father had always made a distinction between him and his half-brothers. The comment of some of my close friends when I complained that one of the other five had given me incorrect information was also illuminating. 'You might have expected that,' said Gi'lahi. 'Naturally, a man never takes much trouble with the upbringing of someone else's child—he doesn't bother to teach him to be truthful. Bastards can never tell right from wrong. Everybody knows this is so, everybody.' A month or two later, during a dispute over the arrangements for a forthcoming marriage, one of the villagers twitted the same man with his illegitimacy and attributed his action to this cause. Bystanders rebuked the speaker for the breach of etiquette in referring to the subject, and he subsequently handed over a gift of food as an apology. But he assured me privately that he had been right. 'You wouldn't give your wife's bastard proper instruction either, now would you?' he concluded.

7

Marriage[1]

YOUNG men are considered to be sufficiently mature to enter into matrimony at an age I judged to be twenty-two, girls at an age I judged to be seventeen; and the majority of the men are in fact wed by the time they are about twenty-four, the majority of the girls by the time they are about nineteen. I knew of no able-bodied bachelor older than about thirty-one and no able-bodied spinster older than about twenty-three or twenty-four. Parents often speak of the folly of delaying a girl's nuptials and in support quote the proverb, 'Pigs set aside for another feast die in the end from snakebite, and then nobody has pork to eat.' Elder sons, if physically fit, must always be married before younger sons, likewise elder daughters before younger daughters.

The natives ban the union of 'men and women who regularly work and eat together and in consequence look upon themselves as brothers and sisters'. These are the *da-tigeng* relatives and in addition, such of the *hu-tigeng* relatives as belong to the lineage or club group. An individual is not allowed to marry the following kin from his own generation level: his siblings, his first parallel cousins, his first cross cousins, and certain of his other cousins (parallel and cross) from farther away. As many as a quarter of the total number of contemporaries of the opposite sex may be forbidden.

People also justify the prohibition by reference to the reserve proper between affines. They point out that a sudden switch from the easy freedom of most cognatic relationships would be awkward and uncomfortable. One man I knew well spoke of his revulsion on discovering that his kinsmen expected him to marry a girl with whom he was thoroughly familiar. She was a second cousin, and the rest of the community accepted the match without criticism, but he told me that he was so ashamed that he vomited. 'I knew I mustn't refuse, but how could I take this girl to my bed? She was my cross cousin, another sister. I'd thought of her like that since we were children. And I called her father "maternal uncle". I'd been going to their house, eating with them, walking along the road with them, and working in their gardens. Now I had to have sexual intercourse with the one and turn the other into a father-in-law.' He added that months went by before his

---

[1] The material in this chapter supersedes that in a paper of mine published in 1946, 'Sex and Marriage in Busama', *Oceania*, Vol. XVII, pp. 119–38, 225–47. Later visits to the village led me to revise several of my early conclusions.

shyness disappeared but now he felt he and his wife were like any other couple.

Two earlier arguments cited against the union of near kin are nowadays out-of-date. The old folk say that it used to be urged that marriage ought to increase if not double the number of social contacts and also that a ridiculous situation would have been created had someone been simultaneously obliged to contribute to a bride price on account of his ties with the husband and entitled to demand the share back on account of his ties with the wife. There is no longer any practical reason, strategic or economic, for spreading kinship so widely, and bride-price payments ceased in about 1912 or 1913.

I found no case of an 'incestuous' marriage within the lineage or club, but twenty years or so ago the son and daughter respectively of a brother and a sister were wedded, why I was unable to discover. The public reaction may be inferred from remarks overheard when the two children of the match died during an epidemic. The villagers whispered that here was clear proof of God's intervening to punish sin.

The senior men make all the marriage arrangements and are under no obligation either to consult the young people or defer to their wishes. Each alliance is worked out in conformity with the principle of reciprocity —just as a man who receives a service or a gift must make an equivalent return, so those who accept a bride on behalf of a young kinsman are in honour bound to bestow another girl on the donors. Like the services and the gifts, too, the marriages do not cancel out, and always the latest recipients are considered to be in debt. Thus each separate union is the completion of one exchange and the prelude to another, a link in a never-ending chain. A gives to B, and B gives to A; then A gives again to B or to B's heir, and B or B's heir gives again to A's heir; and so on *ad infinitum*. That, at least, is the theory. In practice a new series almost always begins each time the chain descends a generation. So A gives to B, and B gives to A; then if A gives again to B's heir, A's heir passes out of the picture in favour of the more immediate relatives of the girl provided by A. These are the persons who can expect to receive the next bride.

The first open moves come from the girl's side, from the persons who are anxious to hand her over in repayment for an earlier bride (one of the words commonly used for 'marriage' means literally 'sending the girl'). 'It's like paying a bill,' a commercially-minded villager remarked. 'You want to keep your money, but you know you'll lose your reputation if you do. People will say that you take things and never even up to the score— that you're the same as a thief.' The responsibility rests squarely on the previous bridegroom's father and paternal and maternal uncles. They prefer to take the young man's sister or, failing her, one of his first cousins. The latter may be one of their daughters or, because in certain cricumstances, to be discussed later, a brother has rights over his sisters' daughters, the daughter of an aunt (as has been pointed out, a maternal uncle may also be

A large trading canoe

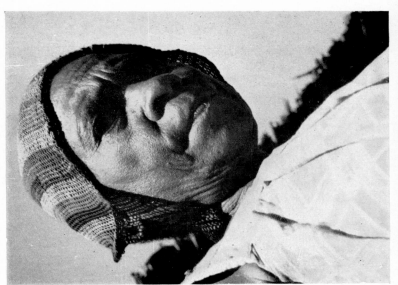

(b) A widow in mourning

(a) Mother and family

a paternal aunt's husband). If the earlier bridegroom has neither a sister nor first cousin available the father and uncles try to secure a second cousin, but more often than not their efforts are unsuccessful.

Opposite, waiting to take the new girl as a wife for one of their sons or uterine nephews, are the previous bride's father and paternal and maternal uncles. Her bachelor brother, if she has one, heads the list of eligibles, and six marriages in every hundred are balanced by the union of the bridegroom's sister and the bride's brother. Her first cousins come next, her second cousins at the tail end.

Obviously the return marriage has sometimes to be postponed for years. On the one hand, there may be a girl but no youth to receive her and, on the other, a youth but no girl to offer him. It follows that a girl's father and uncles could be in arrears to the extent of owing not only her but a couple of her younger sisters and cousins. If then they cannot use her to discharge one liability they divert her to another. Similarly a boy's father and uncles may be in credit to the extent of two or three brides. The chances are that when at length he is old enough to marry, one or other of the debtor units will be able to settle its account.

A man becomes linked in a special way with the sister or cousin, if she is a contemporary, whose marriage made his own possible. They use the regular kinship terms, but their mutual responsibilities are now especially urgent. They exchange gifts of food every few days, he immediately stands by if she is in any kind of trouble, and she comes at once should he suffer the slightest mishap. He also acts as the principal maternal uncle to her children even when their relationship is classificatory rather than real. He takes them to his house from their earliest years, introduces them to his club group, and on all occasions showers them with favours and attentions. Equally, she is the chief paternal aunt to his children, though this relationship is less important. Men without a linked sister or cousin, women without a linked brother or cousin, and such women's sons and daughters are all regarded unfortunate. Ordinarily the situation arises only when a decade or longer elapses before a return marriage can be arranged. The second bridegroom is then too young to behave in a fraternal fashion to the earlier bride—he could belong to the same generation as her offspring.

When there is but one girl available and several potential bridegrooms her relatives are faced with having to choose between them. In some cases her father and paternal uncles have the prior right to decide, in others her maternal uncles.

In earlier days the eldest daughter was said to 'belong' to her father and his brothers. These men also reserved the bride price for distribution among her patrilateral kinsfolk, thus compensating them for expenditure incurred by their forbears when the father was himself married. Ideally the father—or, if he was dead, his eldest surviving brother—initiated the discussions, and in the event of disagreement his views prevailed. Once his

H

brothers had given their approval he was supposed to approach his wife's brothers for formal consent.

At this period the next daughter 'belonged' to her maternal uncles. The principal spokesman, equivalent to the father on the earlier occasion, was the mother's linked brother or cousin, or if she had none, her eldest brother. It was this man's job to raise the subject, convince his brothers or cousins, and secure the confirmation of the girl's father and paternal uncles. Subsequently he caused the bride price to be distributed among her matrilateral kinsfolk.

The infant-mortality rate was so high that probably few families included further daughters. Any that there were 'belonged' to both sides, and neither the father nor the mother's linked brother could claim special privileges. Somehow unanimity had to be achieved with, subsequently, a general sharing of the bride price.

Today the consensus of opinion is that, as the father's kindred were not called upon to make any outlay at his marriage, he and his brothers should surrender to the mother's brothers and instead take the second daughter.

THE SONS OF THE FAMILY

A young man's kinsfolk never ask outright for a girl on his behalf, but the father and mother's linked brother or cousin, and to a lesser extent the paternal uncles and other maternal uncles, have the responsibility for ensuring that he does not remain unwed indefinitely. Two courses are open to them. Which they follow depends on whether or not they have a daughter-niece to be sent as a bride. Should such a girl be on hand they consider their various sets of creditors. When one of these has both an eligible son-nephew and an eligible daughter-niece they offer their girl as a partner for the former in the expectation of receiving the latter as a partner for their young man. They thus return to the *status quo*. But should such a girl not be available they consider their various sets of debtors. If there is such a group with an eligible daughter-niece they seek out somebody closely related to one of themselves and also to either her father or her mother's linked brother, depending on which has the chief say in her disposal, and request him to act as their emissary. They urge him to use his persuasive powers, with hints first and arguments if need be later, to have the account squared.

Today extra confusion occurs because of the shortage of females. Why so many New Guinea societies should have a surplus of young males is not clear, but the problem is often acute. So in Busama in August 1945 there were fourteen single men and only eight unmarried girls. The Army authorities had just released a large number of conscripted labourers, and eight of the fourteen arrived home on the one day. The elders were so worried that they decided to call a public meeting. The villagers assembled in the evening on the beach, and, after prayers for divine guidance, the chairman asked the father and uncles of each of the girls whether they had begun to make any plans. Nobody wished to interfere in what all agreed was a purely domestic matter, he said, but harmony might be more easily preserved if people were aware of what was intended. Several householders expressed anxiety because six of the young men must for the present remain single, and there was some talk about which of the schoolgirls would be likely to reach maturity in the near future. It is possible that as time goes on the average age at which the men marry may go up and that of the women come down.

Occasionally a returning labourer brings back a foreign wife. His relatives at first react unfavourably, but the rest of the people are delighted that a local girl has become available for someone else.

The idea of a Busama woman marrying a foreigner and thus aggravating the situation is, of course, repugnant to all. The only recent unions of this kind that failed to arouse criticism were those of the two daughters of an unpopular Government representative who was dismissed from office shortly after my first arrival. Loose conduct had made the names of these girls a byword, and all their father's efforts to marry them off to the sons of neighbours were fruitless. He therefore sent the elder to a man of low intelligence in Asini' and the younger to the sergeant-major of police stationed at Salamaua.

Youths whose immediate relatives are all dead suffer most from the shortage. Some of them overcome the handicap by attaching themselves to another household and there becoming indispensable, but the rest, especially if they fail to cultivate their kinsmen and spend a long period in employment, may still be bachelors at the age of thirty. 'I sometimes think that when an orphan without a sister is at last married the same thing as a miracle of Jesus has come to pass,' one of my less reverent friends commented. 'It's just like walking on the water.'

Hopeless cripples, deaf mutes (there are two of these), and imbeciles (of whom there is today only one) have no chance. A man partially disabled has to be content with a girl besmirched by scandal or a widow; and a woman partially disabled must make do with a widower.

MARRIAGE DISPUTES

Inevitably such a system creates tensions. Most of the difficulties stem from the fact that the individuals making the exchanges come together in a series of differing combinations. Every person shares an interest in the marriage of his own children with his brothers and wife's brothers, an interest in the marriage of the children of each of his brothers with his brothers and the particular brother's wife's brothers, and an interest in the marriage of the children of each of his sisters with his brothers and the particular sister's husband and husband's brothers: but he is not concerned, except perhaps indirectly, with the marriage of his wife's brothers' children; and, equally, the brothers' wives' brothers, the sisters' husbands, and the sisters' husbands' brothers are not concerned with the marriage of his children. At times the conflicts occur between the paternal and the maternal kin, as, for example, when one of the girl's father's brothers and one of her mother's brothers both have a son. The father's brothers then tend to look upon her as a means of acquiring a spouse for their son-nephew, whereas the mother's brothers see her rather as a source of a spouse for theirs. At other times there are conflicts either among the paternal kin or among the maternal kin, as when two of the girl's father's brothers, or two of her mother's brothers, have a son apiece.

The conventions about the allocation of the main rights of disposal reduce but do not eliminate the friction. The father's oldest brother, accustomed to exercising authority, may seek to impose his will against the father's personal inclinations, and, correspondingly, the mother's oldest brother may attempt to dictate to her linked brother or cousin. Occasionally, too, a member of the grandparent generation intervenes. And although people say that nowadays the eldest daughter ought to 'belong' to her maternal uncles, it sometimes happens that the father and his brothers, acting from selfish motives, arrange her espousals without informing the mother's brothers, who have no opportunity for protesting till too late. On such occasions the culprits justify themselves by posing as the champions of tradition and assert that they are impatient with innovation for its own sake.

Trouble may also arise between debtors and a body of disappointed creditors. People do not mind waiting as long as they can see that payment is impossible, but they may object strongly when at long last there is a girl ready to be married and her father and uncles present her to others.

As a rule, however, quarrels over marriages are soon patched up. A man and his brothers and brothers-in-law have too much in common to break with one another for good, and after a few weeks the losers swallow their resentment and behave as though nothing untoward had happened. This is true also of dissatisfied creditors, who come to realize that continued criticism may still further delay their satisfaction. The situation might be very different if the exchange took place not between varying sets of individuals but between lineages or some other sort of groups that endure through time; though in such conditions the risk of deep cleavages would be so great that a system of never-ending chains is unlikely.[1]

DIVORCE

The complications ensure that marriage is looked upon as a lifetime contract. Frequent divorce would heap trouble upon trouble and lead to chaos.

[1] It seems that in those societies where the marriage rules require an exchange between descent groups the second union always cancels out the first (see e.g. Bohannan, 1953, pp. 69–71; Bohannan, 1957, p. 72; and Elkin, 1954, p. 60). There are also societies with asymmetric systems, where the women of one descent group regularly pass as brides to the men of another in return not for wives but for goods, services, or some other consideration (see e.g. Leach, 1951, pp. 23–25, and Salisbury, 1956b, pp. 639–55).

Yet it is surprising there is no divorce whatsoever. This is true of both Busama and the surrounding villages. The people are agreed that divorce is not feasible, and the elders are never called upon to exert pressure on dissatisfied couples to keep them together.

In the past the fact that the authority of tradition, with the members of the senior generation as its representatives, was strengthened by cruel initiation ceremonies, may possibly have had some influence. But nobody now living has been initiated. On the other hand, the Lutheran missionaries, despite their disapproval of arranged marriages, are as opposed as the old men to divorce. A person who left his or her spouse for a new partner would be suspended from Church membership, a penalty never accepted with equanimity. Yet too much emphasis must not be placed on the new teachings. From time to time individual Busama have risked suspension when tempted to commit such offences as adultery or theft, which are also condemned by both tradition and the Mission; and Lutheran converts from New Guinea communities with different kinds of marriage rules sometimes take the consequences in preference to continuing in a state of unhappy wedlock.

Usually consideration of marriage stability demands reference also to the stability of the family and of the domestic unit. Marriage is stable if divorce is rare no matter how many spouses separate or how many women become concubines; the family is stable if a child's affiliation is fixed once and for all by the marriage of his parents irrespective of whether they remain together; and the domestic unit is stable if the men and women who cohabit, even if they are not legally husband and wife, continue to share a household.[1] In Busama these distinctions are of no account. Here only married couples live in company; moreover, they stay that way till one of them dies. A few young husbands, especially if the wife appears to

---

[1] Cf. M. Gluckman, 1950, p. 190; Gluckman, 1953; and Schneider, 1953. Gluckman put forward three hypotheses: (i) that divorce is rare and difficult in societies with marked Father Right and frequent and easy with other types of organization; (ii) that the divorce rate is a function of the kinship structure; and (iii) that the amount of bride price and the divorce rate tend to vary inversely and both are rooted in the kinship structure—'It is rare divorce which allows high marriage payment, rather than high marriage payment which prevents divorce.' Busama, with slight matrilineal stress and no divorce, contraverts the first thesis, and the material also suggests that the second is not of universal validity. The Busama marriage system itself prevents divorce. Scrapping the on-going exchanges could well lead to frequent divorce without the kinship groups or kinship obligations being seriously affected. (Leach, 1957, in a discussion of Gluckman's hypotheses, pointed out that two categories of 'Father-Right' societies ought to be distinguished. In one the brother-sister tie is weak and a woman at marriage is absorbed into her husband's patrilineal group, which from then on exercises control over her; in the other the brother-sister tie is strong, there is a clearly-defined rule of preferred marriage, and the woman still belongs to, and is controlled by, the patrilineal group of her birrh even after she marries. In the former divorce is probably rare, in the latter common. See also Djamour, 1959, pp. 130–40.)

be barren, may after a year or two re-enter employment, but they always come back again and take up their marital responsibilities.

SOME ACTUAL CASES

In this section I propose to give a few examples of the sort of clashes that occur when the relatives are arranging a marriage. The first case illustrates differences of opinion between patrilateral and matrilateral kin.

Dahungmboa, as the linked first cousin of the woman Mangwi, assumed that he was entitled to dispose of her eldest daughter, a girl named Awibalu. He told me that he intended to use her to obtain a wife for his ward Tabi', the son of another of his female first cousins, a woman unrelated to Mangwi, who had entered his household on the death of her husband some years before. Awibalu was the older, but he intended to pick her a man with a young sister who later on could come to Tabi'. There were two possibilities, two men to whose kindred he and his relatives owed girls, and he was in no immediate hurry to decide between them.

Then suddenly Awibalu's father Gamung announced that he and his brothers intended in the following week to give her as a bride to the youth Ta'angki, to whose relatives they had long been in debt. He made no mention of Ta'angki's sisters but must have had one of them in mind as a probable future wife for the son of one of the brothers.

The public at large were shocked by the news, but Dahungmboa and his relatives could take no steps to prevent the match. Gamung was an affine, and they had to treat him with respect. The only course of action open to them was to signify their displeasure obliquely. Dahungmboa next day set off on a fortnight's visit to Buakap, thereby missing the wedding. On returning he declined to meet Gamung and always walked away ostentatiously at his approach.

Two months passed, and Dahungmboa contracted influenza, which rapidly turned to pneumonia. He now begged Gamung to come to him. ' "If thou bring thy gift to the altar and there rememberest that thy brother hath ought against thee; leave there thy gift before the altar and go thy way; first be reconciled to thy brother and then come and offer the gift," ' he quoted as Gamung entered the doorway (Matthew V, 23, 24). He went on to say that he was seriously ill and, in spite of my sulfa medicine, might still die. Before asking for God's mercy he wished to make his peace by expressing regret at having nursed hatred for so long. Gamung shook hands but did not admit that the fault was really his.

In the second case two men each with a son strove secretly against one another for the same girl (see Figure 4). The prelude was the marriage of Ikawi, only child of Mtung, to Yomsop, only child of Wapa. The obvious bride for the return marriage was Yomsop's cousin Tasuluwi, the second daughter of his father's elder brother Mamang. But to whom should she be sent? Ikawi had no brothers, and all her male first cousins, the sons of her father and mother's brothers and sisters, were already married. But as

it happened there were two bachelor second cousins, second cousins also
of each other, Gaya, the son of Mtung's linked first cousin, and Titu', the
son of another first cousin, this time a male. Urged on by Mtung, Gaya's
father and uncles chose as their spokesman his mother's mother's brother's
son Mingkwa, a true cross cousin of Mamang and Wapa; and within a
day or two the father and uncles of Titu' picked his mother's father's
father's sister's son's son Nga'luasi, a second cousin to Mamang and Wapa,
to state a case for them. The fact that the negotiations were carried on

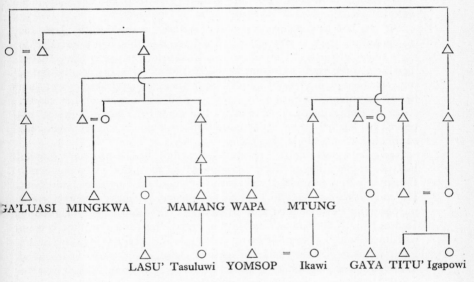

FIGURE 4
The background of Tasuluwi's marriage

separately behind closed doors meant that the ordinary social co-operation
of the parties was not impaired. They were always polite on meeting and
bottled up their anger till later, when in private they did not hesitate to
make spiteful remarks about one another. Eventually Mamang and Wapa
decided to give Tasuluwi to Titu'. Mamang informed me that he would
have been just as satisfied with Gaya but that his wife had said that the
girl preferred Titu'. The other villagers were sceptical. The result had
been a foregone conclusion, some of them maintained. Nga'luasi was not
as close a relative as Mingkwa, but Mamang and Wapa liked him better
and were always seeking his company. Four years later the uncles of Titu'
balanced his marriage by giving his sister Igapowi as a bride to Wapa's
linked sister's son Lasu'.

Another case presented similar features. Mala'sawa when disposing of
his sister's daughter Ambawi was faced with deciding between the lads

Lahilu and Gai, the former fairly closely related to him, the latter more closely related to her father. The girl's paternal uncles constantly stressed Gai's merits and also pointed out that he had a sister who would become available as a wife for Mala'sawa's son Si'bong, a young man already past twenty years of age. But Mala'sawa, drawn to his own nearer kin, continued to hesitate, although Lahilu's sister was but a baby. Finally he requested a cousin to be his go-between and extract the promise of another girl from Lahilu's father. The latter agreed and announced that he would send his niece to Si'bong. A double wedding followed—and Gai's kinsmen were annoyed.

For the last example we must go back to the time of the Japanese occupation in 1943. A rumour had circulated that the enemy intended to place the single girls of the village in a brothel for the use of the soldiers. Terrified, the parents immediately married off everybody over the age of puberty. One of the men, Nga'sele', sent his daughter Dabungyam, then barely seventeen, to the youth Lahung, who was not much her senior. Later, after the Japanese commander had denied the story, Nga'sele' repented his haste and, on being assured that the union had not been consummated, took Dabungyam back.

Nga'sele' is past middle age, and his marriage to Dabungyam's mother had taken place before the abandonment of the bride-price payments, though at a time when cash had already replaced the traditional valuables. He and his father and uncles had not owned sufficient money for the purpose and had accepted a substantial contribution from a neighbour, Dantu. By now Dantu was dead, but his credits had come down to his main patrilineal heir Gwaleyam, the son of his brother. Accordingly, Gwaleyam insisted that he had the right to dispose of Dabungyam, whom he intended to use as a means of obtaining a wife for his nephew Iging. He selected the youth Muengpop as the bridegroom on the assumption that the lad's father, a man named Gase', would subsequently send a daughter for Iging. Gase', however, is undependable and quarrelsome, and before the arrangements had been finally approved he fell out with both Nga'sele' and Gwaleyam. By way of revenge for what he said were their insults he determined to humiliate them, and an hour before the ceremony was to take place he and Muengpop left the village. Dabungyam and all her relatives were thus left in great embarrassment. Next day Nga'sele' tried to hide his shame by taking her on a visit to Lae.

At this point another villager, Salingbo, began taking a hand in the affair. Nga'sele' not only owed him a girl, but they were affines, and he felt sorry at such humiliating treatment. He now approached a distant cousin married to another daughter of Nga'sele' and begged the man to suggest that Dabungyam be sent to Salingbo's classificatory grandson Gi'lahi. Nga'sele' replied that he declined to be caught up in a third fiasco and must first have an assurance that Gi'lahi's other relatives would agree. Unfortunately one of them, Nga'gili', the favourite cousin of Gi'lahi's mother, now deceased, was temporarily absent from the village, but the rest approved and the wedding took place. (Nga'gili', however, was not Gi'lahi's mother's linked cousin.)

Gwaleyam was furious. He called a meeting of protest and declared that unless the marriage was annulled he would demand that the money paid years before by Dantu be returned. Nga'sele' in a dignified speech admitted the claim but said that surely his willingness to allow the match with Muengpop had absolved him from any further obligation. He was not responsible for the churlish behaviour of the boy and of Gase', and he intended to stick to the present arrangements. The villagers, already for a different reason displeased with Gwaleyam, were won over, and the chairman of the meeting pronounced judgment for Nga'sele'.

A week or two afterwards Nga'gili' came back. On learning of recent events he also was angry. Why the hurry, he enquired. Why was the ceremony not postponed until his views had been ascertained? He refrained from making a public attack on Salingbo, his own elder brother, or Gi'lahi's true maternal uncle, but he told them separately in private that they were potential murderers. 'The lad is still a mere boy and not nearly strong enough to stand up to the hardships of marriage,' he averred. 'Soon he will be dead, and each of you will be to blame.' He began avoiding them and choosing other working companions, though within three months the Mission pastor brought them all together and made them shake hands. Nga'gili' offered the excuse for his displeasure that the family honour had been sacrificed. Dabungyam, as a double reject, had lost her reputation and was probably no longer a virgin. We did not learn the truth till later. It transpired that already he had tentatively accepted another girl on Gi'lahi's behalf.

The marriage began satisfactorily, but one or other of the pair proved to be sterile. Gi'lahi blames Dabungyam and in his most recent letter wrote that he wished Salingbo had waited for the return of Nga'gili'.

CHOICE AND NECESSITY

Probably the young people always hope for a partner who will be physically ideal. There are established standards of beauty, and while the girls talk of the attraction of broad shoulders and narrow hips in the opposite sex, the youths speak with approval of firm upright breasts, regular features, a long face, a smooth forehead, a narrow nose, and a prominent chin. (They seldom mention skin colour but dislike medium reddish brown.) The seniors dismiss such talk as nonsense. 'Looking puts no food in the belly,' was one man's expressive comment. 'To eat you must first work, and the proper wife or husband is someone unafraid of mud and sweat.' He went on to say that the wise elder selecting a spouse for a dependant looks for such qualities as industry, adaptability, mildness of disposition, and cheerfulness—all of them more important than appearance.

Yet marriage is so much a matter of accounting that frequently the best-intentioned fathers and uncles find that they have no alternative but to thrust a worthy young girl into the hands of a waster or burden a dutiful youth with a slattern. Lazy Ahi, depraved Biyaweng, neutoric Tusili, and bullying Yomsop, to give only a few examples, have admirable wives; and shrewish Makisa'wi, bad-tempered Dale'wi, unsociable Anggudaluwi, and wanton Mukowi have excellent husbands.

The relatives have grave misgivings when a person's bride or bridegroom is manifestly unsuitable. Sagau', for instance, told a group of us that he would be prepared to imitate Biyaweng and blow off his hand if he thought that by doing so he could secure a more suitable wife than Tapongwi for his son. 'Her mother has an evil tongue, her elder sister has an evil tongue, and before long she, too, will have an evil tongue,' he lamented. 'Besides, her father Tangapi' is a fool. But there it is. He owes us a girl, and if we decline this one where shall we find another?' 'Don't carry on like that,' his brother advised. 'Tapongwi isn't too old to learn. Your wife will teach her how to behave properly.'

Some parents manage to appear complacent, but even these express their fears to intimates. Once, with deliberate lack of caution, I asked the man Gala'bo why was he giving his daughter to such a cockscomb as Alum. 'You could have waited,' I said; 'there are many youths and few girls.' 'Alum's all right,' he replied. 'These silly fellows settle down when they have a family to think of.' Another elder thereupon pulled me aside and reproached me for my tactlessness. 'Don't think you're alone in your concern,' he scolded. 'We, her uncles, are all upset; and Gala'bo isn't sleeping because he's so worried. But he must give his consent—he's weighed down by debt to Alum's uncles for another girl and has also to think of a wife for the next son. Alum, you see, has a sister.'

An old saying recommends the elders to take the young man or woman into their confidence. I was present when Gaiwaku asked his son would he be satisfied with the girl Hipowi. 'I don't know about her uncle yet,' said Gaiwaku, 'but if you like her, my boy, I think we can get Nga'gali to persuade him to let us have her.' (Nga'gali was a prominent villager related to both families.) The boy would scarcely have dared say 'no', and when he had given a favourable answer his father advised him how to find out the girl's views. He suggested waiting in concealment at the edge of the garden till she was alone and then emerging and throwing a twig at her feet. 'If she looks at you and stays quiet we'll go ahead; but if she leaves we'll know tha' she doesn't like us and that we must look for someone else,' he concluded. 'Yes, and where else would they look?' Gi'lahi remarked when I reported the incident.

Consultation, nevertheless, is a counsel of perfection rarely possible of fulfilment. The average young man learns by letter as his term of employment draws to a close that his relatives have accepted a wife for him. The stock proverb to meet the occasion is, 'Prawn in shallow water', implying that an opportunity once lost is gone for ever. Bobob's reaction was characteristic. On hearing from an uncle that the girl Suwi was waiting to become his bride he sent a note saying that he wanted not her but Gaiwi. 'Do not stop us,' he wrote. 'Read 1 Timothy IV, 1 and 3.' ('Now the spirit speaketh expressly, that in the latter time shall depart from the faith, giving heed to seducing spirits, and doctrines of devils . . . forbidding to marry.') His kinsmen failed to see the relevance of the passage and declined to alter the arrangements. Finally, after more pleading, he accepted. 'I couldn't stand up against all that chiding,' he told me. The youths who in recent years have remained stubborn can be counted on the fingers of one hand. They either renewed their labour contract as a sign of determination or, if already at home, went away again to a fresh employer.

These natives offer negative confirmation of La Rochefoucauld's maxim that people fall in love only because they have heard about it. They know nothing of the grand passion and do not expect romance. My account of Antony and Cleopatra proved meaningless to them. How could a man and woman feel strongly about each other without first living together and rearing a family, they asked. Husband and wife become united after years of marriage, not before the ceremony. (It is of interest that my friends thought Othello silly to have murdered Desdemona even though he believed her to have been unfaithful: they sympathized only with his desire to avenge himself on Cassio.)

But if Busama couples fail to achieve an initial ecstasy, they also avoid any subsequent revulsion. Our 'you-were-meant-for-me-I-was-meant-for-you' attitude may lift the newly married to the emotional heights, but living in so rarefied an atmosphere too often becomes intolerable. The Hollywood movie star who changes spouses with the seasons is but the logical development of such a system.

PERSONAL SELECTION

Girls, unlike the youths, cannot go away from the village and therefore find greater difficulty in opposing their relatives' wishes. Yet it is a fact that more of them are prepared to do so.

Awasawi was the first of my acquaintance to display independence. She declared that she would marry Koin and nobody else. He had come from the village of Butala' on the other side of the Huon Gulf and at the outbreak of the Pacific war was working as a medical orderly in the Salamauna hospital. With the entry of the Japanese he fled to some relatives in Busama. Here gossip soon linked his name with that of Awasawi, and when her father Magwalam questioned her she admitted the liaison between them. Magwalam and his brothers refused to countenance her marrying an outsider and sternly bade her keep to herself for the future. This she declined to do, and the affair continued in secret. At length, early in 1943, she became pregnant. Magwalam was inconsolable and said that he would raise the child himself rather than treat such an ingrate as a son-in-law.

Not till Koin promised to settle in Busama permanently did he and the uncles relent.

By this time the allied Armies were close at hand. As soon as they had thrown out the Japanese Koin found himself conscripted for hospital duty in another area. He was now able to send word to his parents telling them that he was safe and duly married. They and his other kinsfolk, as yet unaware of the circumstances, wished him to return to his own place when his period of service was over, and towards the close of 1944 some of his uncles arrived in Busama. A local elder summoned a village meeting, and they explained that they had come to fetch Awasawi so that she could await her husband in his home. As compensation for her relatives they heaped up gifts totalling eighteen pounds in cash, fifteen woven bags, and eleven pandanus-leaf mats. Magwalam and his brothers and brothers-in-law indignantly told them to take the money and goods back again. Koin had undertaken to stay, and they intended to hold him to his word.

The argument had been going on for over an hour when Awasawi arose. She announced that this was her business and that she had decided to leave next day for Butala'. Her father, grandmother, and other relatives tried to dissuade her, but she was adamant. The Mission teachers alone gave her support, protesting that Christians must be allowed to work out their lives in their own way.

At dawn the following morning the Butala' canoe departed with Awasawi aboard. Her father beat his breast and threw himself on the sand, but she turned away and urged the crew to paddle more strongly. Later he appealed for help from the Administration, but the District Officer replied that, as she had left of her own free will, the Government had no power to intervene.

The gifts remained piled up in the centre of the village till noon, when a teacher took them into his house for safe keeping. He tried to pass them over to Magwalam and to each of Awasawi's uncles, but when they all refused he sent them back through the Mission to the donors.

No word came from Awasawi for five months. Then she wrote begging Magwalam to fetch her home. Her mother-in-law had been unkind, and the Butala' women constantly sneered at her unfamiliar ways and called her a good-for-nothing stranger. He was too ill to make the journey and sent one of his sons-in-law to act for him.

Koin when freed from service joined Awasawi, and they have lived in Busama ever since.

This case led to talk of previous incidents. There was Singdahawi who ran away to join Busilim at the Mala'lo Mission, where he was working as a labourer. Her parents had announced that she was to be married to a youth called Mi, whom she despised. She wrote first asking Busilim would he take her, and when he said 'yes' she fled to the house in which he was living. Her parents pursued and demanded her back, but the European missionary reasoned with them. Forced marriages were pagan, he argued,

and Christians must be allowed to decide for themselves. Reluctantly the
father and mother acquiesced.

Then in 1945 another girl, Kwasangwi, refused to accept a widower,
Anggu. Her uncles pleaded with her and beat her, but she remained
steadfast. Meantime she had written to the Mission teacher Ida', also a
widower, saying that she wished to marry him and begging him to take
her away. By sheer bad luck his reply, in which he declined to act because
his relatives had refused to help him, fell into the hands of her brother,
who gave it to their father. The latter at once called a public meeting to
investigate. Kwasangwi, questioned, threatened to commit suicide if her
relatives persisted in their plan. She denied that she had anything against
Anggu personally but protested that he was too old. The village leaders
also interrogated Ida', but he would not answer. Later that week she
followed him to the gardens and persuaded him to have sexual intercourse
with her in order to force the hands of the kinsfolk of them both. She
announced what she had done, and the wedding followed.

Homkiwi was not so fortunate. In 1948 her maternal uncles arranged
for her to marry the youth Anso. She joined him but three days later, before
the union had been consummated, went home to her parents. Her father,
whose favourite she was, allowed her to stay and a month or two later even
helped her to elope to Lae with another man, Nga'singom. But her uncles,
thoroughly angry, pursued and brought them back. Nga'singom then took
a job in Port Moresby, well out of reach.

At this point the father died. The relatives at first made no move, but
after the mourning period was over they began hinting that, after all,
Homkiwi and Anso properly speaking were husband and wife. It was now
the turn of Anso's kin to be angry, and they speedily saw to it that he should
receive another bride.

A year later Homkiwi was discovered in an intrigue with a third man.
Her uncles hoped that his relatives would accept her, but they excused
themselves. Nga'singom also wrote that he was disgusted. Ultimately, late
in 1950, she became the wife of a widower several years her senior.

LOVE AND DUTY

The story of Awimasu and Nga'gili' is the most touching of all. Here at
last was romance even in Busama's arid soil. She was prepared to sacrifice
everything for him, but he put his kinship obligations first and repudiated
her. Yet his affections were so deeply engaged that fifteen years later he
still spoke of her with desire.

My account came from Nga'gili' himself. The story began with Awimasu
approaching him and asking him to marry her. He reminded her that her
relatives had set her aside for Balimboa, at that time still in employment,
but she answered that she wanted not Balimboa but him. He hesitated and
urged her to give him time to think. Her reply was to come that night to
his lodging and insist on sharing his bed. (Normally he slept in the club

with the other youths, but as at this time he had just recovered from an illness he was occupying a small room on the verandah of the house of his guardian Salingbo). The visits continued, and on each occasion she begged him to persuade his kinsfolk to sanction the marriage. At last, when she realized that he would not make the move, she deliberately overslept, thus bringing the affair into the open.

Awimasu's father was Nga'sele', father also of the much younger Dabungyam, subsequently the wife of Gi'lahi. On this occasion Salingbo came to his rescue, just as he did later after Dabungyam had been jilted. He set to work on Nga'gili' and made him promise to give the girl up. The negotiations with Balimboa's kin had gone so far, Salingbo pointed out, that Nga'sele' could not withdraw without great loss of face. Nga'gili' must say goodbye to Awimasu, by letter if he felt too ashamed to tell her directly.

Nga'gili' when I first became acquainted with him was already thirty-two but still one of the handsomest men in the village. Ten years earlier, so people said, he had had few equals. Perhaps it is not surprising then that within a few months he should have a second proposal, this time from the girl Iste, daughter of the quarrelsome Gase' referred to in an earlier section. She sent him a letter which, according to his recollection, read as follows: 'You evil man to bewitch me so that I dream about you. Stop making magic at once. I have no intention of asking my father to let me marry you.' This he ignored, and within a week she sent a second note in similar vein, ending up, 'Alas, I suppose I shall have to talk my father into letting me marry you. Your magic is so strong.' (I am not sure whether she really thought he had been using magic or was making this an excuse for offering herself to him.) Again he took no notice. Then one afternoon as he rode by on his bicycle she ran out of the house and belaboured him with a stick, yelling out as she did so that he was wicked to have worked such powerful spells upon her. He escaped, but that evening Gase' enquired was it true that he had had recourse to magic. On his protesting innocence Gase', who owed Salingbo a girl, said that there would be no objection to the match provided that he received two pigs first as compensation for the unpleasant publicity. Nga'gili' replied that he was without animals of his own and his relatives must do as they thought fit. Salingbo dismissed the demand as outrageous—perhaps Gase' had intended that he should—and the incident ended.

A third girl proposed before Salingbo began to take steps to find a suitable bride. He realized that unless he hurried there might be serious trouble. By judicious angling he managed to secure Nga'angkangwi.

In the meantime Awimasu had gone to Balimboa, who, because of the scandal, was somewhat reluctant to take her. 'She still doesn't like him though,' Nga'gili' maintained. 'They've been married now for a long time, but outside the house you never see her speak to him.' He has not quite learned to control his feelings and his eyes always follow her when she passes along the street. Twice he caught me watching, and on each occasion he shrugged his shoulders, sighed, and made a coarse jest at her expense—I suspect in an attempt to convince both of us of his indifference. Nga'angkangwi proved to be barren, as was mentioned, and once I reminded him that he would have been no better off with Awimasu, who also is childless. 'That's because she refuses to have a son by Balimboa,' he retorted. 'She chews herbs to shut up the mouth of her womb. If she can't have my babies she won't have anybody else's. No, no, she didn't tell me so—nowadays we never speak to each other—but long ago when we lay together in my house I learned her mind.'

Nga'gili' avoids Balimboa unless they have urgent business to discuss. At first he also kept out of the way of the man whom Iste married, though this embarrassment is now over. At the same time, he says that he would find an excuse if they ever invited him into their house.

REASONS FOR THE WOMEN'S BEHAVIOUR

Whence did Awimasu, Awasawi, Singdahawi, and the rest derive their courage? The seniors see the answer in the breakdown of native society. They insist that the members of the younger generation, having discovered that Europeans disapprove of marriages of convenience, trade on the knowledge that missionaries and administrative officials will always give them support. Once at a conference about the projected alliance of a young girl, I observed how one of her uncles seized upon a statement that she had shown a great liking for the lad Sapi. 'Then to Sapi she must go,' he exclaimed. 'New times have come with the white man, and we don't want her appealing over our heads to the District Officer.'

The argument sounded plausible till I discovered that the man had always advocated Sapi as the husband and was grasping at an excuse to press the boy's claims. He showed up in his true colours when at another conference on a different marriage he took the opposite side. On this occasion someone remarked that the girl seemed to dislike his candidate. 'That's of no consequence,' he replied. 'It has always been customary for the father and the uncles to decide on the husband. That is our law, the law of Busama.'

Western civilization is a handy scapegoat, and doubtless the older men are correct in blaming many of their present troubles on the new ideas and values. But in this instance they are wrong. Various stories are told of women who in the last days of the pagan era married against the wishes of their kindred, and in one of them a war followed. Further, even if the young people of today enjoy greater freedom, as is alleged, it would still not be clear why the girls alone should reap the advantages. As in other parts of New Guinea, the females of Busama have no opportunity for higher education, travel, or paid employment, and the result is that they remain the backward and conservative half of the population. I believe myself that the young man conforms because he is aware of his need for the goodwill of his relatives in the future—he knows that he will have to seek their help for most of his activities on almost every day of his life. The married woman, on the contrary, will work either alone or with her husband's kindred and can thus flout her own with impunity.

It seems probable also that the girls are aware of their scarcity value and if strongly moved are prepared to exploit it.

THE PAGAN WEDDING

In earlier times the first step was the appointment, by the girl's father, mother's linked brother, or father and uncles acting together, of one of her senior *hu-tigeng* relatives as a master of ceremonies. This man had the duty of fixing the dates for the different proceedings, giving general directions, and accepting and distributing the bride price.

When the day of the wedding arrived various young women, also of no particular kinship status, came along early and decked the girl out in finery. They rubbed her with coconut oil, painted her face with red and yellow ochres, robed her in new grass skirts, and hung strings of shell beads around her neck. By now a large party of her kinsfolk had assembled. They were not obliged to come, but most of them were pleased to do so. As soon as everything was ready her father or his spokesman stepped forward to give her a last word of advice. She must be mindful of her training and strive to satisfy her husband by working hard and cooking plenty of food; she must obey him and refrain from running away at the first sign of his displeasure; and she should help his kinsmen, who were about to give wealth to have her 'name' transferred to them. At the same time, those who had reared her still looked upon her as their relative: they would never forget her, and she must always remember them. Then her parents and uncles went inside and shut the doors. They took no further part in what went on.

The rest of the people now formed a procession, with the bride in the centre, and set off for the house of the bridegroom's mother. Each one carried a worn-out tool or utensil—a torn bag perhaps, or a cracked pot, a broken knife, or a smashed canoe paddle. On arrival they sat down, and the bridegroom's kinsfolk offered them a light meal. The girl took a piece of taro, handed it to her husband, and the two ate together, thus symbolizing their union.

The visitors, once they had disposed of the food, set out the various objects they had brought. This was the signal for the bridegroom's people to make replacements, a freshly-woven bag for a torn one, a sound pot for a cracked one, and so on. The transaction was known as *mo'asa'*, a word that has no other meaning. There was a good deal of hilarity and joking, but after the bride's relatives had departed she was usually in tears. Her mother-in-law led her away and tried to comfort her.

Payment of the bride price (*buling*) followed within two or three weeks. It consisted of dogs' teeth, boars' tusks, pigs, and baskets of vegetables. The man's father and uncles provided the bulk of the goods, but his other relatives helped, each according to his inclination. I tried to discover the

approximate value of the total, and whether the amount was relatively high
or low, but without success.[1] The old currency had been laid aside for so
long that nobody could recall how much was presented. There was no
haggling, however, and the only considerable variation that occurred was
at the wedding of the son or nephew of an important personage. Such
people always liked to establish their superior status by giving more than
ordinary folk. One old man also said that the bridegroom's kin were extra
generous if the bride came from a distant village. This was to compensate
her relatives for cutting them off from the possibility of daily contact
with her.[2]

The bridegroom's relatives collected their goods and set off for the bride's
mother's dwelling. They erected a small decorative tree in front, hung the
dogs' teeth and boars' tusks in the branches, and piled the trussed pigs and
other foodstuffs alongside. A spokesman now pointed out some of the
valuables as a special offering for the girl's mother. In theory these were the
reward for bringing up her daughter well, though the practical aim was 'to
silence her criticism and shame her into refraining from interfering in the
running of the new household'. The bride's relatives now furnished a
simple meal, which the party ate before returning.

Late in the day the master of ceremonies supervised the slaughter of
the pigs. He had the carcases cut up and the pork and vegetables cooked
and then caused platters of the food to be taken round to all the bride's
kinsfolk with the exception of her parents and uncles. These persons were
in a sense the hosts but were forbidden to eat. The dogs' teeth and boars'
tusks he shared out in the next day or so. If the girl was an eldest daughter,
and so 'belonged' to her father's side, he gave them to the men who had
contributed to the payment for her mother, or their heirs; if she was a
second daughter, and so 'belonged' to the mother's brothers' side, he gave

---

[1] Deciding whether a bridal payment is high or low must always be difficult.
Leach, 1953, argued that consideration ought to be given to the number of objects,
whether they are of one kind or several kinds, their economic cost, the period of
time over which the payment is made, and the number of relatives implicated. A
comparison with the amount of compensation for various offences, including
homicide, might also be useful.

[2] Busama could serve as a model for the many communities of Melanesia that
make bride-price payments. Save in the central highlands of New Guinea, preliminary discussions between the two sides do not occur, and the givers offer as
much as they can, within certain fixed limits, in the interest of prestige. Doubtless
the prevalence of the custom is to be correlated with the widespread rule of virilocal residence (patri-virilocal if descent is patrilineal, avunculo-virilocal if descent
is matrilineal). In such circumstances the woman's birth group, even when her
children belong to it, loses her economic service and prime allegiance, both of
which pass to the group into which she has married. (In Wogeo residence is
optional, and although virilocality is the popular choice, no bride price is paid: and
in Dobu, where couples have to live alternately, for a year at a time, with the husband's group and the wife's group, there are continued exchanges—see Fortune,
1932, pp. 1–5, 189–93. New Ireland is exceptional in that, despite matri-uxorilocal
residence, bride price is paid—see Powdermaker, 1933, pp. 32, 145–8, 157.)

I

them to these relatives; and if she was a junior member of the family he split them up between the two parties. The distribution always took place in the presence of disinterested witnesses who could be appealed to in cases of dispute.

One further ceremony remained, the *buakup* (literally, 'coconut water-bottle'), the formal presentation to the bride by her husband's kin of an outfit of clothing and household utensils. 'The girl arrived with nothing,' the old men explained, 'and her in-laws had to see that she had something to wear and something to cook with.'

The early missionaries saw bride price only in terms of economics and considered it to be an unmitigated evil. They imagined that the bridegroom was reduced to a state of penury and that the woman became his personal property. The absurdity of this latter notion was made plain in a statement by one of the men: 'A wife isn't like a piece of cloth you've bought at the store. The cloth is yours as soon as it's paid for. You can wear it or give it away, or, if you're stupid, tear it up, and nobody is angry. But if you beat your wife there's no end of a fuss.' He then went on to say that the seniors finally yielded to the missionaries' request just because the woman was not a slave. 'They agreed that they'd been foolish to pay for something that, after all, didn't become their own.'

Yet many men are ashamed that they cannot now make a presentation. 'We feel unhappy,' they declared. 'We've taken something and given no return. That's not the proper way to do things, not the way we Busama like to behave. If a man accepts a gift and offers nothing people say he's mean.' They also pointed out that a wife can silence her husband's rebukes by taunting him with the fact that he has not paid his debt to her kin.

More serious is the loss of a means of showing appreciation. It might be argued that, as marriage takes place on the old exchange basis, an additional settlement is redundant. But the natives are accustomed to expressing regard, affection, approval, and esteem in tangible form. The builder of a house feasts his helpers, the labourer spends a share of his wages on his kinsfolk, and visitors always arrive in the village laden with gifts and depart with as much as they can carry. 'If you're away from home and your relatives write to say that they're thinking of you,' Nga'gili' once said, 'that's just ink and paper—there's nothing in it. To prove what they say they must send presents. (You must send them money too, of course.) Again, if friends come it's not the soft words that count; no, it's the betel, the coconuts, and the cooked food. Look, it's like this. If I, Nga'gili', want something from you, Obin, you give it to me; and if you want something from me I give it to you. That's what makes us brothers, not my calling you *nga'duwa* and your calling me *lasing*.' The bridegroom's relatives have been deprived of the opportunity for displaying proof of their gratitude, and they find the experience unpleasant.

Probably the complaints would deserve more attention if marrying outside the village were still practised. Formerly when the parties did not know one another the bride price must have helped them to make their appropriate adjustments.[1] But today bride, groom, and their kinsfolk have all been familiar since childhood.

THE MODERN CEREMONY

The present-day wedding is simple. A night is fixed, generally one near the full moon, and at about eight o'clock the villagers assemble outside the house of the bridegroom's parents. When all is ready a Church leader steps forward and calls out the name of the young man and of the woman. They approach shyly from opposite sides, each supported by a few relatives of his or her own age. He tells them that they are now married and bids them shake hands. If he wishes he may deliver a homily on their mutual obligations and remind them of their continuing duty to their kin, though this part of the proceedings is often omitted. Bride and groom then disappear. They keep out of sight for a few days to avoid teasing by their associates.

At this point the man's relatives produce two or three pigs and sufficient vegetables for a small feast. The girl's relatives wait till the following morning before killing the animals and cooking the meat and other food. They send portions to everyone in the village except the parents and uncles of the bride and groom.

[1] Cf. Evans-Pritchard, 1951, p. 96: 'Bridewealth payments [among the Nuer, where the bride and groom are strangers] may . . . be viewed as a technique for creating new social relations between persons between whom there are no well-defined patterns of behaviour and for maintaining them. They are one of the many ways in which gifts and payments are used for this purpose, and have this function, in primitive societies. Bridewealth may thus be thought of as providing a kind of social scaffolding, a temporary structure of behaviour patterns, which enables the union to be built up.'

8

Husband and Wife

MARRIAGE is supposed to be founded solely on sexual desire, and people often say—unwittingly quoting one of the myths forgotten by all but the older men—that its purpose is to preserve social life from destruction. They explain that, just as rain without rivers to carry the water away would become a flood covering everything, so undirected appetite would lead to chaos. This view is understandable in a society that condemns extra-marital intercourse. The physical aspects of sex are bound to be stressed if gratification is only approved when sought in wedlock.[1]

Yet the young man's relatives begin by warning him that he must not on any account approach his bride till she has learned to adjust herself to her new surroundings. They remind him that, whereas he still works with his comrades and spends his evenings in the familiar club, she has to live with a mother-in-law and garden in the company of strange women. These may all have been her neighbours for years, but adapting herself to their idiosyncrasies, running errands for them, and fetching them firewood inevitably create strain. She knows that, even if silent in her presence, they enjoy pointing out her failures and shortcomings when by themselves.

Not until at least a month has passed does the man's mother set about bringing him and his wife together. The woman insists that he must now sometimes eat a meal at home, take the girl with him to the gardens, and till the ground at her side. Soon they are able to behave naturally and speak freely to each other. They may use personal names, but generally the husband addresses his wife as *awi*, literally 'woman', and she him as *nanga*' (from *nga*' = 'man'). For a few weeks longer the kin urge caution, and usually he postpones his advances unless she gives him positive encouragement.

At this stage the couple have intercourse only in the forest, though the man's mother still urges him to share his wife's mat from time to time at home. The mother then waits until everyone is asleep and fans the fire into a blaze to discover the probable state of their feelings. The girl

---

[1] The Wogeo natives, who are in youth promiscuous, over-emphasize the economic side. The relevant myth tells how the culture heroes ordained the institution of marriage in order that men could eat vegetables, grown by women, and women eat fish, caught by men. (See Hogbin, 1945, pp. 324, 325.)

ought to be lying close to her husband, and if she is separated from him or has her back turned the mother-in-law, enlisting the aid of the mother, lectures her on her wifely duty. Formerly the two women might have told the young man to exercise his rights by force.

Frequent intercourse is thought to lead to loss of energy, and young husbands are expected to hold themselves in check. They need all their strength during the first year or two for establishing their gardens and preparing for building a house; besides, if the woman were to become pregnant too soon she also would not be able to work so hard.

The pair do not have sexual relations regularly till they move into their own dwelling, usually towards the end of the second year. They now sleep together nightly except during the wife's periods. In the pre-European era women at such times did no work and kept away from the menfolk: today they can cook and garden, but the average male is still revolted by the thought of contact with menstrual blood.

The taboo operates once more as soon as the woman has become pregnant. From now till the infant is about a year old she and her husband have to sleep apart. In the beginning they hope to protect the growing embryo from injury, and later they want to avoid a second conception until the first baby is old enough for weaning.

In fact few husbands ever become the wife's constant bedfellow again —'they are ashamed lest the child should see their embraces'. Recently the custom of shaking hands has been adopted, but apart from this the natives avoid all contact in public with a person of the opposite sex. Parents free to resume sexual relations therefore prefer to seek the seclusion of the forest. They choose a spot with thick undergrowth at some distance from the gardens 'for fear that the smell of copulation might contaminate the growing taro'.

Old women give the girls sexual instruction when they first menstruate, but boys have to pick up information as best they can in the club house and elsewhere. The position for coitus is rigidly prescribed, with the woman on her back and the man above supporting most of his weight on his elbows. Any variation is held to be perverted, and a newly-married husband who announced that he and his wife had discovered that they derived enjoyment from standing up against a tree for a change aroused considerable disapproval. The seniors denounced him not only for his indelicacy in raising the subject but also for the behaviour in itself.

Impotence in men and frigidity in women seem to be unknown, and I had difficulty in convincing people that the phenomena occur. They admitted that a person's readiness to perform the sexual act might vary in relation to such factors as physical well-being, which in itself is affected by health and fatigue, but they had never before, or so they declared, heard of men permanently unable or of women permanently unwilling. They even denied that young husbands ever retire unsatisfied after their first attempt at intercourse.

AFFECTION

Most husbands and wives become sincerely attached to each other but take care if outside the house never to express their regard by word or deed. When the police came to arrest the man Isom for alleged collaboration with the enemy during the war his wife simply shook his hand in farewell. She knew that if found guilty he would be imprisoned, possibly for several years, but displayed no visible sign of emotion as two constables led him away.

It is true that a proverb, 'The wife is but thatch; the sisters are the posts', implies that she is not highly thought of; but I have never heard the saying quoted by a husband, only by his relatives. The first occasion was when Nga'gili' was walking away after visiting a sick cousin. He was annoyed to see the woman keeping in the background while other persons nursed the patient. 'It's always the same,' he went on crossly. 'The wife looks after her husband while he's fit to work and as soon as he becomes incapable gives place to his kinsfolk.' Later on he conceded that his strictures had been unreasonable. The wife was carrying out the various routine household tasks that had to be done and, wisely, had left the emergency duties to the visitors. 'Yes, I see that you're right,' Nga'gili' finished up. 'You know, at times like this the husband doesn't complain: it's his relatives who talk about the wife's faults.'

The majority of marriages develop into a partnership. Although in theory the cash belongs solely to the man, every one of my intimates who had been wedded for two or three years invariably handed it over to his wife for safe keeping.[1] She sometimes carried it about in her bag but more usually buried it, often in a place whose whereabouts the man did not bother to discover. Ida' lost £10 through carelessness in this regard. His wife died after a short illness, and at the end, when he realized that she was unlikely to recover, he did not care to trouble her with questions about such a mundane matter as where the money was hidden. Most husbands also consult their wives about how the cash is to be spent, whether on tools, clothing, and other essentials or on such luxuries as cosmetics and extra foodstuffs.

Soon after the couple have a house of their own they begin to acquire pigs. It is the woman's job to feed them, and almost always the husband takes her into his confidence before he disposes of an animal. Several times when feasts were planned I heard of men seeking the wife's opinion on the advisability of donating a beast or for the moment keeping the herd intact

---

[1] In former days the sister looked after any ornaments regarded as heirlooms, which had to be transmitted, along with land rights, in the female line. For the moment the brother owned the objects: but they would be inherited by the sister's sons and so were best kept separate from the goods that would go to the sons. Today the men never ask their sisters to mind property, though a young bachelor or widower may give his money to his mother.

against future needs. One householder, Busilim, actually assured me that nobody ever gives away a pig without conferring first with his spouse.

Some of my closer associates also admitted asking advice in the home about general village affairs, and one or two laid great stress on the wife's discretion, judgment, and common sense. A remark of Ahipum's when he was caught up in some dispute has dozens of parallels: 'Mu'alimawi thinks I ought to call a meeting and have the thing thrashed out, and no doubt she is right. She usually is—you know that. She doesn't babble before speaking, and that makes her a good counsellor.' On another occasion Kisi told me that he thought it wise to prove one's partner first, but if she showed that she could be trusted, then a man ought not to withhold anything from her.

The husband's devotion is often apparent during the woman's pregnancy, when he may take over some of her work. Several men also mentioned that at such times they had offered up private prayers for a safe delivery. Again, the grief displayed after the spouse's death has every appearance of being genuine. Certainly the affinal kin would object if there where no tears, but widows and widowers have spoken to me spontaneously of their sense of desolation.

QUARRELS

Living together inevitably leads to minor irritations, and although most husbands and wives like to conceal their dissatisfactions in the interests of domestic peace, if tried severely by a particular incident they sometimes pour out all their accumulated grievances. Each refers bitingly to the partner's immediate shortcomings and then goes on to enumerate others that till then he or she has passed over. A delayed meal or over-strictness with the children often serves as the spark, but the basic cause of trouble usually appears to be disagreement about the urgency of a purchase— whether the man requires a new axe or his wife a dress or household appliance.

Bangaya's house was so close to my own that I could always hear what he and his wife Yagawi were saying when they had a dispute. One evening he came in from the gardens later than usual. Dinner was still not ready, and he made some enquiry about how much longer it would be. The words were not offensive, but she took immediate exception and replied that he had better ask young Kingsawi to give him something to eat. He had talked to this girl in an adjoining allotment earlier in the day, but their conversation was entirely innocent, and he resented the jibe. 'Kingsawi's sensible anyway,' he answered. 'She's satisfied with a home-made pillow and doesn't pester people to buy one from the shop.' 'You've plenty of money and never buy me anything,' Yagawi interjected, her voice rising. 'It's not only the pillow you refused, but I can't have a dress. I've nothing fit to wear to church except my old red from before I was married.' 'Liar!' was his response. 'You've got three dresses. You think of nothing but clothes

all the time.' 'Yes, and you're lazy: you sleep at night instead of going out
with the other men,' Yagawi went on, pretending not to hear. 'When did
we last have fish? Tell me that. Everyone else eats it often, but I must make
do with cabbage relish for my taro.' The argument continued in this strain
till neighbours went in to shame the pair into silence. Bangaya then strode
off to the club, where he spent the night supperless. When on the following
morning he returned neither made any reference to what had taken place,
and shortly afterwards Yagawi accompanied him to the garden as though
nothing untoward had occurred. She is not ordinarily jealous or ill-
tempered, and her fretfulness on this occasion, so someone said, may have
been the result of a feverish cold.

The women's acknowledged weapon is their tongue, and no man can
match their more calculated acidities. Their favourite thrust is a charge of
parsimony, probably because it is unanswerable. Few husbands earn sufficient cash to satisfy all the family wants, and Bangaya, as Yagawi knew
well, could not possibly have purchased a pillow and a dress as well as the
tools that they both needed. Some wives twist the knife in the wound by
further taunting the husband with his kinsmen's failure to give the bride
price. Such a reproach is stupid, for nowadays her relatives would almost
certainly refuse the payment; but, here again, he can offer no satisfactory
reply.

People do not object if a husband retaliates by cuffing his wife lightly on
the head and shoulders, and she herself rarely expects much sympathy.
Sometimes she runs away for a day or two but always returns of her own
accord. If he goes further and beats her he may incur fresh dangers.
Several times I have seen men emerge from a domestic conflict bitten and
scratched and with valuable possessions smashed. If then they allowed
themselves the satisfaction of destroying the wife's property they only
made things worse—they were obliged to purchase the new utensils and
garments.

A woman who cannot fight her own battles reports the husband's
conduct to her father and brothers. They refrain from making personal
reproaches and are content to leave the case to the seniors for investigation
and, if need be, punishment. At such times kinship ties always count for
more than the women's sexual solidarity. The man's sisters may call him
a fool for temporarily depriving himself of his wife's services, but they
never chide him for cruelty in exercising his superior strength against the
weakness of womankind.

ADULTERY

It is clear that after marriage women retain much of their old freedom.
They still exchange cheerful greetings with members of the opposite sex
and still engage them in light-hearted badinage. The only restriction is that,
if previously implicated in a scandal, they must avoid all contact with the
other party.

The average husband is not suspicious unless confronted with positive evidence of his wife's infidelity. The few men who are by nature jealous give rise to a certain amount of scorn and amusement. The elderly Yabo, who dislikes leaving his now aged spouse Lutuwi alone, is regarded as both pathetic and ridiculous. She was unfaithful to her former husband Sam, dead for many years, but has long lost her attractions, and the young men say laughingly that they would demand £10 if asked to lie with her. Tusili, the man who tried to cut off his hand when he thought his wife might be carrying on with other men, is freely acknowledged, perhaps correctly, as doomed to end his days in a mental hospital.

Jealous wives are also uncommon, though one, Mu'apu', forced her husband to give up his career as a medical orderly because she objected to his attending women in labour; and another, Singgawawi, caused a number of domestic crises. Nobody else has ever suspected her husband Mayeng of conducting an intrigue, but recently she became so enraged at what she described as his outrageous over-familiarity with the daughter of a neighbour that she drove an axe through the hull of his new canoe and almost bit the top off his index finger.

It is significant that many people were at first incredulous when told that Biyaweng had offered his wife's favours to the soldiers of the Signals unit. 'No-one would do such a thing, not even the shameless Biyaweng,' they exclaimed. 'She's his wife—he couldn't.' Two men who had been employed earlier at Salamaua then disclosed that he had prostituted her there. 'He's like a dog or a pig,' was the unanimous verdict.

Several of the married men, however, confessed to dreams about relations with other women. Such nocturnal visitations were the result of natural longing, they admitted. They had noticed the girl's pleasant appearance and had allowed their mind to dwell upon her. They knew that fulfilment of their desire would be fatal and during waking hours had pushed their thoughts 'deep down in their insides'; but at night the will is lulled, and hidden impulses rise again to the surface. Nga'gili' once told me of a dream about Awimasu, the woman whom he had hoped to marry: 'I saw her catching prawns yesterday, and her face lingered with me until after I had set to work felling trees in the cultivations. So later when I slept I dreamed about her. No, I am not going to do anything about it. If I were I'd be too ashamed to talk now.'

As a rule a husband who believes that his wife has a lover does not make accusations until he can produce a witness. First he shams illness and sends her to the garden alone. Then, after a few days' delay to give her a feeling of security, he follows behind and conceals himself in the forest nearby. He whistles when she approaches the fence and watches her behaviour carefully. If she ignores the sound he concludes that his suspicions are without foundation; but if instead she steps outside at the signal, thinking it comes from the other man, he knows that his action has been worth the trouble.

The next step is to catch the pair *in flagrante*. The husband pretends to have business that will keep him for several days in one of the other villages, but each night he returns with a trusted relative to keep watch. If the lover appears he follows him into the house. In former times he would have done his best to kill him on the spot. The relatives of the adulterer, confronted with clear proof of his guilt, accepted the punishment as just and refrained from taking vengeance. But if he was lucky and escaped he had to flee at once and take up permanent residence with a kinsman living elsewhere. In no circumstances could he return home even after the lapse of several decades. The husband beat his erring wife severely, but her life was not in danger.

Today adultery is a criminal offence, and an Ordinance provides for the imprisonment of both the lover and the guilty woman for a period of up to six months. Presumably the intention is to give protection to married labourers who have left their wives at home. Magistrates dislike invoking the law, however, and in most instances dismiss the charges. The natives complain in consequence that the Government has no respect for the sanctity of wedlock. 'The husband's name is upon his wife, and naturally he is angry when an adulterer also tries to put a name upon her,' Ahipum once remarked. 'The rest of us object to marriage being treated as of no importance and give him our support.' 'Quite true,' Nga'sele' interposed. 'But District Officers don't mind: they refuse to imprison the offender. You'd think they wanted people to behave like dogs.'

A wronged husband who has not been able to secure legal redress has to be content with a lesser penalty. He makes a report to the Mission leaders and asks them to take appropriate action. They remind the guilty parties that their sin is a violation of the customs of the ancestors and the commandments of God and then sentence them to suspension from Church membership. This is tantamount to sending them to Coventry, for the other villagers are reluctant to associate with them. As usual, the man can escape to employment, but the woman must face out her shame. At first the husband may refuse to have her in the house, and generally several months elapse before he forgives her. One man, Sam, declined to live with his erring wife and departed for Buakap, where God speedily took vengeance upon him for failing to give her a second chance.

A husband who is absent from home expects his brothers and other close kinsmen to safeguard his rights. But although they ought to take action should his wife be unfaithful, in practice they try to ignore the affair. In 1944 the villagers were gravely shocked when the wife of one of the Army conscripts compromised herself, and for the space of two or three weeks her name was on everyone's lips. New to the place, I enquired whether the seniors would summon her and her lover to answer for their actions. Not unless the husband's half-brother laid a complaint, was the reply. The woman died shortly afterwards—God's judgment again—and the people then assumed, rightly as events proved, that the husband would never learn of her misconduct.

Government representatives are the worst offenders. The European officer responsible for their appointment can seldom afford the time to pick the most suitable candidates, and those selected are often ill fitted to exercise authority. The Busama have had several unfortunate experiences with such petty tyrants. Gwaleyam, for instance, a representative of the Awasa section of the settlement, was accused of adultery no less than three times between 1944 and 1950.

The other culprits, a total of half a dozen during the same period, were each implicated only once. Most of them had the misfortune to be married to childless wives in whom they had lost interest. Perhaps the most interesting case was that of the anti-social Biyaweng. The idle prattle of a small child revealed that he had been carrying on an intrigue for over a year with the most repulsive woman in the neighbourhood. She suffered from nodular elephantiasis and a scaly skin complaint, and the stench from the open sores with which the poor creature was covered was so disgusting that the elders when questioning her ordered her to stand on the leeward side. Here was proof of the infrequency of adultery, people pointed out. It was hardly possible that Biyaweng would have gone to her had someone else been willing.

WIDOWS AND WIDOWERS

Men as a sign of mourning refrain from shaving for a period of about six months: women wear either an old net bag or a woven cap on the head for at least a year. Both men and women as far as possible remain indoors and if compelled to go out walk with eyes downcast. They also intensify the reserve that characterizes relations with their affinal kin, whom for the time being they call by a new all-embracing term, *moasing*. Eventually these latter make a small feast 'in appreciation of the shame'.

A widow is identified with her deceased husband's *da-tigeng* cognates. The prime responsibility for seeing that she and her young children are properly housed and fed rests with them, and if she is strong and healthy they also arrange for her to remarry. None of them can take her as his wife, and they are also forbidden to send her to a lineage mate or fellow clubman of the dead husband. The most likely choice is a widower from among his second and third patrilateral cousins. Such a man is not under an obligation to replace her later with another widow, and formerly there would have been no demand for bride price. If she passes to one of her former husband's more distant cousins he also does not incur a debt; but in earlier days he would have been obliged to make a small payment to each of the dead man's *da-tigeng* cognates.

The deceased husband's kinsmen are angry if his widow remarries without their consent. A case occurred in 1945, when the widower Kaneng wed the widow Amba. Her first partner had been dead for less than a year, and officially she was still in mourning. The couple shook hands in the centre of the village in the customary way, but Kaneng's relatives, disapproving of his haste, failed to provide a feast. Immediately the dead man's brother and sister strode to the front. 'Kaneng, our name rests upon this woman,' the brother declaimed. 'Her husband is still present in our memory, and what you have done is evil in our sight. As for you, Amba, you are the same as an adulteress. We'll never look upon your face again, and I shall take care to prevent your children from visiting your house.' 'It's all very well for you, Amba, I daresay,' the sister began bitterly. 'You've got rid of someone you hated and taken a really good husband in his place—you've buried your rubbish and should be satisfied.' Then, turning to Kaneng, she screamed at him, 'Man, you are evil, a devil. We'll remember this for ever, and I shall never look at your face again.' The brother did not carry out his threat to remove the children, but three years passed before he and the sister relented.

A man whose wife has died within a few months of their marriage, before any children have been born, expects her kinsfolk to replace her, preferably with a younger sister. The dead woman's relatives accept the demand as legitimate (in the past they would not have asked for a second bride price). Thus although a widow cannot marry her deceased husband's brother, a widower is permitted to wed his deceased wife's sister. The natives explain the difference by pointing out that, whereas a woman and her brother-in-law belong to the same club, a man and his spinster sister-in-law belong to separate clubs.

Widowers with but one child would like to return to the marriage market on the same terms as bachelors and become eligible to secure a youthful bride. But they know that females are short, and usually when the time comes they settle for a young widow.

AFFINAL TERMS

The term of reference for 'wife' is *lawi*; for her elder sisters, and also, if a man is speaking, for his elder brothers' wives, it is *lawi-ka*; for her younger sisters, and also, if a man is speaking, for his younger brothers' wives, it is *lawi-saung*: for 'husband' it is *lakweng*; for his elder brothers, and also, if a woman is speaking, for her elder sisters' husbands, it is *lakweng-ka*; and for his younger brothers, and also, if a woman is speaking, for her younger sisters' husbands, it is *lakweng-saung* (*awi*, literally 'woman' = 'my wife'; *awi-ka*, *awi-saung* = 'my wife's elder sister', etc.; *akweng*, literally 'digging stick' = 'my husband'; *akweng-ka*, *akweng-saung* = 'my husband's elder brother', etc.). Sisters-in-law use the reciprocal *halawi* (*ya'wi* = 'my sister-in-law', woman speaking), brothers-in-law the words *halangga'*, 'wife's brother', and *ngimmtu* = 'my sister's husband' (*ya'* = 'my wife's brother', *nga'mtu* = 'my sister's husband', man speaking). When a true brother and sister, or two first cousins of opposite sex, have married a true sister and brother, or two first cousins, and each man is in consequence both a

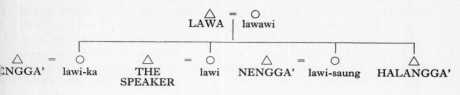

FIGURE 5
Kinship terms used by a male for his wife's relatives

'sister's husband' and a 'wife's brother', *ngimmtu* is preferred to *halangga*'.

Ordinarily these terms are also applied to the spouse's first cousins and to cousins' spouses.

Although a man refers to all his sisters-in-law by the one word *lawi* (with the addition of the qualifying suffixes *-ka* and *-saung*), he is permitted to marry on one side only. As has been pointed out, an alliance with the deceased wife's sister is approved, one with the deceased brother's wife forbidden. Correspondingly, although a woman refers to all her brothers-in-law as *lakweng* (with the addition of the suffixes), she can become the wife only of her deceased sister's husband, not of her deceased husband's brother.

The term of reference for 'father-in-law', 'son-in-law', 'grandfather-in-law', and 'grandson-in-law' is *lawa*; that for 'mother-in-law', 'daughter-in-law', 'grandmother-in-law', and 'granddaughter-in-law' is *lawawi* (*lawang lawangwi* = 'my father-in-law', etc.). These are applied also to the spouse's uncles, aunts, great-uncles, and great-aunts; and to the spouses of the nephews, nieces, great-nephews, and great-nieces.

There are also terms that can be used either in address or for reference for certain of the marriage connections. The men married to two sisters are *nengga*', and the women married to two brothers *dawatang* (*nengnga*' = 'my wife's sister's husband'; *dawatang* does not incorporate the possessive pronoun).

The behaviour considered proper between affines is in basic essentials the same as that between cognates; they too should be mutually loyal, helpful, and co-operative. In the event of a conflict a wife must even take the side of her husband's family against her parents. The approved patterns

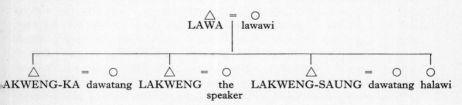

FIGURE 6
Kinship terms used by a female for her husband's relatives

may be gathered from the derivations given for some of the words. *Ngimmtu*, 'sister's husband', allegedly comes from *mtu*, the net used for gathering certain kinds of fruit, and the natives explain that 'support from a man's brothers-in-law prevents him from falling to the ground'; *nengga*, 'wife's sister's husband', is the same as the word for 'blood brother' (see above, p. 50); and *dawatang*, 'husband's brother's wife', was once applied to the co-wife in a polygynous household.

For the most part, nevertheless, affines begin their closer contacts after reaching maturity, and at the outset they may feel uncomfortable in one another's presence. On the one hand, the woman's cognates are apt to resent her being taken from them, and, on the other, the man's cognates tend to think that his wife is not good enough. An elderly man with whom I was discussing the approaching wedding of his youngest daughter made the following observation: 'It's always the same. I'd known from her birth that this child would leave me—hadn't her mother trained her to be a wife? —but I'm still sorry to see her go. I say to myself that she'll not be far away—no marriages into other villages for my girls—and that her husband is a fine fellow and bound to treat her well; yet, there it is, I'll be angry with him for taking her.' I asked had he felt any different when his sons had married. 'Fathers are always suspicious,' he replied. 'Sons-in-law and daughters-in-law—we're on the lookout for laziness and bad temper in all of them. We ought to be easy, certainly we ought; but we can't be, at least not until there are children.'

Usually the arrival of an infant has the desired effect—as the natives point out, a man who begets a son is also giving his father-in-law a grand-child and his brother-in-law a uterine nephew. Yet sometimes a slight prickliness remains, and many a person well on in years has complained to me that the spouses of his children were not as energetic as they should be. As an instance I quote the comment of Nga'sele' when he had to make plans for securing coconuts and betel ingredients to entertain a crowd of guests; 'Here I toil while my son-in-law Balimboa sits idle and makes no move to help.' He made no mention of his two nephews, who ought to have been present, and chose to forget that Balimboa was suffering from a bad tropical ulcer and could scarcely walk unaided.

The difficulty is overcome, as in the case of cross cousins, by declaring that affines are taboo and have a 'bitter touch'. In consequence they treat one another with formal respect. The social barrier is again symbolized by a ban on the use of personal names. Brothers-in-law, sisters-in-law, the men married to sisters, and the women married to brothers can fall back on the kinship terms, but parents-in-law and children-in-law have no alternative but teknonymy—they address each other by such phrases as 'Father of So-and-so'. All affines avoid handling one another's belongings, sitting on one another's beds, undressing in one another's presence, eating from the same dish, and sharing cigarettes and betel lime. In earlier times they also 'ate politely' when partaking of a common meal—that is to say, they covered their mouths from sight. (Why an unshielded mouth should have been thought rude I do not know.) Naturally public displays of anger are proscribed, together with overt references to excreta or sex. In ordinary circumstances they would never ask outright for assistance, but if an emergency arose, and a man was forced to turn for help to his affines, they could not possibly refuse.

The taboos weigh more heavily on the person who comes into the family from outside, on a woman's husband rather than on her parents and siblings and on a man's wife rather than on his parents and siblings. So if a bathing party is suggested and a man and his son-in-law are both present, or a man and his sister's husband, it is always the latter who withdraws.

People take pains not to utter coarse expressions in the presence of two kinsmen-by-marriage; and they are much discomfited if caught unawares. I was sitting one afternoon with Buho'sung on his father-in-law's verandah when a companion of his named Anggu came up. 'Hullo, itchy penis,' said the newcomer playfully as he set down his burden for a chat. Buho'sung at once jerked his finger over his shoulder, and a few moments later the father-in-law made a quiet exit from another door. Anggu gave an audible gasp and quickly vanished. Buho'sung should have gone away and left the older man undisturbed but had hoped the words were inaudible. Subsequently the father-in-law told me that he had wished to avoid embarrassing Anggu and myself.

The natives recognize that a marriage is not fully successful if the man and his wife's cognates, or the woman and her husband's cognates, remain on good terms only by keeping apart.[1] They say that as soon as it is clear that harmony has been achieved the regulations ought little by little to be relaxed. Yet faint traces of the 'bitter touch' are always present. Nga'gili' was caught up in a revealing incident a decade after his alliance with Nga'angkangwi. He and his father-in-law Gilingu' are sincerely attached, much more so than is usual, and they often go out fishing together. One day in 1946 they both suffered a sudden attack of violent diarrhoea. They could not disguise their predicament, but each had to pretend to be unaware of the plight of the other. Time after time on the voyage to the shore they altered the direction of the canoe, changing from bow to stern, ostensibly to take turns at steering but in reality to relieve themselves over the side without being seen (the vessels are double-ended, and in reversing —provided the sails are not in use—the members of the crew have only to face about). Throughout they kept up a polite conversation, speaking loudly in a vain endeavour to drown the noise made by their bowels.

[1] The people laughed scornfully when I told them about Radcliffe-Brown's Australian aboriginal, who, when asked why he avoided his wife's mother completely, replied, 'She is my best friend in the world: she has given me my wife' (Radcliffe-Brown, 1950, pp. 57, 58). He went on, 'I think the answer was logical and adequate. What disturbs or breaks a friendship is a quarrel. You cannot quarrel with a person with whom you have no social contact.' (As a former student of Radcliffe-Brown, I was able to quote the story long before its publication.)

I learned of the affair from Nga'gili' immediately. Emotionally upset and in great pain, he came to me for medicine as soon as the canoe was beached. Several days passed before he saw the humour of the situation and could describe the events as a joke. His hearers laughed heartily but agreed that no other course of action would have been possible. When later I discussed the subject with Gilingu' he also was amused; but he added that in olden days Nga'gili' would probably have committed suicide. 'We two are taboo,' he said. 'We have a "bitter touch", and talk of excreta is forbidden. In the past defecation would have meant death for the son-in-law.'

A man is never quite so reserved with his sister-in-law, and neither is she with him. They are always polite and keep off all subjects remotely connected with sex, but often they disregard the extreme niceties of etiquette. Brothers can thus talk on many topics in the presence of their wives, and sisters can speak freely in the presence of their husbands.

The men married to sisters and the women married to brothers unbend still more, though without entirely forgetting the conventions. The former are as a rule on the best of terms all the time, the latter, also in general agreeable, at odd moments display a certain coolness. This difference can be traced back to the behaviour of their spouses, the sisters in the one instance, the brothers in the other. Women keep up their social contacts more by visiting than by working together, and accordingly disputes between them are so trivial that family relations remain unaffected; men, on the contrary, are apt to become embroiled, and then to implicate their families, just because they so often toil in company.

A brother and sister married to a sister and brother or to two first cousins conduct themselves if alone as they did when younger but moderate their outward expressions of amity slightly 'out of respect' should the spouses approach. Often I was amused by the abrupt change in the spirit of the conversation.

A husband and wife who were already closely related before their marriage, perhaps as second cousins, find themselves in the anomalous position of having cognates, hitherto treated with familiarity, turned into affines to whom they owe respect (see above, p. 103). Each partner feels compelled to reorient himself or herself in regard to the members of the other's immediate family but generally leaves the remoter ties unchanged. The man invariably refers to his wife's father and mother as 'parents-in-law' and to her brothers and sisters as 'siblings-in-law'; but sometimes he continues to speak of her uncles, aunts, and cousins by the old terms. The wife's father and mother and brothers and sisters reciprocate by referring to him as 'son-in-law' or 'brother-in-law', while her uncles, aunts, and cousins go on thinking of him as they did before the match took place.

Quarrelling between affines is rare, and generally if an incident does occur investigation reveals that the persons concerned are also cognates and thus in a double relationship. A real or fancied affront re-establishes the habit of free speech, and the aggrieved party casts the taboo aside and bursts into recriminations. The elders are content to 'leave the offender to his shame'. He feels his disgrace keenly and for a time withdraws from community activities. In the past if he had been guilty of a very serious error, such as openly insulting his father-in-law, he might have committed suicide; but today, the offer of a gift is felt to be sufficient as expiation. By this means 'he chops off the binding cord of humiliation and so walks once more with head erect'.

I witnessed only two disputes between in-laws. On the first occasion Alingam had become angry with his wife and struck her across the face. She was not badly hurt but ran from the house screaming that he was trying to murder her. Someone rushed to the beach and urged her brother Hagalu', who was fishing, to come at once. He flew up the path and immediately began cursing and threatening, though after a few minutes neighbours dragged him away. Next day he left the settlement. On his return a few weeks afterwards he presented Alingam with a new axe and twenty-five shillings. It should be noted that these two brothers-in-law were also second parallel cousins.

The later case concerned Isom, who became incensed when one of his daughters and her husband had an argument. He asked an elder to sum-mon the young man to appear before a public meeting, but instead of staying away, as in decency he should have done, he himself took the lead in administering the reproof. Ultimately his brother pushed him aside and gave him a talking to on the impropriety of his own behaviour. Nga'gili', discussing the incident with me afterwards, explained that earlier on Isom had looked upon this son-in-law as a uterine nephew—Isom's father and the man's maternal grandfather had been brothers. 'So you see now why Isom forgot himself. Those two have only half a "bitter touch".'

9

Supporting a Family

CONSIDERATION must now be given to the way in which married men organize their various tasks. I shall begin with agriculture.

Taro, the staple, is not a seasonal crop, and planting goes on more or less continuously. Each person prepares a new area every couple of months and in a two-year period makes about a dozen gardens. The probability is that six of these will be located on the territory of his own lineage, two on that of his father's lineage, and the remainder on that of the lineages of some of his other cognates and affines. Only if he still lives near his father is the proportion likely to be much different. In these circumstances the number on his own lineage lands and that on his father's lineage lands may be reversed.

Lineage members, once they have reached a decision about which fresh patch of ground is to be cleared, indicate to a few of their kinsmen that any who care to join in will be sure of a welcome and the offer of a plot. On a given occasion one man may be accompanied by a son and a brother-in-law, a second by his father and father-in-law, a third by a paternal uncle and a son-in-law, and so on. An identical procedure is followed next time except that some of the guests will be changed. The man who earlier chose a son and a brother-in-law, for example, now perhaps prefers a remote cousin and a son-in-law, and the one who chose his father and father-in-law perhaps a paternal uncle and a wife's sister's husband. Such hospitality is reciprocated, and the relatives whom a man brings to his own lineage territory return the compliment by taking him to theirs. Accordingly, when a working party sets off the lineage members are in the minority. The rest, who may make up two-thirds of the total, include such people as fathers, grandfathers, father's brothers, father's brothers' sons, father's sisters' sons, mother's brothers' sons, sons, grandsons, remote cousins, fathers-in-law, sons-in-law, and wife's sisters' husbands.

The lineage leader makes the announcement of the day on which clearing is to begin, though often he acts less on his own initiative than at the prompting of his fellows. Hosts and guests then proceed to cut down the larger trees. They leave the timber for a few weeks to dry out and eventually burn it.

Each man now says how much ground he needs, having in mind his own household and any other families that look to him for help or to which he wishes to do a favour—that of a widowed sister maybe, or a sister-in-law or aunt, or some other woman whose husband is ill or absent in employment. Frequent visitors speak for themselves, but those who come on rare occasions beg their immediate host to do so on their behalf. No precise scale of measurement for length or area exist, and a loose description has to suffice. One man says, 'I have only a few taro suckers ready to plant'; another, 'I have a great many and would like to set aside a strip for my sister as well'; a third, 'For myself I want just a piece, not too big, not too small; but there's also my cross cousin whose husband is ill; I am sorry for all their hungry children.'

The leader, or his deputy, next divides the clearing into allotments in accordance with these requirements. He paces across the middle with a pause every few dozen yards. The ground on this side, he calls out, is for So-and-so, that on the other for Such-and-such. All then fall to. They mark the corners with tall stakes and erect flimsy barriers of light poles or bamboo along the sides.

Apart from the erection of the fence to keep the pigs out, the work from now on is done chiefly by the different family groups. The householder first lays a row of saplings crosswise, cutting the allotment into rectangles varying in size from two to three hundred square yards. These he names in order for his dependants and such persons, including possibly his nephews, for whom he feels responsible. His wife, unmarried children, and the older folk living under his roof always receive one each, and, apart from the nephews, he often gives one also to a sister or sister-in-law. He does not keep back any for himself unless he is a widower or intends the garden for some special purpose, as, for instance, to furnish the vegetables for a housebuilding feast. I have repeatedly mapped extensive areas without hearing the name of a married man mentioned once. 'The taro is really the father's,' said Nga'gili', 'but he calls the strips after the women and the children.'

In actual cultivation these minor divisions are largely meaningless. At the same time, the practice has educative value for the children, as we saw, and it is also a useful guide for estimating the size of the garden. If there were no barriers the householder might be at a loss to determine whether the area was big enough, but once the saplings are in position he can tell at a glance if his wants are being adequately catered for. Should he be doubtful he extends the allotment by clearing a small extra strip; and if, on the contrary, he finds that he has too much, he offers a piece to a kinsman.

The men, women, and older children of the household, perhaps occasionally assisted by relatives, tidy up the rubbish side by side, spread the ashes to enrich the soil, and plant the taro suckers and other vegetables. Weeding and harvesting, however, are women's work, and the men take no part.

Fencing is postponed until the pigs begin to be a nuisance. The unseasoned timber, cut straight from the bush, rots away quickly, and the

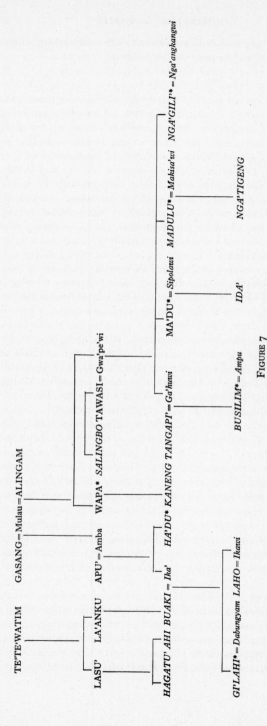

FIGURE 7

A selection of Gi'lahi's relatives

Names of males in capitals, of females in lower case; living persons italicized. Members of the lineage are indicated by an asterisk.

people wish to avoid having to carry out the job a second time before they abandon the garden to the encroaching forest.

EXAMPLES

Gi'lahi in 1950 was twenty-five years of age and had been married for five years. Figure 7 gives his kinship background. The principal living members of the lineage, apart from himself, were his mother's brother Ha'du, this man's mother's younger half-sister's sons Madulu and Nga'gili', and their sister's son Busilim. Ha'du, the head, will be succeeded in order by Madulu, Nga'gili', Gi'lahi, Gi'lahi's younger brothers, and Busilim. The last, although in the classificatory sense a younger brother of Gi'lahi, is slightly older. When I asked would he resent being ordered about by someone born later than himself he replied 'Certainly not' and that he had always called Gi'lahi 'elder brother'. Besides, he added, what could anybody possibly find to quarrel about in gardening?

At the time of the enquiry the group was somewhat unusual in that the houses of the members were not clustered together. I knew the reasons but wished to have Gi'lahi's explanation. He gave the story at length, but a brief summary will suffice here. Several of the men lost their parents in early youth and had been reared by relatives to whom they were still attached.

The man Apu' and his wife Amba had died first, leaving their son Ha'du and daughter Ika in the care of Amba's half sister Gwa'pe'wi. Ha'du was not only older than Gwa'pe'wi's sons Ma'du and Madulu (Nga'gili' was not yet born) but also regarded them as his 'younger brothers'. Ika', however, although genealogically the 'elder sister' of the girl of the family, Ga'huwi, was chronologically her junior.

Then after an interval, Gwa'pe'wi's husband Tawasi had died. Ha'du, Ma'du, and Madulu, all now past puberty, at once entered the household of their maternal uncle Wapa. Ga'huwi, too, was already married and no longer her mother's responsibility. But Gwa'pe'wi still had to look after the orphan Ika' and her own baby son Nga'gili'. Tawasi's brother Salingbo, himself childless and married to a woman who had been blinded in an accident, offered them shelter, and they went to live with him. Thus Nga'gili' grew up with his cousin Ika' and developed a greater affection for her than for his much older sister Ga'huwi. Both children became fond of Salingbo, to whom Ika' was not even closely related. She called him *damang*, 'my father', not *damang-ka*, his correct courtesy title, and later taught her sons and daughters to look upon him as their grandfather.

Ha'du, Ma'du, and Madulu after their marriage erected houses in the section of the village where they had stayed with their uncle Wapa, by that time deceased. Ma'du died in 1944 and his widow and two children then became part of Madulu's household. Nga'gili' may also transfer to this part—he has still not committed himself—but at that period he wished to be near his father-in-law Gilingu', whose dwelling was only about fifty yards from that of Salingbo. Gilingu', an expert carpenter, shipwright, and net-maker, was by native standards fairly wealthy, and, as he had only the one child, there was much to be said for courting his favour and enjoying the fruits of his industry.

Nga'gili' and Ika' did not become linked cousins in the technical sense, but their attachment continued till her death not long before my first arrival in the village. The result was that Gi'lahi considered Nga'gili' a more important maternal uncle than his mother's real brother Ha'du. In 1950 therefore Gi'lahi was saying that he would ultimately live alongside Nga'gili' no matter where Nga'gili' went. But at that stage a move was impossible. His father was an invalid and had moved into the house of the by then ageing Salingbo. The two needed help, and Gi'lahi had chosen to stay near them.

At the time of the investigation Busilim had not long returned from employment. In his absence his wife had lived with her mother-in-law, but Gi'lahi believed that the couple would soon build a dwelling of their own, probably in close proximity to those of Ha'du and Madulu. The prediction was fulfilled early in 1951.

Five years before, in 1945, when Gi'lahi was first married, I had noted that he gardened more often with his wife's kinsfolk than with his own. We were not then nearly such great friends, and it was his father-in-law Nga'sele' who drew my attention to his activities. On several occasions Nga'sele' said he considered himself fortunate in his choice of son-in-law, and then one day when we were visiting the cultivations together we found Gi'lahi already at work. 'Look, there he is with the fence started,' Nga'sele' exclaimed, stopping in surprise. 'I hadn't said anything to him about what I intended to do today. Certainly he's good, very good. And he never fails to send coconuts, or fish if he has any, when I receive guests. Soon we shall be clearing an area along the Buim River, and I must make a point of marking off a big allotment for him. He'll need plenty of taro if he's going to build a house.'

Not long afterwards I remarked casually to Ahipum that Gi'lahi must have received excellent training to be so mindful of the duties to his affines. 'He's all right,' was the reply. 'But you realize why he's being so helpful now? All newly-married men are the same. You see, he wants a house. He knows his own people will aid him—they always do—but he can't be sure yet of his wife's people. So he's taking care to please them. Remember that every time he goes with them they give him another gardening area to increase his food stocks.'

At that time, in 1945, the couple were living with Salingbo but were taking taro suckers for the new allotments from the plots that their families had allocated to them from childhood. At the end of a further eighteen months Gi'lahi, after consulting Nga'gili' and one or two others, decided that he had enough food to provide the series of housebuilding feasts. Accordingly he started preparations.

By 1950 Gi'lahi, now assured of his affines' goodwill, had but one garden on land belonging to the lineage of Nga'sele'. His five other cultivations, each at a different stage of growth, were located on his own lineage land (two), his father's (one), his 'grandfather' Salingbo's (one) and his mother's mother's half-brother's son Kaneng's (one).

The latest of the gardens to have been planted was on the land of Gi'lahi's lineage. Ha'du had made the decision to go there at the instigation of Nga'gili' and Gi'lahi. The two of them when seeking timber for a canoe had walked up the Buyaho valley, where the area was situated, and noted how well the crops there were growing. On returning they convinced Ha'du that this was the place to choose. He immediately informed Madulu and Busilim and suggested that they make a beginning the following morning. Madulu happened to have other commitments, and on that account a short postponement was necessary.

The clearing party that ultimately set out consisted of the five lineage members and twelve of their cognates and affines. Gi'lahi invited his classificatory father Hagatu' and two distant cousins not shown in the text figure; Ha'du his son, his cross cousin Kaneng, and one of his wife's brothers; Madulu his wife's father and his sister's husband; Nga'gili' his father's brother Salingbo and his wife's father; and Busilim a paternal uncle and a brother-in-law. After they had cut down the trees and six weeks later burned the rubbish Had'u assigned the allotments.

The division into plots followed. Each household worked inside its own boundaries, and soon the area was an intricate pattern of oblong shapes. The men then shared these out among their wives and dependants.

Ordinarily Gi'lahi, childless and as yet without mature nephews, had no need to go to such bother. The usual thing was for his wife to take over the complete allotment. But at this period he was partly responsible for his married sister Ikawi, whose husband Laho had not long before taken a temporary job in Lae to earn money for some new tools. Gi'lahi had there-fore run a line of saplings down the centre of the patch so that she and his wife could have half each. The two women were on good terms and did most of their planting together. He dug the holes, and they worked first on one side and then on the other.

Most of the other households had remained apart except for an occasional offer of casual help. Yet relatives were always prepared to come to the rescue in time of need. These same women had carried out many tasks for Gi'lahi's widowed father; and Ha'du and Nga'gili' and their respective wives had taken over the care of the gardens belonging to Madulu, who is a skilled carpenter, when he received a sudden call to repair one of the outlying Mission stations. Busilim's mother and mother-in-law had also planted his wife's taro suckers while she was laid up for some days with malaria.

In January 1950 Gi'lahi's other garden on the land of his own lineage was already four months old. Here again various outsiders had received allotments—one of his patrilateral kinsmen, his brother-in-law Laho (at the time of planting still in the village), Ha'du's cross cousin Kaneng and two of the latter's relatives, Madulu's wife's sister's husband, a man from the lineage of the wife of Nga'gili' and one from the lineage of his father, and Busilim's wife's brother and one of his remote cousins. Gi'lahi could not recall how or why the ground had been selected but said he supposed Ha'du must have decided alone or been prompted by Madulu or Nga'gili'.

One of Gi'lahi's remaining gardens, that with Kaneng's lineage, was very small, not much larger than the average rectangular plot. He explained that Kaneng had invited him to go with the clearing gang but that he was busy elsewhere and had had to refuse. Kaneng had spoken for him, nevertheless, and when the ground was cut up he received this strip.

The other men of Gi'lahi's lineage also possessed extra gardens over and above the two on their own territory. Ha'du owned three more (one with his father's lineage, one with Kaneng's, and one with that of his wife's brothers), Madulu three (one with his father's lineage, one with that of his wife's father, and one with that of his sister's husband), Nga'gili' two (one with his father's lineage and one with that of his wife's father), and Busilim two (one with his father's lineage and one with that of a distant cousin).

Thus these five householders were cultivating a total of twenty-four gardens, ten on their own land, five on the father's, and nine on that of other relatives. The ratio differs slightly from the normal (6 : 2 : 4), but this is not surprising for a particular group examined at one single point of time.

	Own Lineage	Father's Lineage	Lineages of other Cognates	Lineages of Affines	Total
Gi'lahi	2	1	2	1	6
Ha'du	2	1	1	1	5
Madulu	2	1		2	5
Nga'gili'	2	1	1		4
Busilim	2	1	1		4
Total	10	5	4	5	24

Distribution of Gardens Belonging to Men of
Gi'lahi's Lineage, January 1950

Butu will serve as a second example (Figure 8). So far he has stayed near his father. 'I never knew my proper maternal uncle Andi',' he told me. 'No; Andi' died before I was born. So when I married I built my house alongside that of my father. Why not? He and his elder brother Lahi wished to keep me here. I garden with them, too. But don't think I've given up my own land. You'll see me there tomorrow.' Surveys of his gardens in 1945, 1947, and 1948 revealed that out of a total of fifteen allotments seven were on the ground of his father's lineage, two only on that of his own lineage, and six on that of the lineages of various cognates and affines.

Butu's nearest kinsman on his mother's side, Ga'hu, is his mother's mother's sister's son and thus a classificatory maternal uncle. The two are separated by a gap of about three years only, and Ga'hu lacks the maturity that would permit him to act in an avuncular manner. But he shows no resentment and explains that Butu can use the land or not as he pleases.

On the other side there is Tangapi', Butu's father's closest uterine nephew. This man says that although he and Butu are in fact cross cousins, they are the same as 'older and younger brothers' and will go on working

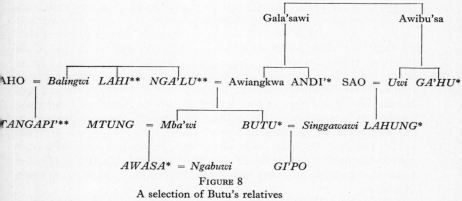

FIGURE 8
A selection of Butu's relatives

Member's of Butu's lineage are indicated by an asterisk, of his father's lineage by double asterisks.

together. 'We are *da-tigeng*,' he pointed out. 'My mother and his father were born of the same woman. Me stop him making gardens? Never!' He also added that Butu was even free to bring guests. Butu has so far ignored this concession, rightly according to other people. If he acted upon it the members of the lineage might reprimand him, or at least criticize behind his back.

On present indications Butu's uterine nephew Awasa will link up rather with Ga'hu and the man Lahung, classed respectively as a 'grandfather' and a 'mother's brother'. Awasa married in 1947 and three years later was still living alongside his father. But examination of his gardens in January 1948 and in January 1950 disclosed that, out of a total of nine, four were with his own lineage, two with his father's lineage, two with the lineages of affines, and but one with Butu and Butu's father's lineage. In 1950 he also said that he had begun thinking about a site for his next dwelling somewhere near Ga'hu's house.

A third case concerned three brothers, the two eldest of whom joined their matrilineal kin in the usual way while the youngest, Gulup, remained with his parents (Figure 9). The father, Bika, freely admitted keeping the last-born back. Two uterine nephews were enough for anyone, he said, and the third boy must stop behind. A further consideration was the fact that Bika's only sister had died without producing a male child, and he

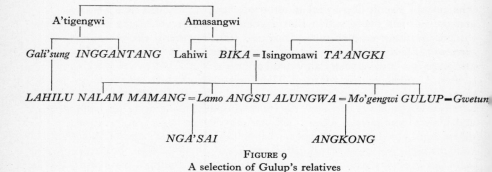

FIGURE 9
A selection of Gulup's relatives

therefore could not hope to have a true nephew 'to make him complete'. There were several young men in the right category, but each one was in the care of a mother's linked brother or cousin.

The brothers' maternal uncle, Ta'angki, sympathized with Bika and agreed that, at least for the time being, Gulup should stay. But usually he added that later on the young man might want to move, particularly after Bika died.

The brothers themselves displayed the usual fraternal feelings. Gulup sometimes insisted that the other two should garden with him and their father, and they in turn occasionally pressed him to garden with them. Of a total of ten gardens, five in 1945 and five in 1950, half were with his father's lineage, two with his own, and three with those of other relatives. On the same dates the two brothers had twelve gardens each, five of them with their own lineage and two with their father's.

It was too early to reach any conclusion about the fate of the brothers' uterine nephews. Gulup, however, was paying great attention to the young son of his linked sister Mo'gengwi, and there is thus some possibility that the lad may become to some extent tied up with his mother's father's lineage.

HOUSEBUILDING

To build a new house well over 200 man-days are required. The supplies have to be obtained from the forest, the constructional work carried out, the helpers fed daily, and three feasts arranged for their entertainment. Men and boys gather the poles, wall timbers, and palmwood flooring; women collect the sago leaflets for the roof; men transport these materials to the village; men and boys act as carpenters and thatchers; women cook the ordinary meals, sometimes with the assistance of a couple of men; and members of both sexes collaborate for the feasts.

For my example I shall take Mamang's dwelling erected in 1948, when he was nearing forty years of age. He was a typical householder with a young family, respected by the people but not yet accepted as a leader. The job took twenty-one working days spread over a period of nine weeks, and the finished house was similar to many others, larger than those of the younger married men but smaller and less pretentious than those of some of the club heads. The interior measured 29 feet by 12 feet 6 inches, and there was a wide verandah down one side.

First I must identify those of Mamang's relatives who appeared to regard the undertaking as their close personal concern. Briefly, they consisted of his *da-tigeng* cognates, the other kinsmen belonging to his club, and his brothers-in-law. These men discussed every step of the work in detail and helped on almost every occasion. Further, each one of them brought along a couple of Mamang's *hu-tigeng* cognates, who, however, were never present continuously. A distant relative lending a hand with the posts, for instance, felt that he was not obliged to be there when the rafters were being fixed.

As technical superintendent Mamang chose Boya, a fairly close classificatory mother's brother. Had the bond between them been remote cash would have had to have been presented as payment, but in the circumstances a large share of the food from each of the feasts sufficed. Boya distributed this among his kinsfolk: money he would almost certainly have kept for himself.

Mamang had begun his preparations months before by cultivating extra gardens. Each time the lineage met to clear new land he had said he needed a big allotment to ensure ample food for the housebuilding workers. His various relatives heard the news and followed suit by planting a strip too. These people also collected their spare nails for him. The quantity proved to be insufficient, and, on Boya's advice, he bought several pounds in Lae.

Then one evening when a group of us were sitting under the trees Mamang said he was thinking of making a start the following week. What about the old posts, someone asked; were they too worn for further use? Yes, he replied, they had been damaged in the wartime bombing and were only fit for firewood. Did he propose to move to another part of the village, another man enquired. 'No, no, I am staying where I am,' came the answer. 'I have you here, my maternal uncles and brothers, in the club with me. Why should I want to change? We'll build right beside the spot on which my old house stands.'

The date for cutting the new posts had first to be fixed, and after dinner most of the club members and one or two of the other relatives assembled. They were mainly concerned to choose a time that was convenient for them all. 'Not Friday,' said one man. 'I've agreed to help Ibaya with his thatch then.' 'And not Monday,' another interposed. 'I'll be clearing land with my brother-in-law.' The club headman listened and finally settled for the following Tuesday.

Later that night Mamang visited his deceased father's club. He had kept in close touch with the father's heirs, his own cross cousins Awasa and Laugwi', and frequently went gardening with them. Now he wanted to let them know what had been decided. The 'bitter-touch' relationship prevented him from actually asking them for aid, and for over an hour he spoke of other topics. Then suddenly he remarked, 'I shan't be able to go fencing with you on Tuesday. Let's leave it for the present. My maternal uncles insist that I make a start on my house. They scold me daily for continuing to risk a beam falling on the children and killing them. I don't think things are as bad as that myself, but you know how it is when people go on nagging. So we're all setting off on Tuesday to cut posts.' Awasa and Laugwi' made no comment, and fifteen minutes later Mamang and I left.

On our way back I wanted to know had anyone mentioned fencing the garden so soon. 'I don't believe so—no, I'm sure not,' Mamang replied. 'Awasa's and my cultivations in the Moapang valley are still safe. The pigs haven't come near them yet.' Why, then, had he referred to the work? 'Awasa and Laugwi' are my cross cousins,' he responded. 'That means we have to be careful what we say to one another. They're willing to come with me, and I'm willing to go with them; but we can't make requests outright, can't even drop a plain hint. Yet I have to let them know—how else can they be there? I do it by speaking round about, beginning with fencing, or fishing, or something of the kind and ending with just a little about my plans.'

During the next couple of days Mamang's other close kinsmen adopted similar indirections for spreading the news, and when Tuesday came eleven persons, all with axes, collected outside the old dwelling. The job was likely to be strenuous, and none of them was over fifty years of age. Mamang's club was well represented, and I also counted the two cross cousins, two sons of his father's brothers, and a brother-in-law. The party went along the coast to the mouth of the Buasi' River and then up towards the foothills, where the lineage bush lands are situated. Mamang indicated the trees that he had been marking during the past few weeks, and the men started work with a will. They finished at about four o'clock and made their way homewards in a body, pausing only for a bathe on the way. Mamang's wife was ready with a meal and now carried over several platters of steamed taro garnished with spinach to the club. She, her young daughters, and the women from nearby (the wives of the club members) had cooked most of the food, but her own sisters, Mamang's sisters, and the wives of his cousins had also brought contributions.

Mamang did not stir from the club that evening, and various people called in to hear how things had progressed and whether the timber was now ready to be brought down. He told them 'yes' and that it was proposed to do the job on the following Friday. The logs must be dragged overland to the Buasi' first and subsequently floated downstream and along the beach. A postponement until the following week was impossible as the tide would by then be too low in the afternoon. The gathering eventually agreed to leave at dawn before morning prayers.

On the Friday twenty-three men were on their way by sunrise. Mamang went with them, but this time two members of the club group stayed behind to gather betel-nut ingredients and to help the women. After collecting the areca nuts and pepper they gave up the rest of the morning to chopping firewood, a job normally left to females. Then in the afternoon they grated coconuts and squeezed out the cream for the sauce that was to be poured over the taro.

The hauling party reached the village shortly after four o'clock and spent the next couple of hours eating, chewing betel-nut, and chatting. Mamang was satisfied although some of his fairly close relatives were missing. 'I've counted and know who's here and who isn't,' he told me. 'But it doesn't matter. We had enough, and extra people would have been in the way. You'll see some of these men dropping out now and others taking their place. Look, there's Sali, but his brother Nga'sele' didn't come. I daresay they've decided between themselves on which days each should attend.' Sali later confirmed that this was so. He and Nga'sele' were morally bound to assist and had worked out a rough timetable in order to prevent overlapping. On this occasion Nga'sele' had been fishing: for the next task he took over while Sali fished.

Mamang called on Boya formally within a day or two and said that the job could start at any time. Shortly afterwards Boya measured up the poles with his rule and marked them for sawing. Mamang borrowed tools from the head of the club, and he and his first cousins and club 'brothers' cut the uprights, stumps, ridge, purlins, and braces.

After a delay of a week word again went around to the various kinsmen that Boya had fixed a day for putting up the frame. Ten men assembled to carry out his orders, and everything was in place within seven hours.

In the meantime preparations were going on for the first feast, which took place towards the end of the afternoon. Mamang felt that he lacked the experience to take charge and asked one of the seniors from the club to act for him. Six men put themselves at his disposal together with nearly a score of women, some of them Mamang's cognates, some his affines. Each member of this party brought a contribution of food and then left to fetch taro, greens, coconuts, areca-nuts, and betel pepper from Mamang's cultivations. On returning they made a joint effort of the cooking on two long fires near the club house. Ordinarily Mamang would have supplied a pig, or possibly two, but the war was not long over, and as yet the herds had not been replaced. He produced instead twenty-four pound tins of meat, fourteen contributed by his *da-tigeng* relatives and fellow clubmen and three by affines.

The men who had helped previously but on this occasion were taking no part began to arrive soon after four o'clock. By then the food was cooked, and the workers had tipped it into a series of bowls, many of them borrowed, which they arranged on mats in a long line. The master of ceremonies first gave one-third to Boya, who directed a few supporters to take it to his club. Various youths then carried the remainder to the waiting crowds, who were sitting in groups nearby on the verandahs and under the trees. They began eating at once and finished the last crumb. All the guests received the same amount irrespective of their efforts or the length of time spent on the job, and those who had toiled from the beginning sat side by side with those who had been present only once.

The work continued in similar fashion. Eight men felled a number of saplings, and the next day six of them, together with seven others, floated the wood to the village. A different set then cut them into lengths for the bearers, joists, rafters, and battens and added them to the frame. The thatch followed. Three men and twelve women collected sago leaflets, and fourteen of the seniors fastened them into sheets. Mamang and a few helpers spread these in the sun for a day or two to dry, and eleven youths afterwards lashed them in place along the rafters. At this point he held a second feast and gave away the same amount of food as on the earlier occasion.

The flooring came next. Palmwood will not float, and twenty-five men had to carry it across the swamps and through the forest. This was the worst of the tasks, and the party did not return till long after nightfall. The wall boards could now be secured, and at last the house was finished. In all about ninety different adults had been engaged, fifty men and forty women, as well as numbers of youths and girls.

A month later the final feast took place. In pre-war days the guests would have expected a joint of pork each, but at this time tinned meat again sufficed. The helpers were spread among five different clubs, and as this was to be the chief celebration each group elected to cook its contribution separately. The members of Mamang's unit worked the hardest and provided the most, nearly half the total quantity, though about half of this came from him personally. Next on the list was the club to which his father's sister's sons belonged. This made a quite considerable offering. The shares of the other three were approximately equal.

Once more Mamang's club senior took control of the proceedings. He had the supplies collected and the pots on the fire by two o'clock, and about two hours later the food was ready for serving. He told the women and some of the youths to turn it into bowls and asked other people to spread out mats and coconut leaves on an open place close at hand. The youths laid the vessels in rows along the top, and the men from the other four clubs arranged their offerings in separate rows below.

Several minutes elapsed while the assembly admired the dishes, and the man in charge then began the distribution. He marked off some of the bowls for Boya and a set each for the contributing club houses, calling out the names of the heads as he did so. Parties of youths now came up and bore the vessels to one side. The guests ate the remaining food as a communal meal. They sat in groups, men in some and women and small children in others. Different workers took bowls across to each, and everyone began. Mamang and his deputy, as hosts, went from circle to circle chatting and looking to see that nobody had been overlooked. Later they offered the men betel-nut and cigarettes.

Boya and the club groups carried their private shares away at dusk, and the seniors subsequently divided the portions among the individual householders. Some of these latter presented an odd platter or two to relatives who had taken no part, men unconnected with Mamang. If pork had been available every part of the village would have received a piece.

CANOES

Each household aims at owning a small canoe for two or three persons. On some occasions the man goes out in it himself, and at other times he sends his sons or nephews. The catch is his, and he keeps enough fish for himself before making presents to brothers and cousins. Less fortunate neighbours occasionally borrow the craft and as acknowledgment of the favour hand over a portion of their haul.

Canoes, like houses, last only for a few years, and new ones are fashioned continually. The usual feasts have to be held, this time when the log has been brought to the workshop, and, as ordinarily pork must be included, a young married man is forced to wait for a craft till his herds have multiplied. Usually he achieves his ambition within seven or eight years, and in January 1950 I counted thirty such vessels, a figure possibly lower than the normal on account of the delayed recovery from the effects of war.

Trees suitable for the dugout hull grow deep in the bush. When felled they are heavy and awkward to handle, and the task of dragging them to the village demands thirty or forty workers. Two or three miles of rough track may have to be cleared and many sets of rollers cut for use over the hills and rough patches of rock. Even then the space is often so confined that only a dozen men are able to pull on the ropes at any one time. Further assistance is needed for the outrigger float, booms, and lashings. Suitable timber is fairly plentiful, but the search for tough durable creepers may take a couple of days.

The work opens with the usual preliminary talks in the club house. The householder or his headman, after listening to the discussion, names the day for the start and then takes measures to see that the news drifts through to the other kinsfolk. The crowd duly assembles, fells the tree, and brings the log down. As before, a few of the relatives remain behind and toil with the women preparing the feast, which follows later in the afternoon. The householder sets aside special portions for the shipwright whom he has requested to superintend the construction. This man also receives a share of the catch for as long as the vessel remains serviceable.

The first crude hollowing out of the log demands little skill, and the owner, his fellow clubmen, and his other close relatives spend a short time at it each day. But the final chipping is done by the specialist. The sides must not be too thick or the craft will settle deep in the water, and if they are too thin there is a risk of the hull being stove in on the reefs. The ship-wright alone knows exactly when to stop; and it is he, too, who shapes the ends. On completing these tasks he proceeds to sharpen the outrigger float, drive the pegs into it, and attach it by means of the booms to the dugout. Long practice and experience have taught him the proportions necessary to ensure that the craft will steer well and not veer to one side.

In addition to these small canoes, there are also a few larger sea-going vessels used for tuna fishing in the open waters of the central Huon Gulf, for visiting, and for trading voyages. When the log for such a craft, fifty to sixty feet long, is to be brought in from the forest a huge team assembles. Two feasts must then be organized to reward them and the other workers, one when the log is safely in the village and the second just before the finished craft is launched. Men of substance alone can sustain the drain on their resources, and as a consequence canoes of this type are mainly owned by club heads and other leaders. In 1950 the sole exception was Nga'gili', who owed his good fortune to the fact that his father-in-law Gilingu' is a skilled shipwright and expected no reward for his labours. Sixty-five men and boys had worked on it, and when completed it required a crew of four and could carry several passengers and many hundredweights of cargo.

The owner of a large canoe has the responsibility of caring for it, arrang-ing for any repairs, and directing how and by whom it shall be used. The members of the club group and the rest of the kinsfolk who helped with the construction can all claim the right to take it to sea but must seek permission first. A householder who wishes to make an expedition to replenish his stock of cooking pots, for instance, enquires when the vessel will be available and then gathers his crew. Similar proceedings take place during the tuna season except that the full catch always goes to the owner for distribution. He gives the crew the best fish in recognition of their efforts and apportions the rest among the clubmen.

SEINE FISHING

Ordinarily there are three or four seines in the village. The net itself, apart from the stout rope to which it is fastened, is some sixty fathoms long by a fathom deep. Floats of balsa wood or cork line the top, weights of clamshell or lead the bottom. A large body of men and youths is necessary to operate such an appliance, some to cast the net around the shoal of fish and others to haul on the ropes. They form a semi-permanent voluntary association based on this one specific activity.

In earlier times certain individuals had the special knowledge, inherited from their forbears, of the magical ceremonies that accompanied the weaving of a new net. Each magician was associated with a private following of fishermen eager to do his bidding and so to win a share of the spoils. He called them together to help make the net, which was then regarded as his property, an honour carrying the usual responsibilities.

As with so many skills, net making has been forgotten, and the seines must now be obtained from outside. The cost is always high, well over £100. Nobody has as much money as this, and collaboration is essential. A leading elder initiates the scheme. He announces his intention and starts the fund off with a substantial contribution, perhaps £12. Any of his relatives who wishes to join in does so with as much cash as he can spare, and as soon as the amount is fully subscribed the elder makes the purchase. He becomes the owner and thereby fulfils the same functions as his magician predecessor. He or a deputy decides when the net is to be taken out, where it is to go, and which men are to carry out the different jobs. He also divides the haul and subsequently makes certain that the gear is properly dried, mended if torn, and stowed away.

The only conditions of membership of a seine-net group are payment of an initial contribution and a willingness to go on forming part of the working team. The members are all related to one another but by a wide variety of bonds.

10

Fulfilling Obligations

BUSAMA are so drilled during childhood in the moral obligations under-
lying kinship ties that when grown up they help one another almost as a
matter of routine. Yet they are also fully conscious of their mutual dependence and of the risks they would run by defaulting. Ha'du and Nga'gili',
on undertaking the management of Madulu's cultivations after his sudden
call from the Mission (see above, p. 143), explained that they were not only
thinking of him but also of themselves. This aid ensured that at some
future time he would attend to their concerns. 'Today I wanted to go
fishing with Gilingu', but by staying here I am making certain that
tomorrow, or the next day, or the day after that, Madulu will do my
planting,' Nga'gili concluded. Equally down-to-earth was Busilim's statement about why he was giving a hand in the repair of Gi'lahi's thatch.
'It's enough that we two are older and younger brother. But if I didn't
come now, how do you think I'd get along later? Gi'lahi would pay me
back by stopping away from my work.'

Several men grumbled at different times about receiving inadequate
help, but a little probing soon disclosed that they were at the moment
tired, out of sorts, or disappointed by having to shelve some cherished
project. If taxed subsequently with unreasonableness the majority were
shame-facedly prepared to agree. As an instance I quote Titi's remarks
when declining to accompany me on a trip to the pot-making villages in
the south. 'I'd like to go but have to say "no". Nga'lu is building a new
house, and as he and I are *da-tigeng* I've got to be there. You know, this
sort of thing is always happening to me. Nga'lu and I are *da-tigeng*, so I
work on his house; Gwaleyam and I are *da-tigeng*, so I work on his;
Gwe'tam and I are *da-tigeng*, so I work on his. Yet not one of them was
here to help me. Nga'lu said he was ill, Gwaleyam said he had business for
the Government in Lae, and Gwe'tam—I forget now what it was with him,
but he wasn't present. They're good-for-nothing loafers, that's what they
are, fattening in idleness while I sweat.' If he felt so strongly why did he not
tell them so to their face, I asked. 'I couldn't do that,' he replied. 'They'd
be very angry and perhaps never help me any more. I'd be too ashamed.'

A few weeks afterwards I was able to remind Titi of his words. A party
of his kinsmen were dragging a great log from the forest to make him a
canoe, and although he had taken no part in bringing in Gwe'tam's log,

there was Gwe'tam now well to the fore. 'I was mourning for my sister. Nobody expected me. They knew I couldn't come,' Titi snapped, thoroughly indignant. But in a few minutes he looked up and admitted, with a cheerful grin, that the earlier charges had been unwarranted. 'I must have been in a bad temper at not being able to go with you. And it's just as well you didn't tell anyone what I said. There'd have been a great fuss if Nga'lu, Gwaleyam, and Gwe'tam had come to hear.'

In earlier days sorcery was another factor to be reckoned with. The fear of black magic spurred people to overcome temptation and meet the legitimate claims of their kin; and, in addition, it served as an innocuous outlet for feelings of irritation. By this means the man harbouring a grievance obtained satisfaction without jeopardizing his position, hurting his enemy, or upsetting the life of the village.

The rites were of two types—one, known as *bula*, believed to be lethal, and the other, *mwi'sinang*, supposed to result in illness only. *Bula* was performed by a handful of specialists, but everyone of standing possessed a pair of *mwi'sinang* spells, the first to cause some specific ailment (perhaps malaria, tropical ulcers, toothache, or diarrhoea) and the second to cure it. He guarded the details to hand on to his nephews as part of their inheritance but made no secret of the fact of his knowledge. Thus the villagers knew which of their fellows could induce and treat each of the various common diseases.

When, rightly or wrongly, a man considered that his neighbours had affronted him he retired to some secluded spot and there invoked magic against them. He took care to conceal himself well lest they should become suspicious and take action against him either directly or by means of counter sorcery. Once the rite was completed he was convinced that they would soon begin to suffer, a supposition that subsequent events seemed to confirm. New Guinea is not a healthy country, and there is much sickness. In the normal course therefore the sorcerer's 'victims' did in fact fall ill. At times no doubt his spells for, say, malaria apparently resulted instead in an attack of tropical ulcers or toothache, but for this he could always find a simple explanation. He assumed that he had recited the words of the spell incorrectly, or that his magic was working itself out in a new way, or that another sorcerer had forestalled him.

The procedure when someone became ill was for the relatives to request a magician known to have inherited an appropriate curative spell to undertake the treatment. Any of those available served the purpose, and no attempt was made to identify the sorcerer. Where, indeed, could a search have begun? The rite, if carried out at all, had been performed in the depths of the forest or under cover of darkness.

Here again later happenings seemed to support popular belief. More often than not the patient built up a natural resistance to the passing infection and recovered. If he did not, then, as with the sorcerer, he fell back on another interpretation—that the spirits were punishing him for omitting a sacrifice perhaps, or that he was suffering the effects of ritual contamination.

If in spite of every remedy the illness proved fatal the survivors concluded that the other type of sorcery, *bula*, must have been responsible. They were obliged to avenge the death and as an initial step consulted a specialist who possessed the magical skill to persuade the ghost to reveal the name of the killer. It was taken for granted that no normal person would want to murder a regular helper from the village, and mostly the culprit who was selected lived at a distance in some hostile community. Whether the avengers speared him or were content with bewitching him with *bula* spells largely depended on the social status of the dead man.

It is impossible to decide if discord among kinsfolk has increased since the people renounced sorcery, but my feeling is that the situation is relatively unchanged. The natives continue to regard disease as a supernatural manifestation but now look upon it as God's judgment on sin. They resort to prayer as a substitute for magic, black as well as white, and when aggrieved beg the Almighty to visit His divine wrath on the wrongdoer; and if sick, instead of approaching a magician, they call in the pastor, confess their faults, and ask for forgiveness.

DISSENSIONS AMONG CLOSE KIN

Rare as quarrels are, they occur more commonly between true brothers than any other type of relatives. Brothers become irritated by the strength of the link uniting them and strive to break free. Yet they cannot do so and after a few days have to admit defeat.

Within my personal experience the most serious fracas was that between Gepo and his younger brother Gangga'. Afterwards I discussed the incident with their brother-in-law Ida', Nga'gili', and Gi'lahi. Ida' made the following comment: 'If Gepo wants aid who does he go to first?—to Gangga', who can't possibly refuse him. And if Gangga' wants aid he goes to Gepo. Well, constant calls of that kind are irksome and disagreeable— you feel that you'll never escape from them. So now and again, perhaps because they've been provoked by something else, their anger boils up inside them, and they say terrible things to each other, words they wouldn't dare utter to other people. Then suddenly they remember that they're *da-tigeng*, born of the same woman, and shame shuts them up. They realize they've done wrong. Besides, if they separated where else could they turn? So next day, or the day after, they're asking for aid as usual.'

Nga'gili' pressed the argument home with an analogy. 'Look at that fat child playing over there. Older and younger brothers are like his two legs. The limbs are useless separated—they can't walk by themselves—but I'll be bound that he's chafed in the crutch by using them together.'

'Yes, or think of two people with long hair sleeping on the same mat. The strands become entangled, and neither can move without pulling at the other,' Gi'lahi added.

The disagreements, even if brief, are likely to be bitter, and bystanders sometimes feel obliged to interfere lest the parties should injure one another. Certainly Ida' was correct also in saying that brothers use language that in other circumstances would be unthinkable. Yet the seniors never have to deal with the matter at a higher level. The two men go their separate ways muttering threats and imprecations only to meet again without any apparent ill feeling.

The Gepo-and-Gangga' squabble had started over some coconuts. Gepo, returning thirsty from the gardens, had gone searching for a green nut to drink. He then discovered that Gangga' had gathered them all, and in a rage he felled the palm tree. Still holding the axe, he strode across to where Gangga' was quietly sitting and spat in his face. 'Greedy dog,' he shouted, 'Why did you take the nuts? Why didn't you ask my permission? I'm the elder, and the palms belong to me.'

'I'm no dog,' Gangga' replied. 'Who ever heard of seeking permission to take his own nuts? You yourself are at fault. That tree belonged to the pair of us, and now you've destroyed it. You've always been the same, taking my things since we were boys together. What about my pig when you built your house long ago? I'm the one who gives and gives and gives —you just hold fast, hold fast to everything. Mean, hungry, and shameless, that's what you are.'

'Shut up, you bandicoot,' Gepo screamed. 'I'll split you open with this axe. You hate me because I'm the elder.'

'Big words, big words as usual,' came the answer. 'Easy to talk when you have plenty of breath. Why not? You sit there idle all day while I tire myself out working for you. We'll see who'll do the splitting open. I own an axe too. Perhaps I won't have an elder brother soon.'

The two of them began dancing round with weapons poised ready to strike, but at that point the men near at hand rushed in, threw them to the ground with a flying tackle, and took their axes away. Gepo walked off and kept out of the way till the next morning, when he called for Gangga' to come and repair the thatch of a house belonging to an uncle. An hour later I saw them laughing together over some joke. 'Yesterday's trouble forgotten?' I enquired. 'That! Why, we weren't serious,' said Gepo. 'You didn't write down what we said in your notebook, I hope. We're just older and younger brother, that's all.'

A month or two after this a fight took place between the brothers Bu'da' and Muengpop. They had had a slight tiff earlier in the day over a damaged canoe, for which each blamed the other, and were still on edge when the second event took place. Their neighbour Bangaya started them off by throwing a coconut at one of the children of Bu'da'. The boy deserved a beating, for he had been crying loudly for over an hour, but he retaliated by hurling rubbish into Bangaya's house. The latter, now really angry, came out and gave the child a hard slap. Then Bu'da' descended also and began abusing Bangaya, calling him an ill-tempered fool. At that point

Muengpop interrupted and told his brother not to be so silly. The child was a nuisance, and Bangaya, a close relative, had every right to correct him. 'As for you, Bu'da',' he added, 'you've no sense at all—taking the boy's part! That's just the sort of stupid nonsense you engage in all the time.'

'You keep your nose out of this,' said Bu'da'. 'He's my son, and if he wants to cry, he may.'

' "Old idiot Bu'da'," ' Muengpop sneered, turning away. 'It's no wonder that's what people call you "If he wants to cry, he may"! Elder brother, indeed! You're crazy.'

'So I'm crazy, am I?' Bu'da' stormed. 'Let me tell you, the only crazy thing I've ever done was supporting you in your adulteries—defending you when I knew what people were saying was true. You disgusting reprobate, dragging our good name down.'

'You strike me on one cheek,' Muengpop countered. 'Well, I obey Jesus and turn the other.' He then advanced, exposing the left side of his face. The offer was too much for Bu'da', who knocked him down. As usual, several men interposed and led them away in different directions.

Muengpop had been an adulterer, but his offence had taken place long before, and the villagers seldom mentioned it. The reference was humiliating to him, nevertheless, and for a couple of days he kept out of sight. But on the third or fourth morning he set off together with Bu'da' for the gardens.

Quarrels may also break out between a man and his parallel first cousins on either side. It is said that such disturbances are even less frequent than those between brothers, but my figures are too low to have any statistical significance, and I cannot confirm or deny the statement. It is definitely true, however, that, although cousins usually manage to avoid the extremes of violence, their breaches take longer to heal. The bonds between the sons of brothers and between the sons of sisters, being a little looser than those between the sons of a married couple, do not exert the same urgent pull, and a week or ten days may pass before relations return to normal. Outside intervention is seldom necessary, but there are times when a senior kinsman has to give the pair a lecture and insist on their partaking of a common meal.

During the parallel cousins' early manhood most disputes are the result of failure to seek permission before borrowing a tool or appliance, damaging or losing it, keeping it too long, or being absent from some communal task without reasonable excuse. But they can also come to blows on slighter pretexts. Once Nga'gili' attacked a patrilateral parallel cousin, a man named Apilum, after the latter had unintentionally insulted him. The District Commissioner in Lae had not long before invited the people to assemble for a great dance during the forthcoming Christmas festivities. The elders were doubtful whether they should accept, for the Mission disapproves of such entertainments, but Nga'gili' felt that at least a small party ought to go. When visiting some relatives in another club house he therefore began testing the hand-drums to see if a new tympanum was required. Apilum, at that period a staunch supporter of the Mission viewpoint (though less from moral conviction than purely personal motives), heard the noise when walking by. He poked his head inside but in the gloom failed to recognize who was there. He called out in pidgin-English, 'Keep quiet, you bastard; we want some sleep.' Then, seeing Nga'gili', he immediately apologized, saying that he had assumed some young lad was responsible. Nga'gili' brushed the explanation aside and sprang upon him. They struggled together till Salingbo reached the scene and threatened to punch them both soundly. At this they separated and withdrew. A week or so later Salingbo called upon them to share his dinner. Nga'gili' had no valid reason for being so touchy. Perhaps he was uneasy about the dance and hence over-anxious to justify himself.

As parallel cousins grow older marriage arrangements can be a further source of conflict. I have dealt with this subject in an earlier chapter, and there is no need to go into it again.

Cross first cousins have almost as many interests in common as parallel first cousins and, as we already know, a greater number of things to quarrel about. The various rights and privileges to land are the source of the extra difficulties. The taboos associated with the relationship are a constant reminder of the need for caution, a sort of warning bell, and as a result troubles are practically unknown.

This same 'bitter touch' also has the effect of preventing wrangling between affines.

Female relatives seem to bicker only in defence of their menfolk and children. As we have seen, their tasks seldom bring them together as working units, and their interests are largely focused on their own homes or the affairs that occupy their husbands, to whom they are in a sense an economic appendage. A tactful wife can exert great influence behind the scenes, but she does not take the lead in any of the village concerns and consequently never meets the members of her own sex as a competitor. It is of interest to note, nevertheless, that the wives of two brothers who have had a misunderstanding may keep apart long after the men have composed their difference.

DISTANT KIN

Remote cousins, because they are not obliged to combine every day, lack the immediate compulsion to overlook offences, and trouble between them can have more disturbing effects. Each one, too, may be supported by his brothers and first cousins, and possibly also by his brothers-in-law, often without much thought of the rights and wrongs of the matter or of what is at stake. Nga'gili' plunged straight in, for example, when he found his brother Madulu and their third cousin Tibalum quarrelling. Subsequently he admitted that at first he had gone to see who was making the noise and had then attacked Tibalum while still having no notion of why Madulu was angry. Ha'du ran over also, and Tibalum might have been badly hurt but for the efforts of a couple of seniors. As it happened, his annoyance was justified—Madulu, in felling a tree, had broken one of his areca palms. Again, Lukas and Galop threatened a man who, not unreasonably, was abusing their brother for having through carelessness damaged one of the outrigger booms of his canoe. A third case presented unusual features, though clearly similar motives inspired the behaviour of those implicated. The youth Butu had seduced a young girl but on discovering that his father Boya planned to find him another bride immediately abandoned her. Much distressed, the girl's parents and uncles publicly chided both Butu and Boya, who departed in shame on a protracted visit to Lae. At the time the villagers were building a new school under Boya's supervision. Now, therefore, they had to find a new specialist. From the day of this man's appointment all Boya's *da-tigeng* kinsfolk refrained from taking any part in the work.

In earlier times a man injured by a distant relative endeavoured to secure redress by personal retaliation. He assembled such of his *da-tigeng* cognates and closer affines as were his contemporaries and marched to the wrongdoer's house to punish him and, if possible, secure compensation. In the meantime the offender's *da-tigeng* cognates and closer affines gathered to protect him. If a clash occurred, and it seemed likely that someone might be badly hurt, a village headman despatched a couple of seniors to stop the fight. He then ordered the contestants to submit the case to judgment by the body of older men. That evening, or on the evening of the following day, he called the meeting together and either himself sat as chairman or requested a fellow headman to do so. Ideally the person taking charge was not a near relative of either of the parties. It was felt that by this means partiality could be avoided and an unbiased decision assured. Stories are told of leaders who, contrary to custom, supported their closer kinsmen in the face of the evidence, but such tales always conclude with the people revolting and choosing another headman.

Elders whose loyalties were divided could stay away from the gathering if they wished, but often they were responsible for the affair being satisfactorily concluded. They wanted the matter settled and accordingly suggested a compromise solution.

The plaintiff led off with his account of what had happened and was then followed by the defendant. Each now called his witnesses, including kinsmen who vouched for his good character. The elders asked questions and later discussed whether the charges had been sustained. If they thought that this was not so the chairman dismissed the case. But if they were satisfied that the plaintiff was in the right they moved on to consider the appropriate penalty, generally payment of dogs' teeth, pigs, and other valuables. The chairman allowed them to go on speaking till they had reached unanimity, when he announced the verdict. Both parties submitted, partly out of deference to the public opinion, of which he was the spokesman, partly because they realized that they could not afford to go on being enemies.

Similar meetings were held to deal with civil disputes. Villagers who disagreed about such matters as the precise location of a land boundary or the settlement of debts arising out of marriage payments asked a headman to arrange for a deliberation at which the conflict could be resolved.

Informal courts of this kind still take place in modified form. The chief difference is that, as the office of headman no longer exists, a special chairman must be chosen for each occasion. Any experienced senior is regarded as satisfactory, and the plaintiff picks out a neighbour with whom he is on good terms, perhaps a Government representative, a Mission leader, or somebody else noted for sound common sense. Obviously he has to rule out his close relatives, and often the man he first approaches declines to act.

My account of the earlier tribunals is necessarily based on hearsay, but, as recorded elsewhere, I have often attended the present-day assemblies.[1] The chairman calls the people together by blowing a series of blasts on a conch-shell trumpet late in the afternoon, and they begin to arrive in front of his club house as soon as they have finished their meal. The men seat themselves on one side and kindle small fires from which to light their cigarettes, and the women go across to the other side with the children. He then rises to his feet, relates what he knows of the case, and summons the plaintiff to give further details. The defendant also tells his story, and the witnesses, including most of the close relatives, make their contributions. No elaborate system of etiquette is observed, and those who want to interrupt do so as often as they please. The chairman calls for order only if a speaker is hysterical or so diffuse that the issue has become obscured.

Once the facts have been sifted the seniors rise and give their views. They may take some time to make up their minds, but eventually it becomes plain either that they are agreed on the guilt or innocence of the accused or that their opinions are irreconcilable. In the latter event the chairman adjourns the meeting for two or three weeks. He hopes that by that time the strong feelings engendered will have simmered down so that the incident can be seen in proper perspective.

If the elders decide that the man charged is blameless the chairman tells the accuser that he must have been mistaken and had better apologize. When, on the other hand, they find the guilt proven, they go on to advise about the penalty. Usually they are content with scolding the wrongdoer, though if the offence is really serious they may urge the injured party to take him to a European magistrate for trial.

OBLIGATIONS AND REPUTATION

The few men who give their kinsmen more help than custom demands win the reward of public approbation. Alingam is today the prime example.

[1] See Hogbin, 1951, pp. 166–80.

He seems to be less interested in praise as such than in physical exertion for its own sake and is almost always on hand for jobs even when his relationship with those directly concerned is remote. People used to say laughingly that he was incapable of sitting still, but his own explanation was that he preferred company to being by himself. The villagers welcomed him with pleasure everywhere, spoke of him affectionately, and, most significant, minimized his faults—a hasty temper and a tendency to talk too much.

The opposite types, those who consistently fail to live up to their obligations, whether through ill-nature or laziness, are referred to with contempt as 'the rubbish that destroys the good name of the village'. Ahi, already mentioned (pp. 85, 86), is acknowledged to be among the worst. He appears to be strong and healthy but is temperamentally incapable of maintaining a family. His wife in consequence is often forced to ask his relatives for taro or to help herself from their gardens. They submit to her demands unless already exasperated from some other cause, when they may become abusive. 'Ahi has never learned what shame is,' his brother Hagatu' sighed. 'The rest of us would hang our heads—perhaps commit suicide—if anyone upbraided us as I sometimes scold him. But he only laughs. What am I to do? I can't see his children starve.' Other natives compare Ahi with the village idiot. Why waste words chiding him, they ask, when nothing makes an impression on him? 'Ahi speaks like other people, but there's something wrong with his inside, and he's really insane,' Gi'lahi once told me. He then added that men like this can count on the support of a brother but that once the latter dies they are destitute. 'An elder brother will look after a younger brother born of the same mother throughout their lifetime; but other "elder brothers", born of different mothers, in the end become impatient, and the man must then steal to keep himself alive.'

Till now Ahi and his wife when taking food have confined themselves to the cultivations of their close kin and thus escaped the epithet of thief. Once they begin to look beyond these gardens they will be treated as criminals. In earlier days somebody would have killed them, but in present circumstances they will be brought before a magistrate and given a gaol sentence.

Equally unpopular is a man named Yakob, though he perhaps has a better reason for neglecting his kinsmen. He runs his own trade store and has not time to busy himself with their undertakings.

Yakob went away as a labourer like everyone else at the age of about seventeen but had the good luck to choose an employer who trained him as a skilled carpenter. He earned high wages and was able to save, relatively, a considerable sum of money. Then on his return home in 1947 he received cash due to him as compensation for war damage done to his property. A couple of orphaned nephews and nieces might have expected his help, but they were already absorbed into the households of other uncles and aunts. Thus his wife and children alone were directly dependent upon him. He determined to invest his money in a shop, the first establishment of the kind in any of the local villages. He obtained building material from an old Army camp and almost unaided put up a house with an extra room in front for his customers. The next move was to buy the stock. Lack of capital forced him to limit himself to the cheaper goods for which there would be a ready sale, but as he is on the spot he feels he can safely charge higher prices than those current in Lae. Although the people complain that he robs them, they continue patronizing him for the sake of convenience.

Not more than 1,300 natives live within a radius of five miles, and Yakob's profits are inadequate to support him fully. He and his family eat a good deal of rice and tinned food, but he has several small taro gardens to eke out his supplies. His relatives have given up helping him with the fencing and clearing, and he finds that he must now do all the work alone. 'My kinsmen forget and leave me to garden and repair the house by myself,' he lamented. '*Da-tigeng* kin, and *hu-tigeng* kin also, ought to stand together, but I have to do without mine. They leave me out of their feasts and won't help me bring a log down from the forest so that I can hollow out a canoe. What happens? I have to pay for the hire of a vessel when I want to bring back more things for them from Lae. They envy me and make me waste my money.'

The villagers reply that Yakob has only himself to blame. They point out that he never helps other people in their work and consistently ignores his other kinship responsibilities. On not one occasion has he contributed to the marriage feast of a relative or sent a tin of meat when somebody was ill. A neighbour once told me that they were all wondering what would happen when Yakob's house had to be rebuilt. The timber from the Army camp was all gone and without this it would be impossible for a man to erect a dwelling unassisted. 'If he expects us to do the job we'll want wages—£20 or £30, something like that.'

Yakob's case, so far as Busama is concerned, is unique. The expert carpenters and shipwrights, like the craftsmen of the past, practise their skills in their spare time and hence never earn much. For parallels it is necessary to go to the settlements on the outskirts of such European towns as Rabaul and Port Moresby, where a few individuals have incomes derived from cocoa or copra production or some business activity. Usually they own large houses furnished in Western style but so far have preferred to use their money to improve their position in the traditional social system rather than to cut loose from it. Instead of sending their children to be educated at Australian schools and universities, for instance, they devote surplus cash, after daily wants have been met, to entertaining their neighbours in the old-fashioned way at a feast.[1]

[1] Belshaw, 1957, p. 147.

11

The Last Years

OUR study has brought us to the years of maturity, when the man's children may be expected to be old enough to marry. In the earlier chapters I have frequently referred to the part the seniors play in the village life, and we can therefore pass quickly over the final period. One subject only, the way in which special distinction is won, demands detailed consideration. Four fields are open, and a man may gain prestige in any of them. If he has the necessary qualifications he can decide to be a craftsman or a club head, or he may seek appointment as a Government representative or Church leader. A few may even gain double renown, perhaps as a craftsman and club head, perhaps as a club head and Government representative.

THE VILLAGE NOTABLES

Certain of the old crafts have disappeared as European contact has increased. Stone tools are no longer valued, for instance, and I never met anyone who could fashion them. In 1945 people regretted the loss of the art of net making, but this was a temporary phase. All the seines were burned during the war-time bombing raids, and the men were saying that if only the ancestors had passed on their skills new ones might have been woven from home-made ropes and cordage, Gilingu' alone knew what to do but despaired of training a sufficient number of pupils to carry out the work in reasonable time. Shortly afterwards, however, the Army withdrew, and the Fisheries units disposed of their equipment, including several large nets.

The services of eight or nine carpenters, on the other hand, are in constant demand for directing and supervising village building operations, such as the erection of dwellings, clubs, and schools. Probably these men possessed innate ability, but they also had to be trained. The local school teachers selected two of them in early youth as likely candidates and sent them for instruction to the Mission technical college, then located at Finschhafen. Mission and Government authorities still call on them occasionally when extra buildings are needed. One gave a good deal of help in Lae after the war, and the other was away for six months during 1949 and 1950 working on a new hospital in Madang. A third carpenter, Alingam, served his apprenticeship with a European contractor, who early recognized his talent. Alingam says that when his master became seriously ill he took charge and completed the construction of an aeroplane hangar from the blue prints and specifications. A fourth, Buaki, learned his craft in the traditional way by working at home with men who were acknowledged experts. He is partially crippled by elephantiasis, and employers may have been chary of accepting him into their labour line. Such men own expensive kits of tools. One of them lost his set in the war, and when making a claim for compensation he estimated the value, at the prices current in 1940, as upwards of £50.

There are eight expert canoe builders, the 'shipwrights' as I have called them. This craft, having no European counterpart, must be wholly learned in the settlement. A man who feels that he may have a natural gift for it attaches himself, usually during his twenties, to a master who is also a relative. He chips away at the dugout with this person during the early stages and later helps him with the booms and outrigger. Canoe experts cannot explain the guiding principles in abstract terms, but I have often heard them giving practical advice on particular points. 'For a canoe like this you want the booms to reach to that spot there,' one man told his pupil. 'If it were to come to here the canoe would be no good at all, and if it were cut off at that knot you'd turn over in the first wave.' (The absence of the comparative forms 'longer' and 'shorter' means that in translation such statements always sound clumsy.) A scale of measurement would lessen the difficulties, but this work, unlike housebuilding, is so much governed by tradition that even today rulers and squares are not in use.

After about ten years or more of apprenticeship, the novice takes the step of constructing a canoe for himself without supervision. If this is satisfactory, as it always seems to be, he has passed the test and accepts commissions.

Canoe building is an activity for the hours of leisure rather than a full-time occupation. The food with which the expert is presented as a reward for his services is always cooked first, and, because it cannot be stored, he makes a distribution then and there among his fellow clubmen and other relatives. Thus to support himself and his family he must have the same number of gardens in cultivation as other people. He is therefore forced to spread the work on a dugout over several weeks. Often, indeed, he is so much concerned about his clearing and planting that he does not approach the job for the space of ten days or more.

Sufficient young men are still coming forward. They are attracted most by the opportunity to display their skill, though being in a position to dispense food to a wide circle of kin is also an inducement.

Two or three of the carpenters, and two or three of the canoe builders, are also heads of clubs, an office for which industry and temperament are more important than specialized skills. The man must cultivate an extensive area of garden land and keep a large herd of pigs. He can then hold lavish feasts on his own account and also offer contributions to the lesser festivities of his followers.

The biggest feasts take place when the club house is on the point of falling down and a new one has to be built. Till recently the structures were higher and roomier than the dwellings and so required greater effort and more labourers. Correspondingly, the payments in food had to be bigger. The other club groups to which the head's kinsmen belonged donated the posts, for example, a favour demanding return gifts of pork and other supplies. In 1938 a man who rebuilt a club house paid out seven pigs, five tons of taro, and rice, bread, and tinned meat to the value of £4. On this occasion his followers as a whole helped to the extent of four more pigs, five tons of taro, and European foodstuffs costing £3.

Headship of a club is not a popular office. The man exercises limited authority and has to work so hard to achieve it. He cannot sit back after giving one set of feasts but must go on piling up wealth for further distributions. 'His hands are never free from earth, and his forehead continually drips with sweat,' said Gi'lahi. 'He isn't like a foreman on a plantation strolling round with a stick telling others what to do; he carries out the tasks himself.' Only when the club head has looked after the affairs of the group for years and grown old in service is he allowed to relegate the bulk of the physical work to those younger than himself.

Sensitivity to criticism is a further curb on ambition. The natives detest being sneered at, and mostly they try to avoid giving the neighbours a chance to deride their failures or poke fun at their arrogance. They keep to the middle course and hesitate either to rise too high or sink too low.

GOVERNMENT AND CHURCH

In recent years District Commissioners have permitted the natives to choose their own representatives, but this is an innovation. Till 1944 the European officer made the selection. In the initial period of contact he picked one of the traditional headmen, but after these disappeared he preferred a man with some experience of the white-man's world, often a retired member of the police force.

The job is onerous and in some respects unpleasant. The representative has no legal power but is expected to maintain good order. If persuasion fails the only course open to him is to report the offenders to the district station so that they may be arrested and brought to trial. Other duties include regular consultation with the Commissioner to receive Government orders for transmission to the people; organization of the villagers for such public works as weeding the bush pathways, repairing the bridges, and cleaning the settlement; supervision of the construction of latrines; enforcing the law that persons who become gravely ill must be taken to hospital; and assisting any Administration officer in transit, native as well as European, by providing food, carriers, or canoes. The penalty for laxity, or what the Commissioner regards as laxity, is imprisonment.

Yet there are compensations, especially for the unscrupulous. As in other colonial territories, the European staff is overworked and cannot spare the time to become thoroughly acquainted at first hand with the affairs of every village. Patrol officers spend only a few hours each year in the various settlements within their jurisdiction and of necessity rely on information supplied by the native representative. It follows that if a conflict arises they tend to support him against the people. Again, although every villager has the right to make a complaint against his fellows at the district station, the Commissioner usually calls for a report from the representative on the spot and often accepts the advice given when making his decision.

Religious affairs are in the hands of half a dozen Church Elders, all of whom have had special training in one of the main centres of the Lutheran Mission. Generally they are either retired school teachers or 'black missionaries', men who have spent several years in spreading the Gospel in those areas of New Guinea that are still pagan. The people themselves elect their Elders and are careful to consider only those with a blameless record.

Church Elders preside over the daily prayer meetings in the village and any special services, as at funerals; attend the annual Mission council, when questions of policy are decided; and sit in judgment on sinners. They have the right to suspend those guilty of any form of serious wrongdoing from membership of the congregation but in practice reserve this punishment exclusively for adulterers.

The Busama are fortunate in having so many channels for exploiting their talents. There is even scope for seniors of no more than average attainments. Any householder can speak at the public meetings, and a man who makes a positive contribution is sure of an attentive hearing and of praise for his wisdom afterwards. The village includes a few nonentities, persons who pass almost unnoticed and are rarely quoted, but these would scarcely have made a mark in other settings. In 1950, when there were twenty-six men over middle age, only about eight could be dismissed as without social significance.

THE END

Deserving members of the senior generation continue to enjoy the respect of the rest of the community, and even the most futile is treated with courtesy. Old people always work for as long as it is physically possible for them to do so, though they usually take a long rest in the shade during the hottest part of the day. Grandmothers are more useful as nurses than as cultivators, but they like to tend a plot or two. One old lady of my acquaintance, who, judging from the age of her grandchildren, must have been over eighty, was at the time of her death caring for five different gardens.

Husband and wife retain their own household till one of them dies, when the survivor moves in with a daughter or son, or, if the children are all dead, with a niece or nephew. A man prefers to sleep in the club but eats most of his meals in the dwelling and keeps his personal possessions there. Widows and widowers therefore are from now on dependent, and their offspring have to discharge in full the obligations for upbringing incurred during childhood.

When at last death comes the ceremonies are more elaborate than those heralding the birth of an infant. The whole village attends to mourn the passing, nowadays almost the only occasion when Busama-Lutu and Busama-Awasa unite.

Such emphasis on funeral ritual is in primitive societies usual; moreover, at this time it is customary for the various kinship obligations to be given tangible expression. The structure is suddenly visible, crystallized out as it were. Each separate group may be obliged to carry out particular kinds of duties, which are allocated strictly according to the kinship categories of the members. The actual interment, for example, is often the respon- sibility of the dead man's mother's patrilineal clansmen as a whole, with her brothers, real and classificatory, dealing with certain of the tasks and their sons with certain others. The Busama, however, concentrate ex- clusively on the broad distinction between the *da-tigeng* cognates and the rest of the kin. They ignore the matrilineage, the club, even the categories of kindred. If an action requires the presence of only a few persons then any of those belonging to the right set—on the one hand, the *da-tigeng* or, on the other, the *hu-tigeng* and affines—are allowed to perform it.

In pagan times the deceased's male *da-tigeng* cognates at once destroyed some of their property. The father, uncles, brothers, and first cousins (for an older person the brothers, first cousins, sons, and nephews) cut down several coconut palms and drove an axe through the hull of a canoe or smashed a number of clay cooking pots. The female *da-tigeng* cognates then bathed the corpse, arrayed it in a new loincloth, and placed ornaments upon it. By this time the other relatives, pregnant women and young mothers alone excepted, had assembled outside the house. Here they sat down, and for several hours the women wailed and the men chatted. At last one of the seniors suggested that some of the young people had better dig the grave. He spoke to those who happened to be sitting near him, and their precise kinship status, provided they were either *hu-tigeng* cognates or affines of the dead, was of no importance. Two or three other men, again *hu-tigeng* cognates or affines, then volunteered for the burial. They placed weapons or string bags alongside the body (depending on the person's sex), wrapped it in mats, laid it in the grave with a basket of taro for the spirit to eat, and filled in the hole. Other *hu-tigeng* cognates and affines now built a hut nearby whither the da-*tigeng* kindred could retire for a period varying from a week to a month or even longer if the person was somebody of note. The distant relatives fed them during their seclusion and kept them sup- plied with wood so that they could keep a huge fire burning as comfort for the spirit. They ate everything raw, nevertheless, and refrained from washing and cutting their hair. Meantime the villagers carried out only essential work—they cleared no new land, built no new houses, and made no overseas voyages. Finally, on a day agreed upon, the *da-tigeng* kindred burned their hut and distributed the dead person's food supplies to the other relatives. This was the only time that quantities of pork and vegetables were given away uncooked. 'The death had doused the fires,' it was explained. The spirit had now joined the ancestors and from that point onwards never impinged as a separate entity on the life of the community.

Today when a death occurs the senior man of the *da-tigeng* kindred is expected to take charge, though he may ask a brother or a cousin to act for him should he feel unfit. If all the cognates and affines are not already present his first task is to send messengers to bring them in. He then tells the *da-tigeng* womenfolk to make the body ready for display. They wash it with soap and water, close the eyes, and bind up the jaw. Next they dress it in white clothing and lift it on to a length of white calico. Most households have sufficient material on hand, but if not neighbours come to the rescue. White is chosen 'because the disciples and the three Maries robed Jesus's body in white; and because white is the colour of the angels'.

While this work is going on the master of ceremonies sends the *da-tigeng* menfolk to the cultivations for food, areca nuts, and betel pepper. The youths also bring in green coconuts for drinking.

By now the *hu-tigeng* relatives, affines, and other villagers have assembled. The men proceed to the dead person's club, but the women crowd into the dwelling or sit just outside. For about an hour they wail in long-drawn-out cries, and then somebody begins singing one of the old German chorales, the words of which the missionaries have translated. Others take up the tune, and the chanting continues till the evening, chorale following chorale.

The men neither enter the house of death nor take part in the singing. They sit throughout the day chatting and smoking with the male *da-tigeng* kindred of the deceased. Etiquette compels them to refer briefly to their regret, but most of the conversation turns on other topics. From time to time the *da-tigeng* kin excuse themselves and go off to cook light refreshments, some of which they take across to the women. The remainder they hand around to the men, together with coconuts, betel-nut, and cigarettes.

Unless there is an epidemic, burial is delayed till the next morning. The *hu-tigeng* kin and other villagers return to their homes at dusk, but the *da-tigeng* kindred remain for the night. The women are by now too hoarse to sing, and they once more take turns in wailing.

At the request of the master of ceremonies, the carpenter most closely related to the dead person is up at dawn sawing boards for the coffin. Generally he has it finished by about nine o'clock, when he sends word that it is ready. Some of the *da-tigeng* kindred bring it to the house, lift the body in, and nail down the lid; and later one of them sews a piece of white calico on as a cover.

The master of ceremonies now asks a couple of the *hu-tigeng* relatives

M

or affines—the first his eye falls on—to go ahead to the cemetery and dig a grave. The people follow behind in twos and threes, leaving some of the *da-tigeng* men to ferry the coffin by canoe.

The cemetery is half a mile from the village close to the main road and thirty yards or so off the beach. It is surrounded by a hedge of bright croton bushes, and at the entrance a tall wooden cross has been fixed. The graves are arranged in rows, each bordered by white coral boulders or clam shells. A few have a headstone made from concrete with an inscription recording the person's name and the year of his death, and others are marked by ornamental shrubs.

The villagers as they approach change into clean white clothing and then sit awaiting for the arrival of the corpse. Usually the members of the bereaved family are in attendance, but sometimes the women feel that the ordeal would be too much.

The men sitting nearest step forward to unload the coffin from the canoe and carry it on their shoulders to the grave, where they rest it on two logs. A service, led by one of the Church Elders, now begins. The people sing a hymn, and at the close the preacher recites a prayer and delivers a short sermon. He refers to the bliss of heaven ordained for those who repent and warns of the punishments in store for the ungodly. Usually, too, he takes the opportunity to make an harangue on the evils of sexual immorality, the sin with which the Busama are so obsessed. A general prayer comes next and the funeral hymn after it. While this last is being sung the grave diggers, assisted by those nearby, draw the logs aside and lower the coffin on ropes. The children now run forward and throw in sprigs of croton and flowers. The diggers fill the grave in, and the members of the congregation sing a final hymn.

The *da-tigeng* kindred remain indoors for several days, during which other relatives bring them food. Even after they feel free to come out they refrain for a few months from taking part in any public gatherings. The men may also stop shaving.

CONCLUSION

At the beginning of the book I said that the social structure of Busama has survived fifty odd years of European contact. It will be apparent why there have been so few changes. As yet money, Government, law, and Christianity have had little effect on the basic elements of the people's subsistence. The present-day native eats the same foods as his remote ancestors and protects himself from the weather with the same type of shelters. He cultivates taro, digs with a stick, cooks in a clay pot, keeps a herd of pigs, fishes with line or net from a canoe, and builds a house of timber and palm leaf. Collective effort is therefore almost as much in evidence as ever. Kinship and marriage continue to supply the framework for the essential co-operative units of family, household, *da-tigeng* and *hu-tigeng* groups, lineage, and club.

References

BARNES, J. A., 1954. *Politics in a Changing Society*. Oxford.
— 1960. 'Marriage and Residential Continuity.' *American Anthropologist*, Vol. LXII.
BATESON, G., 1932. 'Social Structure of the Iatmül People'. *Oceania*, Vol. II.
BELSHAW, C. S., 1957. *The Great Village*. London.
BOHANNAN, L., 1952. 'A Genealogical Charter'. *Africa*, Vol. XXII.
BOHANNAN, L. and P., 1953. 'The Tiv of Central Nigeria' in *Ethnographic Survey of Africa* (ed. D. Forde). London.
BOHANNAN, P., 1954. 'Expansion and Migration of the Tiv'. *Africa*, Vol. XXIV.
— 1957. *Justice and Judgment Among the Tiv*. Oxford.
CAPELL, A., 1949. 'The Concept of Ownership in the Languages of Australia and the Pacific'. *Southwestern Journal of Anthropology*, Vol. V.
— 1951. 'Two Tonal Languages of New Guinea'. *Bulletin of the School of Oriental and African Studies*, Vol. XIII.
COLSON, E., 1958. *Marriage and the Family among the Plateau Tonga*. Manchester.
DJAMOUR, J., 1959. *Malay Kinship and Marriage in Singapore*. London.
ELKIN, A. P., 1954. *The Australian Aborigines*. Sydney.
EVANS-PRITCHARD, E. E., 1951. *Kinship and Marriage among the Nuer*. Oxford.
FIRTH, R., 1936. *We, the Tikopia*. London.
FORTES, M. and EVANS-PRITCHARD, E. E. (eds.), 1940. *African Political Systems*. Oxford.
FORTES, M., 1953. 'The Structure of Unilineal Descent Groups'. *American Anthropologist*, Vol. LV.
— 1958. 'Malinowski and the Study of Kinship' in *Man and Culture* (ed. R. Firth). London.
FORTUNE, R. F., 1932. *Sorcerers of Dobu*. London.
GLUCKMAN, M., 1950. 'Kinship and Marriage among the Lozi of Northern Rhodesia and the Zulu of Natal' in *African Systems of Kinship and Marriage* (eds. A. R. Radcliffe-Brown and D. Forde). Oxford.
— 1953. 'Bridewealth and the Stability of Marriage'. *Man*, Vol. LIII, No. 223.
— 1954. 'Political Institutions' in *The Institutions of Primitive Society* (ed. E. E. Evans-Pritchard). Oxford.
GOODENOUGH, W. H., 1955. 'A Problem of Malayo-Polynesian Social Organization'. *American Anthropologist*, Vol. LVII.
— 1962. 'Kindred and Hamlet in Lakalai, New Britain,' *Ethnology*, Vol. I.
HOGBIN, H. I., 1934. 'Culture Change in the Solomon Islands'. *Oceania*, Vol. IV.

— 1935–6. 'Adoption in Wogeo'. *Journal of the Polynesian Society*, Vols. XLIV and XLV.

— 1937. 'Hill People of Northeastern Guadalcanal'. *Oceania*, Vol. VIII.

— 1939a. *Experiments in Civilization*. London.

— 1939b. 'Native Land Tenure in New Guinea'. *Oceania*, Vol. X.

— 1943. 'A New Guinea Infancy'. *Oceania*, Vol. XIII.

— 1945. 'Marriage in Wogeo'. *Oceania*, Vol. XV.

— 1946. 'A New Guinea Childhood'. *Oceania*, Vol. XVI.

— 1951. *Transformation Scene*. London.

— 1958. *Social Change*. London.

HOGBIN, H. I. and WEDGWOOD, C. H., 1952–4. 'Local Grouping in Melanesia'. *Oceania*, Vols. XXIII and XXIV.

KROEBER, A. L., 1909. 'Classificatory Systems of Relationship'. *Journal of the Royal Anthropological Institute*, Vol. XXXIX.

LEACH, E. R., 1951. 'The Structural Implications of Matrilateral Cross-Cousin Marriage'. *Journal of the Royal Anthropological Institute*, Vol. LXXXI.

— 1953. 'Bridewealth and the Stability of Marriage'. *Man*, Vol. LIII, No. 279.

— 1957. 'Aspects of Bridewealth and Marriage Stability among the Kachin and Lakher'. *Man*, Vol. LVII, No. 59.

LOUNSBERY, F. G., 1956. 'A Semantic Analysis of Pawnee Kinship Usage'. *Language*, Vol. XXXII.

MALINOWSKI, B., 1929. *The Sexual Life of Savages*. London.

MEAD, M., 1935. *Sex and Temperament in Three Primitive Societies*. New York.

— 1938. 'The Mountain Arapesh'. *Anthropological Papers of the American Museum of Natural History*, Vol. XXXVI.

MURDOCK, G. P., 1949. *Social Structure*. New York.

MURRAY, J. K., 1950. 'Science and the Future of Papua and New Guinea'. *Australian Journal of Science*, Vol. XIII.

NADEL, S. F., 1951. *Foundations of Anthropology*. London.

— 1952. 'Witchcraft in Four African Societies'. *American Anthropologist*, Vol. LIV.

POWDERMAKER, H., 1933. *Life in Lesu*. New York.

RADCLIFFE-BROWN, A. R. and FORDE, D. (eds.), 1950. *African Systems of Kinship and Marriage*. Oxford.

RADCLIFFE-BROWN, A. R., 1952. *Structure and Function in Primitive Societies*. London.

READ, K. E., 1946. 'Social Organization of the Markham Valley'. *Oceania*, Vol. XVII.

— 1950. 'Political System of the Ngarawapum'. *Oceania*, Vol. XX.

RICHARDS, A. I., 1950. 'Some Types of Family Structure among the Central Bantu' in *African Systems of Kinship and Marriage* (eds. A. R. Radcliffe-Brown and D. Forde). Oxford.

RIVERS, W. H. R., 1914. *History of Melanesian Society*. Cambridge.

SALISBURY, R. F., 1956a. 'Unilineal Descent Groups in the New Guinea Highlands', *Man*, Vol. LVI, No. 2.

— 1956b. 'Asymmetrical Marriage Systems', *American Anthropologist*, Vol. LVIII.

SCHNEIDER, D. M., 1953. 'A Note on Bridewealth and the Stability of Marriage'. *Man.* Vol. LIII, No. 73.

SELIGMAN, C. G., 1910. *Melanesians of British New Guinea.* Cambridge.

TODD, J. A., 1934. 'Research Work in Southwest New Britain'. *Oceania,* Vol. V.

WHITE, L. A., 1958. 'What is a Classificatory System?' *Southwestern Journal of Anthropology,* Vol. XIV.

WHITING, J. W. M. and REED, S. W., 1938. 'Kwoma Culture'. *Oceania,* Vol. IX.

WILLIAMS, F. E., 1930. *Orokaiva Society.* Oxford.

Index

LONDON SCHOOL OF ECONOMICS
MONOGRAPHS ON SOCIAL ANTHROPOLOGY

Titles marked with an asterisk are now out of print.